GOLDFINGER

By the same author

In Search of European Excellence
The Business of Winning

Contents

Acknowledgements

Many people have contributed to the ideas put forward in this book, above all the entrepreneurs named in its pages, to whom I am especially indebted for help and inspiration. Many other entrepreneurs have enlightened me down the years, both personally and in books like those cited here, written by Mike Bloomberg, Hal Rosenbluth, Sam Walton, Ricardo Semler and Albert J. Dunlap.

I also owe a great debt to the thinkers whose work has enriched everybody's knowledge of the dynamics of business enterprise. My heartfelt argument, that smaller businesses can learn much from books directed at larger enterprises, is strongly supported by Peter Senge's *The Fifth Discipline*, Gary Hamel and C.K. Prahalad's *Competing for the Future*, James Champy's *Reengineering Management*, T. Bradley Gale's *Total Customer Satisfaction*, Daniel T. Jones and James P. Womack's *Lean Manufacturing*, Faith Popcorn's *The Popcorn Report* and Clayton M. Christensen's *The Innovator's Dilemma*.

Dave Patten's *Successful Marketing for the Small Business*, on the other hand, contains lessons that many large company managers could absorb to their benefit. That was certainly also true of Sir John Harvey-Jones's trenchant investigations of smaller firms in the *Troubleshooter* programmes on BBC TV. In this multimedia age, video is also a significant business tool: Tom Peters's *Service with Soul* (Video Arts) is both entertaining and highly informative.

Management consultants have made a major contribution to my thinking and knowledge. Fred Buggie of Strategic Innovations International is outstanding in his field. I have worked especially closely with Michael de Kare Silver (whose own book, *Strategy in Crisis*, is a powerful and practical study) and the Kalchas Group: the latter's bulletins and surveys have proved most valuable. I owe a great debt to other admirable surveys from PIMS Associates, Bain & Co., and the

London Business School: the latter's research, in association with Pulse, Binder Hamlyn and Arthur Andersen, has provided excellent insight into the motivation of private companies.

I am most grateful to the Royal Society of Arts for transcripts of personal accounts that Julian Metcalfe of Pret a Manger and William Sieghart of Forward Publishing gave to a lively seminar. Path-finding work has also been published by the Department of Trade and Industry, whose collaboration with the Confederation of British Industry has had admirable results. I am most grateful to the DTI publication *Winning*; with its excellent information and interviews, it is a model of its kind. So are the Business Intelligence surveys that I have cited.

Drayton Bird, who features among the book's entrepreneurs, is also the author of the authoritative *How to Write Sales Letters that Sell*. Not only was this a prime source of wisdom for this book: it has also helped with promoting the newsletter, *Letter to Thinking Managers*, for which I teamed up with Edward de Bono. I have found his insights and methods (such as Six Thinking Hats) both brilliant and effective: he also introduced me to many other eminent thinkers, including Professor Sidney Parnes, whose methods are equally valuable for entrepreneurs.

I have drawn on many publications. In America, the heartland of entrepreneurial capitalism, the *Wall Street Journal*, *Fortune*, the *Harvard Business Review* (where I discovered the findings of Professor Dov Eden), *Forbes* and *Inc.* have been indispensable. In Britain, as one would expect from its all-round excellence, the *Financial Times* has been an invaluable source. I am also indebted to *Worldlink*, the *Independent on Sunday*, and *Real Business*; the latter is an example of how British journalism is rightly devoting more attention to the SMEs – the small and medium-sized enterprises which are crucial to economic progress.

The *Mail on Sunday* was among the first to spot the importance of this sector, and I am, above all, grateful to Clive Wolman, then the editor of the Business section, for asking me to write about SMEs. This book sprang out of my *Mail on Sunday* columns, which featured many of the case studies included here. Writing those columns was a highly educative and enjoyable experience.

So was working with Lucinda McNeile and her team at HarperCollinsBusiness, to whom many thanks are due – as they are to my patient secretary, Pathika Martin.

Introduction

The entrepreneur is the hero of capitalism, the object of envy and admiration, the mainspring for the private sector, the stuff of commercial legend, the source of new companies, new products, new industries. In Britain, New Labour followed Old Thatcherite Conservatism in courting the entrepreneur. Yet entrepreneurship is still treated as something of a mystery, a divine gift, like faith-healing, dowsing or the laying on of hands.

Myriad books and courses aim at managers and claim to improve their management, and many of them actually succeed. But books and courses on entrepreneurship are very few and far between – possibly nobody teaches the subject because nobody believes it can be taught. That is patently untrue. Every entrepreneurial father who has ever nurtured the next generation of entrepreneurs disproves the idea. Business may or may not be in the genes. But business know-how is in the teaching, training and experience.

Consider the nature and definition of the entrepreneur, or enterpriser. He or she turns a business idea into a new business, or injects new vitality into an old business. At every stage – from the thinking that produces the Big Idea through planning to implementation and beyond – the entrepreneur can benefit from the examples of others, people who have been there before. Their experience establishes clear precepts and practices, from which others, as in any discipline, can learn.

True, there are also entrepreneurs who are apparently without discipline, who seem never to have needed a lesson, who have acted from instinct rather than intellect. Track their ascents, though, and their actions invariably follow a pattern. They act on logic and observation as well as intuition, and their plans, decisions and execution are controlled by methods which can be easily understood, described – and imitated. If it sounds too simple, so it should. As Mr Bernstein, the factotum for Citizen Kane, remarked: 'It's no great trick to make a lot of money, if all you want is to make a lot of money.'

So what explains the many business failures, or the failure of far more would-be entrepreneurs even to start on the road? Many dream, but don't act; they are unwilling to make the sustained efforts, on all dimensions, that success demands. Once you understand what those efforts entail, and how to make them, however, the effort seems more and more feasible. Once you understand, moreover, what explains the innumberable setbacks of those who start and fail, the better equipped you are to take that risk and avoid the traps.

Dodging the traps, such as going bankrupt, is among the subjects covered in these pages, after the basics (like managing cash), the key methods of moving onwards and upwards, and the most important technique of all – which is getting the best out of people, including yourself. The excellent boss generates excellent employees, who in turn produce better than satisfied customers. The latter are the key ingredients of end-century entrepreneurial success. No consultant or guru will tell you any different.

Listening to consultants and gurus, in person or in print, is a relatively easy way of mastering the arts and crafts needed by the entrepreneur. Expert knowlege is especially valuable in marketing, where today's business may well need, not just national, but global market abilities. In the markets of the millennium, in which small high-tech firms can become international stars almost overnight, the world may be anybody's oyster. Entrepreneurs have no frontier other than their own ambitions.

Far more than large company sagas, tales of small companies that think big should encourage people to cross the frontiers that separate would-be entrepreneurs from their ambitions and to achieve their personal and business ends. If this book provides the understaning and the incentive needed to turn ambition into achievement and desire into reality, it will have met its own objective.

1

The Rules of the Game

How It Became Fastest

The cardinal difference between the entrepreneur and the corporation is that entrepreneurial success is essentially personal. Out there, hoping and hunting for business breakthroughs, are living, thinking, striving individuals whose companies are expressions of their personal drives. Their motivations are generally powerful and simple – witness one who wrote to me as follows:

> Dear Robert Heller
>   With a strong urge to become a millionaire in the next five years, and £100,000 cash available, what would you suggest?

This book is an answer. Many people believe that millions cannot be found between the covers of a book, but another reader strongly disagrees. David Craven, joint managing director of NST Ltd, told me in 1995 that the dozen principles embodied in my acronym IT BECAME FAST had 'provided the basis of my approach to running my own business'.

In ten years, NST had grown from £1 million turnover to £15 million as Britain's largest operator of educational tours. The precepts contained in the acronym – or the Clean Dozen – are straightforward and do indeed govern the game of outgrowing others and doing so profitably:

1 Improve basic efficiency – all the time.
2 Think as simply and directly as possible about what you're doing and why.
3 Behave towards others as you wish them to behave towards you.
4 Evaluate each business and business opportunity with all the objective facts and logic you can muster.
5 Concentrate on what you do well.
6 Ask questions ceaselessly about your performance, your markets, your objectives.
7 Make money; if you don't, you can't do anything else.
8 Economize, because doing the most with the least is the name of the game.
9 Flatten the company, so authority is spread over many people.
10 Admit to your failings and shortcomings, because only then will you be able to improve on them.
11 Share the benefits of success widely among those who helped to achieve it.
12 Tighten up the organization whenever you can – because success tends to breed slackness.

So one small firm had risen to leadership in its industry by applying principles found by the boss in a management book. On the whole, entrepreneurs don't read management literature, most of which seems to be written for large corporations. After all, there is a vast gulf between a company that employs at most 100 people and an organization whose payroll runs into the tens of thousands. A large company can turn over £1 million, not in a good year, but in an hour. In terms of basic management principles, though, the discrepancy in size makes no difference at all. Every time I talk to an audience that includes the bosses of small businesses, they query whether the principles that apply to IBM or ICI apply to them too. The answer is always the same: of course they do. I have long maintained that even start-ups can benefit from the big-time lessons.

Large companies have more sophisticated systems, naturally (or sometimes unnaturally), and more complex tasks. But the fundamentals of business and management are invariable – and entrepreneurs who exploit the insights peddled at seminars and in management books gain immeasurably. Everyone is well advised to study examples from big-time business and the theories and practices that have been proved (or disproved) in that arena.

The Clean Dozen, for example, weren't plucked out of thin air; real life inspired the IT BECAME FAST acronym. All big companies have to start somewhere. In this case, the source was a middling-sized British engineering firm, which was exhibiting the faults that killed off many of its breed and which still plague most small businesses: restricted product range, overdependence on the local market, low reputation, inadequate management.

Three young managers realized that not only the company but also their careers were on the line – and they moved decisively to correct all four faults. I came across their amazing results when, out of the blue, the firm turned up at the summit of the Growth League in *Management Today*, the magazine I founded in 1966.

The new star's name was BTR, and from its modest beginnings it had already multiplied its profits thirty times on a five-fold rise in turnover. It powered on to world-class size (£10 billion-plus of sales) and fame, before hitting the buffers in the 1990s. The highly effective management principles of its former excellent leader, Sir Owen Green, became the basis of my book *The Business of Winning*, and thus came to underpin the growth of Craven's Blackpool-based firm, which, very wisely, has 'kept everything very simple'. That's precisely what another acronym famously lays down: KISS, which stands for Keep It Simple, Stupid.

Moreover, by 'constantly looking to minimize costs and improve efficiency', David Craven believes, NST has stayed well ahead of competitors. He has concentrated on better quality business and higher profit margins, while the product range and market reach have been extended. Turnover has consequently risen to £20 million. All this success has been widely shared, through performance-linked bonuses, with 'very highly motivated, skilled staff'. That sharing policy has been very important, not least in retaining skilled people: 'Hardly anybody has ever left us.'

Another major pillar of Craven's philosophy is the absolute prohibition of the familiar, conservative killer: 'We've always done it that way.' That utterance used to be a 'fineable offence'; nobody talks about fines now, simply because the issue 'doesn't arise any more'. But the principle remains wholly valid. If you don't ensure that what you preach is practised, the preaching is worthless.

That is the real lesson of NST's success. It is not that those dozen principles are the right or only way to grow a business; the lesson is rather that theory can always be put to practical use. What makes the difference is determined application. 'We still follow the same basic principles,' says Craven, and for a very simple reason: 'It's working.'

That should delight some of big-time management's leading gurus. For the Clean Dozen include six of the leading contemporary management theories, all of them well worth applying: continuous improvement (1), fact-based management (4), core competences (5), business process re-engineering (8), delayering (9), even key aspects of Total Quality Management (10). To sum up the six:

- you aim at higher and higher standards for all operations
- train *everybody* in reaching decisions on the basis of accurate data
- concentrate on what you do best
- revise processes to reduce the time and money involved from end-to-end
- strive for the minimum levels of hierarchy (three can be perfectly adequate)
- and build all activities backwards from the goal of satisfying customer wants.

Such standards constitute a tall order, but one that the natural entrepreneur fills by instinct, through an intuitive feeling about what is right, not just for the business, but for its people. The reason why much of today's 'new' management theory is contained in the Clean Dozen's hundred-odd words, written some seventeen years ago, is that the basics of successful management are rooted in human nature. That is the same within ICI as in a mini-market.

The major difference is that largeness imposes unnatural behaviour on natural people, with the usual counter-productive results. Entrepreneurs, true, can breed bureaucracy, stultifying procedures and internal politics just as efficiently (or rather inefficiently) as big-time corpocrats. But the entrepreneur's relative smallness and closeness to the front-line mean that failings are much easier to identify and cure.

So even giants are now trying to think small; dividing into smaller units, each commanded by a single boss with the authority (in theory) of the owner-manager. Within the best mammoths, you can find self-managed manufacturing cells where half-a-dozen workers operate as flexible teams under one-man or one-woman leadership. *They know their products and their customers, and are expected to contribute and embrace new thinking of all kinds to enhance individual and group performance.*

Many small businesses fall well short of that formula. Like the IT BECAME FAST precepts, though, it applies generally. Its three elements now need adding to the original dozen, and with equal prominence:

13 Enable everybody in the business to use their individual powers to the fullest possible extent.
14 Serve your customers with all their requirements and desires to standards of perceived excellence in quality.
15 Transform performance by constantly innovating in products and processes – including the ways in which the business is managed.

Neatly enough, the three additions turn the acronym into IT BECAME FASTEST, thus injecting a necessary note of urgency and ambition. Both are required if you truly want to outwit the competition by the better use of better ways to manage and grow, whether they come from books or seminars or mentors or previous employers or your own experience. Only the individual entrepreneur, by providing the driving force, can make the business become fastest.

Big-time or small, the more you deliberately drive the principles that suit you and your business into effective application, the higher profits and growth will be; witness the fifteen-fold, ten-year expansion of NST.

Thinking It Through

The most valuable tool of the entrepreneur is all in the mind. Think better – and absorb the thinking of others better – and astonishing growth, even quadrupling the business in three years, is perfectly possible *if* you turn thought into deed. Action creates growth and wealth, but thought comes first. Every great business is born in somebody's mind.

Since before there is a business there must be an idea, time spent on better thinking must be highly profitable. How can you find a true winner, a better idea than anybody else's? Are there any methods which mine the mind more effectively? The answer to the second question has to be Yes. Any human activity, from sport to cyberspace, is susceptible to improvement through better methodology.

The thinking doesn't stop at genesis. Once a company is up and running, the need for ideas is just as pressing, and the payoff for effective thought is just as high. The more and better the ideas, the bigger and better the business, and the more effective its operations. This does not mean that all successful entrepreneurs are great thinkers – rather, they're often great thieves.

As many entrepreneurs have demonstrated, it saves much time and trouble to steal ideas from somebody or somewhere else. That's how supermarkets and countless other businesses crossed the Atlantic to Europe. The traffic in stolen ideas is two-way. Thus, a sharp-eyed citizen of the Pacific Northwest, Howard Schultz, spotted the little stand-up espresso bars that proliferate in Milan, adapted the idea to American tastes, and generated a $630 million chain named Starbucks. The chain has over 1,000 outlets and a growth rate of 61 percent annually, which does indeed quadruple a business in three years.

Thought consists of two essential elements: observation, which collects the necessary data; and synthesis, which turns the data into ideas. But even after observation and synthesis, the Starbucks brainwave still had to be processed through the entrepreneurial brain. That process included the adaptation, the sites, the name, the offering, the design – all the elements needed to marry the Italian idea with a quite separate perception: that American coffee was awful and that Americans would pay for something better.

So, even for idea thieves, the key is thinking – the ultimate management technique. Like any technique, as noted above, it can be improved, which is why people attend meetings on the subject (there is even an International Conference on Creative Thinking held in Malta), write and read books about thought processes, and study the lateral thinking methods devised by Edward de Bono. One brilliant idea is all you need to justify the effort.

Meetings in Malta may seem a far-out way of spending time and money, but being far-out and far away holds one of the keys to bigger and better ideas. Louis Farrugia, a Maltese businessman, cogently illustrates the point. He travelled all the way to Scotland for a management seminar, carrying with him a weighty problem. His brewery on the island was not re- sponding to his efforts to achieve profitable change. His initia- tives were getting through to some people, not to others.

The Scottish seminar gave him the idea that broke the logjam, though not directly. The visiting guru, Tom Peters, provided no specific answers to the brewery problem, but his far-out management thinking, deliberately provocative, provoked Far- rugia into producing some brand-new ideas of his own. He went 'outside the box', a phrase that has become popular in manage- ment as people realize how circumscribed and channelled their thinking has become.

The box is the *status quo*, the situation as is. Going outside the box means that you no longer accept that situation. Some parts of Farrugia's brewery, such as distribution, were performing marvellously, but the parts were not recognized or organized as

distinct operations. Everything was piled together as an indivis-
ible whole, a single company. That was the box. Everybody was
confined within the same system. But that did not result from
some immutable, divine law.

Farrugia rewrote the man-made rules. The answer was to
divide and conquer. The brewery was split into units, none larger
than 100 people, each headed by a general manager who was
made responsible for meeting financial targets and was rewarded
accordingly. It worked like magic: sales and profits both shot
up.

That particular approach to improving performance generally
does work. It's another idea that may be well worth stealing.
People respond to both the responsibility and the incentives –
and to their identification with a particular team. But the main
point of Farrugia's happy experience is that thinking differently
is encouraged by exposure to different thinking – and being
different is often the golden key that makes all the difference
between brilliant success and nothing at all. You can, sometimes,
succeed as a 'me-too', imitating exactly what somebody else
does; but it's far more promising to do a Starbucks, providing a
product or service (excellent coffee) that is not available elsewhere, and doing so in a way that is also unique.

The Aroma chain in Britain is following a quite similar strategy
– again, adapted to different local circumstances in a way that
differentiates the business from other coffee shops. The differentiation is crucial. That's where bigger businesses often go astray;
many fail to differentiate their companies from their competitors. It makes them vulnerable to attack from smaller firms
which know exactly why they are special, and which are often
specialists.

The big boys simply haven't thought. The specialists have –
and it goes on paying. Howard Schultz, for example, has thought
through and refined his formula, so that he can say proudly,
'Starbucks is not a trend. We're a life-style.' While he has diversified into coffee ice-cream and alliances with powerful operators
such as United Air Lines, the Barnes & Noble bookshop chain
and Pepsico, he rejects vastly more propositions than he accepts.

Schultz's thinking is that the growth rate must be sustainable:

excessive growth will risk both quality and that up-market life-style image. Mind you, growth of 61 percent per annum and opening as many as 335 bars in a single year is hardly pedestrian; but the thinking management installed as Starbucks grew from start-up to mega-chain understands that even sustainable growth generates new needs. The president, Orin Smith, told *Fortune* that attention had shifted more to the bottom line, as opposed to the top – to profits as opposed to revenue: 'We're looking at efficiencies in manufacturing and distribution. We're reengineering.' In other words, they are rethinking.

Any of the ways to help you think, or rethink, better will work. That's because thinking about thinking of itself develops improved processes. 'Mind-set' is an obvious demonstration of this truth. If you form a project, and set out to realize that plan, your set mind will spot useful contributions, often decisive ones, that would otherwise have been missed entirely.

One of the de Bono techniques is a perfect illustration: the Six Thinking Hats approach painlessly changes your mode of thinking. You have an idea for a new enterprise. With the Black hat on, you look for disadvantages and dangers. Then, switch to the Yellow hat, and seek out the benefits. Perhaps you don't have enough information, so put on the White hat to find out more. If the ideas are stuck 'in the box', the Green creative hat may release them. Maybe you are going about the thought process in a less than ideal way: don the Blue hat to study the process. And don't forget that emotion, feeling and hunch play their part; that's a Red hat job.

Another method is 'visionizing', as recommended by Professor Sidney Parnes. The processes evidently overlap with the Six Hats.

First, envision your desire.
Second, find all available facts.
Third, identify problems, writing down many ideas for solutions.
Fourth, examine and re-examine the ideas until you reach the 'more workable, acceptable, stronger, more effective' idea-solutions.
Fifth, and critically, take early action to turn wishes into deeds.

As Parnes says, one constructive action is worth a hundred New Year resolutions. Yet this is the greatest stumbling block for would-be entrepreneurs. Once I launched a newsletter for such people under the title *Business Fast Lane*. It achieved a spectacular response rate to the first direct mail campaign (see Chapter 5), but the renewal rate was so feeble that the letter died an early death. The excellent mailing, it transpired, had tapped a large audience of fantasizing Walter Mittys. Like Macbeth, they were not without ambition, but they lacked 'th'illness should attend it' – the urge for action. *Business Fast Lane* explained the techniques and tools of turning ambition into achievement, which brought the Mittys face to face with hard reality. They gave up too soon. The fantasy is fine. That's 'envisioning'. The next stage is thought and that's also fine.

How can the vision be realized? What steps need to be taken, when and by whom? As these questions are solved by good thinking, the inhibitions should dwindle away. Build on the vision by intelligent, directed thought, and the necessary actions will come to seem more palatable and practicable until, eventually, farewell Walter Mitty. The entrepreneur and the enterprise are born.

How Planning Pays Off

Great oaks from little acorns grow, and companies as large as Hewlett-Packard or Apple Computer began as two men in a garage. That is how it has to be. Although entrepreneurs may think big, they don't usually have the resources to start big. But why do the vast majority of small entrepreneurs stay small?

Most business acorns, even if they survive, never grow beyond sapling size. One reason is simply that the proprietors, whatever their entrepreneurial urges, lack the professional ability to manage more than one shop or workshop. Many more people certainly believe that of themselves – which is a self-fulfilling and self-limiting prophecy.

The young Charles Forte took a different, and surely right, attitude. He reasoned that if he could run a single milkbar profitably, he could handle two; if two, four and so on, in a numerical progression which led to a world-wide catering and hotel empire and a peerage. Forte, of course, was a brilliantly able young man, who also had the gift of hiring others who could grow with the business, but little talent is required to learn his lessons.

Any would-be entrepreneur is perfectly capable of applying Forte's insight on a smaller scale and of mastering the simple management technique which enabled his business to grow. Knowing his figures in detail, he could work out what ratios of costs to sales would leave his first milkbar in profit. Apply the same ratios to each new outlet in turn, and you have the golden key to control and expansion.

Even if everybody can follow that principle, would everybody want to? The difference between Forte and the proprietor of a single café, between the growing and static small firm, is ambition. It's also the difference in mentality between the small firm and the big company. The latter's managers expect to grow sales and profits. They often fail, sometimes miserably, but their motto is onwards and upwards.

Small entrepreneurs may settle for staying put – a perfectly legitimate, but self-limiting choice. In one branch of engineering, wire-drawing, several small companies used to operate in the South of England. One alone invested in the latest machinery and sought to excel and expand. His competitors (if that was the right word) looked at him without envy. One observed: 'Me? I'd rather take the dog for a walk.'

As it happens, the hare, over-dependent on business from Ford Motor, went bust; virtue is not always its own reward, but the dog-walking tortoises can't have won any races, either. They were simply not trying. Yet a little effort makes so great a difference that it is surely worthwhile. Most entrepreneurs in charge of small businesses rarely write down their ambitions. Do that, on a single sheet of paper, and you're on your way.

The management gurus would call the piece of paper a Mission Statement. It merely involves saying what you want to achieve and when. Convert that into a 'How' statement, complete with facts and figures, and implement simple controls to check your journey. On that foundation, any business can grow wondrously.

Take the example of one small company, a contemporary art gallery. It had journeyed on for seventeen years, neither making a profit nor providing its founder with an income. She was far more interested in nurturing her artists and their art than in her money, and built an enviable artistic reputation. The business was only kept alive by small infusions of capital from a few admiring backers, and the future apparently offered no better prospects.

Nobody looked at that future, however, until one of the loyal investors became anxious about his investment. He sat down with the owner and her general manager to devise a three-year plan. Few small businesses do any such thing; I've heard quite successful entrepreneurs protest forcefully that working out sales and profits in Year 3 is a meaningless exercise. But futurology is not the purpose. Rather, planning forces you to concentrate the mind, and gives you targets and checkpoints. Anyway, you don't start with figures. That three-year plan began with words. Stop losing money in Year 1. Pay the general manager a decent salary in Year 2. Give the owner (who had never taken any monetary reward for her labours) a sensible income in Year 3 and, at the end of that year, move to larger, better premises.

These verbal aims were translated into simple figures, and simple controls were installed to monitor progress: a weekly cash report, a weekly management meeting, an annual month-by-month budget, a monthly profit-and-loss statement. The results were spectacular. The three-year plan targets were met in two. After dodging a three-fold rent increase by moving to much bigger premises in a far less fashionable area, the business was soon selling more in a month than its best previous annual performance.

Slightly bemused by this upsurge, the backer, who knew Lord Weinstock of GEC, mentioned it over lunch one day; he described the simple changes, and said: 'That's all we did.' Britain's greatest maestro of financial management looked at him and replied: 'That's a lot.' That delighted the backer – actually me; and the company, the Angela Flowers Gallery, has supported the maestro's judgement ever since.

Those primitive early disciplines, of course, have been left far behind. Today the accounts and the systems are computerized and highly efficient. The bigger premises in Hackney to which the gallery moved have doubled in size, and a dozen staff now work in a business that Mrs Flowers once ran solo with a part-time assistant. Some 150 shareholders own the company thanks to fund-raising operations under the old Business Expansion Scheme. In 1997 the investors were rewarded for their patience by sales of £2.3 million and profits of £124,000.

The foundations of this success lay in that three-year plan. For most start-ups, Weinstock was absolutely right: what was done so successfully for the gallery is a lot, less in terms of effort than of willpower. It is difficult, until you try, to believe that planning the future improves the present. Time and again in studying big companies, however, I have found that planning for ambitious breakthroughs five years hence pays off in the here and now – even when the planners are expecting no such thing.

The changes and improvements that must be made today if the future plans are to be realized tomorrow will produce immediate benefits. Also, the new mind-set captures opportunities that would otherwise go begging. What you want is what you see. Yet if you listen to many successful entrepreneurs, you would jump to the conclusion that methodical approaches are anathema, unnecessary and even the antithesis of the entrepreneurial ideal.

Thus, Julian Metcalfe of the Pret a Manger fast-food chain told a Royal Society of Arts audience: 'We didn't really plan anything and seek professional advice . . . we still open shops without any analysis at all.' But he also noted, correctly, that 'it takes a long time for a business to succeed, and you've got to think long-term. We always try to think a year ahead.' If that is not planning, what is?

Metcalfe's contradiction suggests a degree of confusion that is also typical of the entrepreneur mentality. An entrepreneur is a typical 'can-do', 'up-and-at-'em' type. When Metcalfe's partner, Sinclair Beecham, assesses a task, though, he truly does plan: 'My partner's way of assessing a risk is to work out that, if we can afford to lose the money, it won't be a big problem. Mine is to do it, anyway, because if you feel passionately about something, it's probably going to work.'

The results of passion, on Metcalfe's own admission, were not all wonderful. They included the creation, 'at vast expense', of a whole new range of sandwiches: 'Customers didn't like it, so we had to abandon it.' Then there was the enormous store in Slough, 'the most expensive store we'd ever opened'. He had 'got fed up with people telling me Pret a Manger would never work outside London'. In actual fact, the store 'didn't work very well. In the end it went'.

Revealingly, Metcalfe puts this sorry incident under the heading 'Getting Carried Away'. Intelligent, common-sense planning is a defence against being carried away and going over the top. The entrepreneur can still be impulsive, but the knack is to confine the impulses to the warm areas of the business; above all, to pleasing the customers. If you act impulsively in the cold areas, you deserve what you get:

> At one time we gave 25 percent of our company to some consultants on the basis that they were going to take us from three to 300 stores and make us rich and famous. It didn't work, and it took a great deal of money and inconvenience to get the company back.

There's an equally powerful lesson to be learned from the career of Sir Mark Weinberg, king of the unit-linked insurance entrepreneurs. He was resentful when American owners forced him to compile a massive five-year plan. To his surprise, however, the exercise threw up a potential disaster in Year 5, which swiftly converted Weinberg to planning.

The dangers of failing to look ahead in an organized manner are too perilous to ignore, while the rewards of thinking and planning ahead are simply (the operative word) too great to ignore. And you can still walk the dog.

The Family Way

'We're trying desperately to hang on to that early successful formula of a very small company.' In case after case, that formula includes family ownership and management. The desperate hangers-on in question, in this example, are the Smurfit family, Ireland's packaging kings. The *paterfamilias*, a rough diamond named Jefferson Smurfit, built the first-stage success, and left the next stages to his four polished sons, headed by Michael.

The formula was so successful that the group is now valued at £2 billion. Companies that start as a family business and stay that way sometimes do carry forwards the original entrepreneurial urge with a consistency and energy that non-family firms find hard to match. Yet nepotism has a bad press: 'From clogs to clogs in three generations' is one famous gibe.

In truth, it is rare for successors to match or surpass the founder's talents, certainly not with the brilliance of Smurfit's second-generation chairman. The 1996 Pulse Survey of UK private companies fully supports this sad observation. In the first generation, families kept up well with the growth rate of non-family companies over the period 1990–94. The second generation fell significantly behind the non-family pace, the third slipped further still, and the fourth grew (on both employment and profits) slowest of all.

As the Survey comments: 'The most likely explanation for these findings is that certain attributes of the founder(s) are associated with, and critical to, a company's success.' Nevertheless, it is wrong to ridicule the family business, despite its unbridled nepotism, in which (to quote one famous Hollywood joke) 'the son also rises'.

Another way of looking at it was expressed in a crack about Robert Sarnoff, the former head of RCA. Bobby, it was said, joined the company at the bottom, but then his father took a fancy to him. The son dissipated General David Sarnoff's splendid legacy by ridiculous mismanagement, notably a half-billion-dollar loss in computers. Once the king of thermionic valves, too, RCA somehow let the semiconductor revolution pass it by.

For every effective dynastic succession (Thomas Watson Sr to Jr at IBM, Israel to Marcus Sieff at Marks & Spencer), big business has seen many notorious hereditary flops of the Hoover variety: Herbert Hoover Jr performed so poorly that his professional management team persuaded the family to eject him. That still didn't save the firm from takeover. The same fate befell Forte: Sir Rocco, following in the footsteps of his father, Lord Forte, lost his takeover battle with Granada.

In smaller firms, innumerable collapses show how often parents misplace their trust in their offspring. But non-family promotions can also be dismal failures – witness John Akers, in whose hands the Watson inheritance fell to bits at IBM. The extraordinary fact is that the family head, Tom Watson Jr, the giant who took the company belatedly but brilliantly into computers, sat on the board of directors during a decade of mismanagement without, so far as any outsider knows, uttering a word of criticism. That was poor family management. Like any other variety of management, it must evolve to meet changing circumstances, knowing what family habits to keep and which to drop, as it takes the expansionary path. With this proviso, the family firm can exploit many advantages. One is that its inheritors literally know what they are doing. They don't have to decide from scratch what business they want to be in.

John and James Martin, for example, inherited the clearest possible mandate: to make the best ejection seats in the world. Their mechanical engineer father, another James, started Martin-Baker to build aircraft, but his plane designs never achieved commercial success. The company changed direction successfully after his test pilot partner, Valentine Baker, was killed in one of the prototypes. That spurred Martin's interest in airborne safety: the first ejection seat resulted at the very end of the Second World War.

By April 1997, according to the *Financial Times*, Martin-Baker ejection seats had saved 6,577 people, gaining 75 percent of a world market where giant companies, mainly American, are dominant. Among aerospace companies, Martin-Baker is unusual in the narrowness of its single-product field. That has been enough to generate sales of £65 million, finance £8 million of annual spending on R & D, and employ 800 people. Such narrowness is far from rare among family businesses, which tend to stick to father's, or even grandfather's, last.

Devotion to a single market or product should be a source of substantial strength. The beloved product or service receives devoted attention, from which it greatly benefits. There is a parallel risk, of course, if anything goes wrong with its single market. The sudden arrival of a new and better technology, for instance – Martin-Baker could be ejected from its king-of-the-market seat as rapidly as any saved pilot.

A family may become blind to trends and changes that are making the business obsolete. For instance, the founding genius of the word-processor, An Wang, fatally missed the PC revolution and handed over a poisoned inheritance to his son. Sometimes it's the father, not the heir, who justifies the 'clogs to clogs' gibe.

Turning an inheritance into a goldmine, rather than a bottomless pit, may require exactly the same talent which An Wang first exploited and then lost: imaginative awareness of the trends. Thus, the coup which created Howard Hodgson's fortune didn't lie in buying his father's funeral business at a bargain price of £14,000 in 1975; success sprang from seeing that the application of efficient business methods to Hodgson & Sons, and then to a series of acquisitions, would create an undertaking, you might say, of major size and significance.

The £6.5 million which Hodgson pocketed from selling his shares to the French was the reward for what two admirable academics, C. K. Prahalad and Gary Hamel, call 'reinventing' your industry and 'regenerating strategy'. That means taking an entirely different approach to the industry and to the way in which you manage your business.

Just as Hodgson made a multiple chain out of funeral parlours, so the Sainsburys built their family firm into one of the country's largest retailers by turning small stores in the Southeast into a nation-wide chain of great supermarkets. Effective family management is always hands-on, however, and that of the Sainsburys grew less formidably effective as management grew apart from 'that early successful formula of a very small company'.

Yet the chain still possesses another valuable attribute of the family firm: the name over the door is personified, and the eponymous person is in an excellent position to lift morale and performance by the personal touch. Family succession can build on this base. It inherently provides a bundle of attributes that every business needs, large or small: a focus of loyalty, an instinct to preserve and enlarge the inheritance for the next generation, and an innate pride in the name and reputation of the firm. A good family business does not know the word 'short-termism'; it builds for the future.

At the same time it never forgets past virtues, and it never undermines both future and present by promoting incompetents. In Japan, which is dominated by family businesses, the matriarchs make sure that only the ablest members of the family run the business. Four IFs govern whether the son or daughter (or niece or nephew) should follow in the family footsteps. That should only happen . . .

1 If they want to
2 If they have demonstrated their ability inside the firm – and preferably outside as well
3 If they are respected by and work well with their ablest non-family colleagues
4 If they are equipped by education and development to lead the firm onwards and upwards.

Michael Smurfit, for example, was sent to Harvard Business School, which equipped him to overcome that dangerous second stage of entrepreneurial development, when the entrepreneur urgently needs reinforcing by professional management. If you can obtain that reinforcement from within the family, the necessary systems and methods can be grafted on to the elements that have brought first-stage success – such as the Smurfit family's marketing platform: 'We got our orders by camping out on doorsteps and keeping very, very close to customers.'

The cons and pros of family succession in fact balance each other out. CON: genetics has no bearing on managerial ability, but (PRO) you're selecting from candidates who have known the business, and been attached to it, all their lives. CON: you can't get the best managers to join a business which will always keep them from the top jobs, but (PRO) the family tradition, built into the fabric of a company, provides an environment of continuity and two-way loyalty that brings out the best in hired hands.

Within that environment, family firms have to follow rules that are no different for non-family entrepreneurship:

1 Promote only on merit.
2 Insist on retirement from operations by 65 at the latest.
3 Promote young talent into positions where it can make a difference while still young.
4 Use elder statesmen (and women) to watch over and guide the young.
5 Keep close to the customers . . .
6 . . . and to the employees.
7 Wage open, critical debate on strategy and tactics.

The final rule, to quote the Pulse Survey, applies only to family firms: 'Consider options other than "hereditary management" when planning the founder's succession.' Absolutely right. The family entrepreneurship can never count on having the good fortune of the Smurfits. If that blessing does occur, though, the presence of uninhibited critics, born to the rule and the role, is another nepotistic asset. As Michael Smurfit has observed, he's subject to review: 'Look, I have highly aggressive, successful and very rich brothers. They need watching, too.' The family way can be OK: but it always needs a great deal of watching.

What the Troubleshooter Shot

Why lay yourself open to criticism by inviting somebody like television troubleshooter Sir John Harvey-Jones into your business? Because criticism is the seed of improvement; because every business can be improved, often radically; and because you can never have too much expert prodding or experienced outside advice. Nor is there any sense in rejecting that advice if it contains criticism. You might as well tell a doctor that your leg isn't broken, whatever the X-ray says.

Broken-legged companies, however, often do just that. Take the interesting case of ACT, the software company which not so long ago disappeared into the embrace of rival Misys. In a previous existence, ACT was known as Apricot Computers: this was the PC business which failed in its brave attempt to become a British Apple. The failure included a foray into Apple's home territory that fizzled out completely.

The absolute, blatant folly of such grand ambitions was argued forcefully by Harvey-Jones when Apricot was featured in the BBC's first *Troubleshooter* series. The trouble that needed shooting was chairman Roger Foster's commitment to the PCs that had originally brought him fame and fortune. Successful entrepreneurs often are overly attached to their origins. Foster boasted about 'some twelve years of continual growth in both sales and profits'. He didn't want to admit, even to himself, that the market had changed to his profound disadvantage, and that the good times had gone for ever. He was very reluctant to take the great man's advice.

Harvey-Jones, though, was right. Willy-nilly, Foster eventually did as bidden and abandoned his own PC ambitions. While the PC side was sold to Mitsubishi of Japan, the remainder prospered enough to fetch £212 million from Misys. Yet the myth persists that, in the cases submitted to him, Sir John's TV troubleshooting somehow failed: that for all his experience and knowledge, ICI's former chairman did not make the right diagnoses and therefore couldn't suggest the right cures. Skills mastered in big business, it was alleged, did not transfer easily to smaller situations – so there. This plain untruth was encouraged by the obvious indignation of some of those (like Foster) whose troubles were shot. Some chinaware brothers resented being chided for their low investment in design. And the Morgan family was angered by the exposure of the inefficient production and under-pricing that helped to explain the huge waiting list for their beloved cars.

However, if you charge too little for a product which you can

make only in very limited quantities, it is not difficult to drum
up excessive demand. Yet even this somewhat bizarre formula
(one which is difficult to emulate) does not justify throwing
money away through sheer inefficiency. For all their pro-
testations, both Morgan and the chinaware company took steps
to remedy some of the more obvious defects revealed by Harvey-
Jones.

The chinaware brothers upped their spending on design. The
managing Morgan learned some more about production engineering, and increased output. All these were obvious and obviously beneficial steps. Any consultant will tell you that their
most powerful recommendations generally are obvious, but
somehow invisible to the managements concerned. Managements may, however, have an unspecified feeling of unease,
which explains why they turn to consultants. After all, Apricot,
Morgan and the other firms studied by Harvey-Jones had volun-
teered for the victim role. But many companies which call for
help actually expect congratulations coupled with some push-
button remedy that will magic away whatever prompted their
SOS. Life is not like that.

Turning to an expert outsider for assistance makes sense,
though, even when the business is flourishing. Expertise adds
a new dimension, as does a detached, objective view. Unlike
you, the outsider has no vested interest in the *status quo*. Every
entrepreneur forms his or her own opinion about the strengths
and weaknesses of the business; many entrepreneurs, however,
see only the strengths. 'The way we do things round here'
becomes set in cement, as it so often does in major corporations.

One of Harvey-Jones's great contributions to ICI was to drill
away at that cement in an attempt to free up the company's
reactions. His entrepreneurial zest, like his naval bluntness, was
among the qualities that made this long-haired maverick an
unusual inhabitant of ICI. The management process on which
he insisted should be basic to any business of any size: collecting
accurate information, analysing what you learn, diagnosing the
faults that need correction and implementing the recommendations.

Using this methodology, a good troubleshooter will uncover

not only the problems that are apparent to the management
(like the ones that bothered Apricot and Morgan), but others
which are unsuspected or tucked out of sight, either consciously
or unconsciously. These sins are unlikely, by the way, to be
subtle matters. Usually the unsuspected discoveries are so blatant
that it is hard for anybody – save the boss and his managers –
to avoid falling over them.

The remedies will probably go far beyond the actual issue
presented, which is often only a symptom of a condition that
requires sweeping change. That's the catch. Major change in
things as they are entails upheaval and a degree of risk, which
always accompanies change, and it implies criticism of the past
and present management of the business. Objections on either
count are purely emotional. That makes the objections stronger,
but it does not make them right.

If the world and market around you are changing, standing
still involves change – and possibly fatal change – in your *relative*
position. In times when markets moved slowly, this relativity
only worsened gradually, too. But these days markets move very
fast. Today very few businesses can ignore change as blithely as
Morgan, whose cars once attracted this comment in *What Car*
magazine: 'Queue here for delivery in next century. Morgans
make no apologies for taking motoring back 50 years.' Mind
you, those prices seem to have advanced into modern times. A
Morgan Plus Four costs roughly the same as a Honda Prelude
VTi, which is faster and comes equipped with all manner of
goodies that the Morgan-makers eschew. But nobody would
queue for a Prelude – it just isn't a Morgan. By ossifying in a
rapidly changing car market, Morgan achieved a rarity value (as
a fossil or a kind of coelacanth in cars) which gave it a Unique
Selling Proposition, a differentiator, but one which guaranteed
that its market niche would remain minute.

Businesses which are many miles removed from the Morgan
cachet still cherish the belief that, like Morgan, they have some
special property that makes them 'different'. When saying this,
though, the managements concerned are not referring to some
reason why the customer should buy from them and not from
somebody else; they mean that the 'difference' justifies the way

in which they manage, no matter how absurd it might seem to a logical external eye.

The first part of the proposition is true: every business, every industry, and every market does differ from every other. But the second part is dangerously false. Every business is also similar to every other in material respects, and the similarities are vitally important. That's where troubleshooters earn their reward and should earn the victim's respect.

Using their wider experience, the troubleshooters cannot only spot the defects that disfigure all businesses and all strategies, and suggest possible cures; they can also lay bare the emotional blockages that have prevented therapy from being applied earlier. The bigger the blockage, the greater the temptation to seek comfort in denial, and to shoot the troubleshooter for bearing the bad news.

Every business needs a Cassandra, a fearless critic who challenges existing policies and actions. It is rarely easy for these to function inside the firm. People who will not take criticism from the former chairman of ICI are not going to accept it from some whipper-snapper of a manager, even if (or perhaps especially if) he is their son. The cure is to build troubleshooting into 'the way we do things round here'.

Deeply wounded by its failure in Vietnam, the US Army developed a process called 'action review' for correcting its mistakes and sustaining its successes. The process amounts to no more than 'reviewing what happened and applying its lessons', according to the Harvard Business School. The lessons, moreover, are passed around to all concerned, so that nobody suffers from the Vietnam Syndrome; allegedly, the USA did not fight its war against the Viet Cong for nine years, but for one year nine times.

Similar failure to correct failure explains the problems at the troubleshot companies – and, indeed, at ICI itself. Significantly, Harvey-Jones had long been a thorn-in-the-flesh critic inside the company before he was elevated to the purple. His heresies helped in his promotion to chairman, because the company had lurched into loss, and radical reforms were clearly required.

Firms which want their troubles shot usually seek help only

when the wolf is already snarling at the door. Good entrepreneurs know that good advice is cheap at any time – including the days of wine, roses and prosperity. The moral is clear. Get your troubleshooting in early, and there should be no real trouble to shoot.

Why Cash is King

'Back to basics' is a far safer rallying cry in management than in politics. The return to basics is the stock-in-trade of turnround managers, company doctors and other revivalists. Even in the most sophisticated businesses, difficult times may reveal the fact that the basics have been improperly executed. Very often, even reformed systems have deteriorated over time.

Which basic is most fundamental? The answer has to be cash. Visiting a business school once, I was told that a sentence of mine was pinned to the bulletin board. This immortal truth consisted of just six simple words: 'Cash in must exceed cash out.' As the academics plainly knew, many managers in large companies never master this concept, simple or not. At ICI, for instance, Sir John Harvey-Jones discovered, on taking firm hold of a loss-making behemoth, that nobody was adequately managing the cash.

The concept of proper cash management is simplicity itself. You get in cash as rapidly as possible, pay out precisely when obligated (not too soon, not too late), keep cash-eating items (such as inventory) as low as possible, and earn the highest going rate on the safe deposit of your funds. Big-time executives are sheltered from these realities of cash flow by the finance director and his cohorts. In smaller companies, there is no shelter: if the cash runs out, the rains pour in.

By the same token, if the flood consists of cash, the business can stay viable despite absence of reported profits. For instance, Time Warner, the media colossus, has not made a profit since the over-priced, over-borrowed merger which created the company years ago. But its free cash flow – the money its managers have available to spend – is ample for their huge daily needs. It was also an adequate base for the multi-billion takeover of Ted Turner's CNN. Cash is not only king, it finances empires.

At the other end of the corporate scale, the truth about cash was brought home to me sharply in the early months of the *Management Today* enterprise. The monthly accounts – the first I had seen for any of the publications on which I had worked – predictably showed start-up losses. But cash was piling up in the corporate coffers. How come?

Subscribers were paying in large numbers, but their cash (conservatively and properly) was being divided between the twelve months of their subscription. The cash balances told the truth: the magazine had got off to a flying financial start. Yet few businesses, large or small, are managed with cash first and foremost in the managing mind.

Trevor Grice, whose initial turnround of Wace Group, a graphic arts business, was very effective, took a different, robust and highly entrepreneurial stance. His managers' bonus payments, for instance, were linked to both operating profit and cash generation; if the managers failed one test, they failed both. The logic behind this iron rule is that increasing efficiency always shows up in the cashbox.

In Grice's philosophy, business strategy is a simple three-legged stool. Entrepreneurs have a natural orientation towards the first leg, sales expansion, the target of all the marketing effort and product plans to which they devote so much splendid energy. Many an entrepreneur has discovered that, without the other two legs, expanding sales may not prove such a warm and wonderful experience. This vital pair are cost reduction and price increases. Combine the two, and profit margins must rise delectably. Combine that with a successful assault on working capital, and the result will be a warming pile of extra cash. Let the costs and the capital run out of control while expanding sales, though, and the cash will also go into a tailspin. Ruin can swiftly follow. Note the reference to working capital, which is intimately involved with both cash and efficiency.

The definition of working capital is the money tied up in stock of all kinds, plus the difference between creditors and debtors. At major US companies, the resulting sum averages around 20 percent of sales. That average may be grossly excessive. According to *Fortune* magazine, working capital zealots are now aiming at a target of zero. The secret lies in speed. Use stock more rapidly, fill the customers' requirements faster, get the payment in sooner, and you require less capital and generate more cash.

Asian wonders such as just-in-time delivery and *kanban* stock control (which operates by a simple coloured card system) work the necessary magic rapidly and are neither mysterious nor complex. Yet there is an even simpler speed-up approach. The true entrepreneur instinctively cuts out 'hand-overs' (when work or paper passes from hand-to-hand) and eliminates second-guessing, in which approval is mandated all the way up the line.

Big bureaucratic businesses love to breed hand-overs. Take the example of an insurance company where a straightforward life policy had to pass through some fourteen head office departments; a well-staffed extra process was needed just to keep track of the paperwork's journey. The net result: issuing this standard product required twenty-four days, when only ten to thirty minutes was necessary.

That example comes from Jim Champy, a high priest of re-engineering. His new-sounding management religion can also work wonders but, again, without using any magic that is unfamiliar to the entrepreneur. The key principle is to identify and examine the processes which are vital to the business, to work through them to find the bottlenecks – hand-overs, second-guessing and so on – and then to work with all concerned to reduce cost and increase speed.

Speeding-up is grist to the mill for cost-cutters like Grice, but he is equally emphatic about the price side of the profit margin equation. Allow managers to take over the pricing job, and usually they do not seek to exercise control over realized prices. They give away profits and cash with price-cuts, discounts, promotions and over-generous terms of trade, all in a feverish effort to retain or gain business.

Rather, they should ask the entrepreneurial questions: What percentage of business will be lost if I raised my realized prices by x percent – or gained if I cut them? How much business can I lose before damaging profits – and how much must I gain to compensate for x percent lower prices? If these critical (and easily answered) questions are not posed, the most common result is not over-charging but under-pricing. That is not going back to basics; it is going forwards into failure.

Getting the cash right, however, isn't the only essential in going back to basics. The Clean Dozen growth principles on page 2 form a set of fundamentals, too. The financial numbers, including the cash flows, are the result of effective management of people, non-financial processes, strategy and tactics. Treating accountancy as the supreme guide to better non-financial management is the ultimate basic.

Some of the guidance will be provided by 'rules of thumb', basic but powerful principles founded on experience. The thumb is a most useful digit, and its messages should never be ignored. I'm especially attached to one promulgated by an exceptionally sharp financial manager, Harold Geneen, builder of the ITT conglomerate. He discovered that if a budget was missed in the first quarter, the deficit was never made up over the rest of the year, no matter what promises and protests the managers made.

The fundamentals and the rules of thumb always speak for themselves. Like the principles of cash management, though, they are honoured at least as much in the breach as the observance – especially if the economy or the company is booming. The tendency is for the entrepreneur (gung-ho for expanding sales, remember) to forget about the basics, concentrate on meeting the booming demand, and never mind the costs or the cash.

In fact, the cash position is particularly vulnerable at times of rapid growth. The entrepreneur can readily plunge into the trap known as 'over-trading'. It is as easy (if not easier) to go broke by selling too much as it is by selling too little. A business that greatly expands sales will also greatly expand the expense of sales – and that can be a fatal trap if the gap between the two flows of cash (in and out) becomes too large.

Normally, the expenses of sales (including wages and supplies) have to be met before the income from sales is received. If the business expands too rapidly, it simply runs out of ready cash, cannot meet its bills, and collapses. That's why up-front businesses (like *Management Today*, with its subscriptions gathered in advance) are so attractive. The money is sitting happily in the bank ahead of need.

Devices such as discounts for partial or complete early payment have a similar function. Getting money up-front always helps as an antidote to over-trading and over-zealous banks – as that superb entrepreneur Henry Ford once demonstrated in spectacular fashion. When the banks attempted to put the squeeze on him, Henry broke free in a single bound by making Ford dealers deposit cash in advance if they wanted any of his cars to sell.

Using the customers as sources of up-front working capital is fine. Never rely, however, on delaying payment to suppliers for the same purpose. Entrepreneurs sometimes use this deceptive route when their own capitalization is inadequate, often combining the ploy with trying to accelerate receipts from customers. Whenever that happens, a chill runs down my spine, and I mournfully order the funeral wreath. That isn't cash management: it's skating on thin ice – and thin ice easily cracks.

2

The Methods of Midas

Use Your Ingenuity

The single most important asset of the entrepreneur is one which most of the breed possess: persistence in the face of obstacles and setbacks. Year in, year out, come rain, come shine, the entrepreneur labours on. The quality is admirable, but needs to be used to its full advantage. To make the cause a truly winning one, other attributes are essential – and ingenuity is high among them.

Often entrepreneurs show a persistence that makes Robert the Bruce's spider seem positively weak-willed. Consultant Michael de Kare Silver of the Kalchas Group tells the story of Lawrence Eisenstadt, who took over his uncle's coffee shop and then came up with a very ingenious idea: repacking the tea landed at the nearby docks into small bags. This innovation gave Eisenstadt a successful local business, but the big food companies joined him and beat him.

He kept on searching for new product ideas that would pay much better than the café. Aged fifty, he invented sugar sachets, packages with just enough sugar for one cup. He built another successful business, but the big sugar companies joined him and beat him. Eisenstadt still wouldn't give up. Another idea came from a diabetic friend who liked his drinks sweet: the entrepreneur turned into a chemist, found the right saccharin mixture by trial and error, patented his development, and the branded Sweet 'N' Low finally made his fortune.

As Eisenstadt's story shows, the ingenious product idea is

not enough on its own. Kalchas research unearthed 130 British entrepreneurs who started up with bright innovations in the early 1990s. Of that number, just twenty were outstandingly successful, with significant profits, seven-figure turnovers, one-man band status left behind, and professional management, systems and procedures in place. Silver identified three common characteristics of these founder-entrepreneurs, not one of which involved the idea in itself.

1 They had worked in the industry for many years.
2 They clearly saw the gap in the market and had deeply researched its potential.
3 They had obtained solid finance from banks, which backed the start-up and were fully persuaded of the business case.

Persistence and experience, as in Eisenstadt's case, went hand-in-hand. To give some examples from the Kalchas research:

'I'd been a butcher all my life, and I'd been experimenting with speciality sausages for years until I realised I could make a business out of that alone . . .'
   'After years of experience of house-building, I reckoned there would be little competition for low-priced, easy to assemble home lodge units . . .'
   'Despite mistakes and setbacks along the way, we all along knew there was a need for our speciality store products.'

Coming up with unconventional ideas, even improvisations, makes the difference between breaking through, plodding on, and maybe breaking down under the weight of those mistakes and setbacks. When it comes to ingenuity in the face of adversity, in fact, you cannot beat a truly determined entrepreneur.
   Especially when starting up, a business will probably lack vital elements such as: sales leads, office space, staff and management know-how. All these can be bought, of course, but that requires the most common (and serious) missing ingredient of all: money. If you lack the backing of supportive bankers, making

do without wealth is where persistence and ingenuity really prove themselves. Real-life examples include a wily fellow who won badly needed sales leads by hanging around and nabbing visitors to the trade fair stands of large competitors.

For office space, the neat solution is barter: swapping services rendered for square feet. If you need cheap labour, to make letter-box drops, say, what about making a charitable donation to some educational establishment in exchange for student services? Even management know-how has been found on the cheap by becoming a guinea-pig for a research project: academics descend on the business to obtain material for their research, and in the process you get free consultancy.

Money remains the largest problem. Again, there are useful wrinkles. In retailing, have you thought of waiting until Friday to pay bills, after estimating weekend receipts? Generally, try paying bills in person, rather than by post. According to the American magazine *Inc.*, from which these examples are taken, that enabled one hard-up entrepreneur to extend his credit from a week to a full month.

On the other side of the cash hurdle, debt-collection, another hard-pressed business billed for payment within thirty days and charged 1.5 percent interest for every thirty days over the deadline. When trade had become sufficiently solid (which took five years, a fact that proves the value of persistence), this firm insisted on up-front payments of 25 percent. The up-front payment does wonders for cash flow, and is nice work – if you can get it.

What you need to get most, though, is permanent capital. Often the sums required are small. The group of businesses studied by *Inc.* prove the point. They covered an enormous range: sporting goods, waste petroleum services, computer networking, pizza restaurants, distributing skin-care products and gifts, health foods, on-site health programmes for employees, and sandwich shops. They had grown to sales totals ranging from $1 million to $355 million (with two franchise operations weighing in respectively at $164 million and $2.2 billion). But none had raised more than $4,000 in start-up capital.

One woman had started with no equity at all. Her solution

was to apply for seventeen credit cards, borrowing up to the hilt on all of them. In financing their drive for success, these businesses substituted obstinate, ingenious persistence for the resources they didn't have. The sandwich shop owner, for instance, chose completely the wrong site for his first shop. Rather than give up, he didn't pay his suppliers and got away with the risky game: they inadvertently financed a second shop in a better location (thus demonstrating a further essential adjunct to persistence, the ability to learn from your own mistakes).

Another man, needing to give the impression of a sizeable business, invented a whole cast of phantom employees and functions. Another went round suggestion boxes, and stuffed them with notes demanding his products. Cutting corners in that style, if taken too far, goes beyond the bounds of absolute honesty. But the entrepreneur is often desperately hard-pressed, drawing no salary, and is reduced to expedients such as raiding dustbins for usable materials, or, very possibly, using home as office and the family as unpaid help.

The better answer is to ensure that you are adequately financed from the start, though that is easier said than done. Many start-ups compound the problem by reluctance to give away equity. One brilliant electronics expert for that reason turned down an offer of finance from one of Britain's wealthiest family companies. The expert actually boasted about how he financed the business by getting swift payment from his customers and delaying payments to suppliers – the lethal trap identified in the previous chapter. The business failed, naturally.

The same stumbling block afflicted one man who wanted a relative to guarantee a £2,500 bank loan, but didn't want to surrender any shares. Then that saving ingenuity came to the rescue. He offered the guarantor a £300 'equity' reward upfront. That left the business the £2,200 needed for the launch – and everybody lived happily ever after.

Once you've overcome the start-up difficulties, ingenuity is just as important. The more successful a business becomes, the more it faces a serious obstacle: conventional thinking. For instance, it makes sense to keep production runs as long as possible by forecasting demand and serving the customers from stock. Right? Wrong.

'When you build to customer order rather than to inventory, you no longer have to make a production forecast. You also eliminate the cost of making the wrong stuff and having to discount it in order to sell it,' writes James P. Womack, co-author with Daniel T. Jones of a book called *Lean Thinking*. Much of their advice, like this, is counter-intuitive. It is not what you expect to be true. Really, the supposedly intuitive opponent has not looked at the facts with an open mind, is not prepared to go against the crowd, and prefers convention to logical truth. That's the exact opposite of the true entrepreneur.

Entrepreneurs rely heavily on intuition, but that means *their* intuition, not the shared preconceptions and misconceptions of the mass. Their intuition tells them, among other crucial things, that going with the crowd is far less likely to lead to major rewards than finding an individual path. The logic of methods like making only to order would appeal to them instantly – especially when they see how much manufacturing time and inventory can be reduced (very likely, by two-thirds and 70 percent).

Take another common problem: the business with seasonal peaks in demand. You deal with that by hiring temporary staff at the busy periods, don't you? Wrong again, according to an American music wholesaler. His ingenious solution is to work the full-time staff all hours and all days in the busy season. In other periods, they work short weeks. Moreover, every worker is expected to tackle any job – and that includes the boss.

Give in to the difficulties and limitations that confront every business and business idea, and you'll get absolutely nowhere. Persist in finding ingenious ways round the obstacles, though, and the ingenuity itself can be the mainspring of major success.

How to Buy Success

Buying a business is easier than building one, and much, much quicker. Properly controlled, acquisition is an important weapon which suits the aggressive mentality of the entrepreneur. It is no easier route to entrepreneurial victory than organic growth, however, unless certain plain rules are followed. Break the rules – as most buyers do – and the deal is likely to be broken-backed.

The most important of those rules, therefore, is obvious enough: keep the rules. This was brought home to one management expert when acting as a non-executive director of a public company. Its executive directors, entrepreneurial and eager, were burning to expand, using their shares and any money they could borrow, through acquisition. The expert's rules, which he had long advocated, are plain common sense:

1 Only buy businesses which you fully understand – never businesses about which you know little or nothing.
2 Never buy businesses which are a long distance away geographically unless you can put your own capable management in place.
3 Don't buy management – buy the business. The business stays, but the management may go, or fail, which is worse.
4 Don't do complicated deals – Keep It Simple, Stupid.

The expert found himself approving, with the rest of the board, a business which was almost wholly unfamiliar, located far away, entirely dependent on the management efforts of the vendors, and purchased through a deal of labyrinthine complexity. It was, naturally, a total disaster, whose only contribution to the purchaser was to help bring the group to its knees.

It is important to bear such horror stories in mind because, sooner or later, the notion of buying somebody else's business occurs to every entrepreneur. That may well mean bucking the odds. It is notorious that big companies get half of such purchases wrong. Actually, it is worse than that. According to one study, another third make only marginal returns, leaving a mere 17 per cent that truly pay off.

With smaller firms, the mistakes are certainly no fewer. The hit/miss ratio of one very sophisticated City investor is typical. It created a fund to win higher returns by picking unquoted companies – the very kind of business which is liable to tempt the entrepreneur. Over fifty buys were selected, no doubt with

all the conscientious investigation that the City calls 'due dili-
gence'; a third of these beauties got sold for losses, five of them
whoppers. Almost as many investments yielded a profit, and the
remainder are by no means all among 'the living dead' (an
eloquent description). But the overall aim of outdoing investments quoted on the stock market was missed – for when smaller
firms fall, they can drop a long way very quickly. There's no
cushion of cash or assets on which the entrepreneur can fall
back.

That's why venture capitalists set such apparently greedy
targets: they aim to multiply their money no less than ten times
in five years. That's their cushion and they need it badly, to
make sure that the successes outweigh the inevitable failures.
Their avaricious formula has lessons for everybody who is thinking of buying a business.

What do you want it to be worth in five years, say? Divide
that sum by ten, as the venture capitalists do, and that's your
target for after-tax profits five years on. How will that bullseye
be hit? Can it be done at all? Unless the goal and the gold are
within reach, and the buyer knows how to get them, the potential buy had best be shunned like several plagues – at the price
on offer, that is.

The alternative is to work back from the truly feasible profits
to establish a yardstick for offering less to the eager seller. He
may refuse – but what have you lost? Learn a lesson from the
world's most successful investor, Warren Buffett, who built his
billions from investments as far apart as a furniture supermarket
in Nebraska, which he owned outright, and Walt Disney, Coca-
Cola and Gillette, where he bought substantial stakes.

Buffett was never in a hurry to buy; rather, he refused to
invest until he found a real bargain (as those all were). If the
buying urge becomes burning, or even addictive, serious mistakes are inevitable. First time round, the investment house
mentioned above rushed in where Buffett would have feared
to tread. Second time round, starting a new fund, it was less
foolish and stood a reasonable chance of being more successful
overall. All the same, a third of this second batch of investments
were sold for losses.

The entrepreneur who is making a one-off company purchase can't afford such odds. It is possible, however, to achieve 100 percent hit ratios by following the non-financial safeguards that are clear from the fund's experience – and everybody else's. First, never invest in strategic weakness: ensure that the business is well placed in its market, or will reinforce a strong position in your own sector. For example, Ted Fortsmann made his fortune by obeying that first principle. He became excited about a company making, of all things, porcelain miniatures, solely because it dominated that market. That worked out fine. Fortsmann had his early disasters, though, including a company whose recording tape dominated nothing. A fellow victim not long ago sent Fortsmann a chunk of the offending tape with this message: 'Never, ever, ever forget your roots.'

In other words, learn from your mistakes. You should make fewer errors if you follow the rules and only buy a business which you know almost as well as your own (if not as well). Otherwise, it requires much homework to divine the target's true strength. People are often tempted to brush the issue of strength aside, buying a business with a weak market position, poor assets and feeble management – on the assumption that their genius will wonderfully improve all three. Sometimes the magic works; mostly it doesn't.

It is obviously far better to buy strong businesses with strong managers, provided (see above and below) that the price is right. If the management is not strong enough, its defects may not appear before purchase. If the managerial faults surface thereafter, remove or reinforce the defective managers without delay. Missed budgets and falsified forecasts are always an ominous sign. Remember Geneen's Law (page 27): a missed first quarter's budget is almost certainly a missed year.

The fund's paramount lesson, however, is elementary common sense: don't overpay. An old rule of thumb is to pay no more in capital than the target company earns in sales – and preferably much less. That leaves room to recover if a mistake has been made, and skeletons start tumbling out of cupboards. That principle would outlaw the great majority of big-time corporate buys, but given the often awful results of these purchases, that would be wonderful news for shareholders (those of the buying company, that is).

All the same, there is a place for the company buyer. Just as war is diplomacy by other means, so good acquisition is organic growth by other methods. How is organic expansion achieved? The answer is a growth formula which is also a clear guide to intelligent acquisition. Organic growth rests on three prime ingredients identified by *Fortune*:

1 Strong management teams.
2 Heavy ploughback into the product or service and the relevant technologies.
3 Recruitment and intensive training of the best people you can find for all positions.

If an acquisition already has these three basic characteristics, buying into its growth potential saves a great deal of time and trouble. The purchaser can expand much faster than by organic means alone – if, that is, the serious potential man-traps are recognized in advance and avoided.

The first snag is that it is easy to be wrong about the quality of another firm's management; although, in close-knit industries, competitors and your own colleagues usually have a clear idea of where the genuine talent lies.

Second, opinions on the quality of the purchased technology can also be misleading, but, again, experts who know and live in the sector should be in a far stronger position to make an excellent judgement.

Third, since you're buying management, the logic largely vanishes if the key people do. Don't be deceived by monetary devices designed to retain their services. If your new managers (which is how they should be viewed) are staying only because they are held by golden chains, they are the wrong people.

The financial problems that almost destroyed Saatchi & Saatchi, then the world's largest advertising agency, were partly caused by the pressure of final payments to ex-proprietors who promptly retired with their loot. Many a company, similarly beguiled by the 'earn-out', in which the ultimate payment depends on post-acquisition results, has found itself paying vast final cheques to the vendors *after* a year which met the target but *during* the following year, when the results have already savagely deteriorated.

The earn-out was an apparently clever way of taking the risk out of acquisition. There are no such ways. The risk is always that the profits earned by the acquired company will not cover the cost of the capital employed for the purchase – meaning the cost of equity (whose owners will expect a handsome return) as well as that of cash and loans.

This concept is so basic that, naturally, the clever minds in the City ignored it for years, blithely encouraging deals that undermined many a balance sheet. If the cost of capital is not covered, the equity is being eaten away. Eventually the simple arithmetic sank in under the smart name of Economic Value Added. If the potential EVA (basically the extent to which true profits exceed the real cost of capital) is non-existent, the deals now tend to fade away.

That may explain why merger and acquisition booms always unexpectedly lose impetus. Keep that simple thought – that buys must pay for their cost – in the front of your mind at all times, remembering, too, more simple knowledge. The bad news will come before the good. No buyer of smaller companies will tell you any different. As an immortal phrase has it, 'Lemons ripen faster than cherries'.

The Franchise Affair

Some entrepreneurial routes are easier than others; and in theory the franchise should be easiest of all. When you jump on somebody else's bandwagon, whether the franchise sells wedding wear, woollens, hamburgers or cleans drains, you are not gambling on the market or the product or service; you can see, use and touch whatever the franchise sells.

Everything already exists, and the basic cost is predetermined. Since the franchisor, moreover, has a vested interest in achieving success much broader than yours alone, you have a disproportionate benefit from all his marketing expenditure and other investment in the brand. Troubling questions of supply and customer choice don't arise, either, since they are pre-ordained as part of the agreement with the franchisor.

The latter, however, is in control. The franchise gambit has been successful in many markets at creating two whole classes of entrepreneur, the franchisor and the franchisee; but it is all too clear which is the upper class. Witness the Benetton supremacy. The family could never have developed its worldwide retail expansion to the power of n without using the franchise method to help finance and generate the growth. The result was to turn the Benettons into commercial aristocrats.

In the mid-1990s they enjoyed over $1.5 billion of sales – light years away from Giuliana Benetton's first woollens, made on a home knitting-machine and sold shop to shop by brother Luciano. The first factory opened in 1965, the first store three years later. Brothers Gilberto and Carlo tasted the honey and joined a firm which by the late 1980s had 3,500 stores in fifty-four countries expanding by the phenomenal rate of one per day.

Jumping on a bandwagon that's moving with such un-exampled global vitality offers several advantages, in addition to those listed above, to the franchisee. For example, you are protected to some extent against your own failings. Poor performance by the franchised entrepreneur will damage the brand and the franchisor's revenues, so managerial and other assistance may be available if required. There is a catch, of course: unless the brand is truly powerful, you won't have a powerful outlet.

In hard fact, losing both money and the business is perfectly possible. Buying a franchise from a marvellous multinational name such as Benetton or McDonald's should, of course, be a win–win, great for both sides, but *caveat emptor* must apply – the buyer has to beware. Like any other entrepreneur, a franchisee is investing hard-earned and hard-borrowed money in a business. If the right key questions get the wrong answers, the basic rules of any business will be broken, and somebody – the franchisee – is bound to suffer.

The first hard truth about franchises is that they are sure to benefit franchisor more than franchisee. If the latter could make more money by operating his own outlets, he would (and does). Especially in the early days, however, when resources are scarcest, the franchising entrepreneur is only too happy to grow faster by tapping other people's finance. The franchisee is in part a banker who pays for the privilege of financing the franchisor.

The latter's benefits aren't confined to the capital kindly supplied by the purchaser of the franchise. The franchisor also gains from the hard work of a self-motivated, self-managing entrepreneur. It's a fair exchange, in the best cases, for the latter buys into a business which is backed by national advertising, equipped with efficient systems and complete with a strong customer base.

A group like McDonald's, by winning another restaurant to add to its 23,000 total (expanding by six a day world-wide), with 18,000 franchises and affiliates, expands that base. Adding maybe another £1 million of sales after a year, the new franchise spreads the costs of those efficient systems over still greater turnover. As for the new franchisee, he joins over 12,000 colleagues – some 80 percent of Mcstores are franchised world-wide, although the percentage in Britain is far smaller.

Joining this hamburger legion doesn't come cheap. McDonald's charges franchisees a varying rent plus an invariable five percent of net revenues; investment in equipment and décor will cost from £40,000 to £500,000; and a long time will be spent in training. But you win control of a not-so-small business for twenty years, and probably a successful one. The successful will join McDonald's heroes like Mike Charles and Clive Aronson.

Aronson, a trained accountant, didn't stay content with a single outlet in Glasgow; he expanded to three, one of which was the first 'drive-thru' in Scotland. The novelty introduced an unusual and significant element of risk. In fact, the drive-thru needed help from McDonald's itself to recover from a false start. Aronson's experience emphasizes that franchise profits don't fall off trees. As with any business, you have to work for your success.

The franchise entrepreneurs come from all manner of backgrounds. Charles was working for British Airways when he decided to get a franchise. His management know-how, though, wasn't acquired in the air, but on the ground at McDonald's management programme. This provides several of the skills whose lack causes small businesses such grief: how to budget, how to understand accounts, how to motivate staff, and how to market. You can't say it's a free education since you pay for the franchise; but it is education with a prompt pay-off.

Chains with reputation, experience and success even within hailing distance of McDonald's, of course, are few and far between. When looking at other franchise possibilities, would-be franchisees want to ensure that they get the same high-class treatment. These are some key questions which must be rigorously pursued:

1 What do you think of the product or service? Is it really good? Would you buy it yourself?
2 Will you get high standards of training, guidance and marketing support? (McDonald's intensive four-stage training takes up to nine months full-time, two years part-time.)
3 Did the former franchisee (if any) prosper or perish?
4 Are existing franchisees happy with the relationship and their results?
5 Is the franchisor's own company rich, successful and growing?
6 What happens when you've got grievances?

If the franchisor simply gets the market wrong, so do you. Even a McDonald's can stumble over its marketing. The UK boss, Paul Preston, admitted that a 1991 survey revealed a 'horrifying' gap (since corrected) between McDonald's self-image and the views of those who count, the customers; they thought McDonald's 'loud, brash, American, successful, complacent, uncaring, insensitive, disciplinarian, insincere, suspicious and arrogant'.

The saga of McPloughman's, a cheese-and-pickle variant, was a particular horror: 'Customers didn't want the product and our staff were embarrassed even to have to say McPloughman's.' You can't blame the staff, but you can blame McDonald's for not having researched the product adequately. In the end, the

small businessman in the franchise depends on the big businessman in the head office – so make sure that there's an open
channel for your views about any McPloughman of a brainwave.

The dependence on head office can turn sour. If a substantial
group of franchisees become disaffected, that will have an effect
on the business – happy customers don't emerge from unhappy
shops. For example, the franchisee wants a substantial catch-
ment area to himself, but in the US Benetton shops were opened
too close to each other, and were allegedly under-supplied with
goods. The number of US outlets at one point fell by a spectacular
two-thirds, leaving many litigious, angry shopkeepers.

Benetton has also faced legal disputes in Europe, for a different
but equally threatening reason. Those sensational ads featuring
gory images upset the retailers, giving German franchisees
(whose sales were tumbling) an excuse to withhold payment for
goods. They in turn were sued by Benetton. Over in McDonald's
home territory in the mid-1990s, the native franchisees were
also restless: sales figures sagged as the management lost its
touch and the formula its magic.

Over-expansion affected the decline, too, and brought more
complaints. McDonald's decided to close 115 smaller outlets. In
the last analysis, though, a corporation with $8.28 billion of
sales and $1.57 billion of profits is unlikely to be moved far
by a group of disgruntled franchisees, let alone a single upset
individual. Franchises are formula-based companies, and in
business a winning formula tends to become Holy Writ, even if
the victories are ebbing away.

Benetton, for instance, stayed wedded to only two collections
a year at a time when rivals were changing fashions every few
weeks. The risks of such a strategy, in the fast-moving fashion
trade, are obvious, but Luciano called his system 'perfect'. Since
nothing is ever perfect in business management, the word is
perfectly worrying in itself.

If mismanagement and disgruntlement can develop in great
and successful franchise operations, much worse can follow in
minor and less well-managed ones. Since you are becoming, in
effect, part of the corporation, it is crucial to be as happy with
its ethos, management style and policies as if it were your own

business. But the connection also has some characteristics of the employee relationship: as with any career, make certain that you work only for an excellent employer.

Finally, never forget the get-rich-quick acid test. If the franchisor is dangling the bait of small risk and tiny investment for a whopping return, run for the hills. That is precisely the kind of offer that comes from a smooth (or rough) operator who is more interested in selling the franchise to you than goodies to the customers. Accept, and you are liable to be sold in more senses than one.

Mastering the Sharp End

Behind every resounding entrepreneurial success lies a vital transition to managerial excellence. This moment of truth comes quite early in the enterprise's career. The problem is that fast growth puts a heavy strain on processes and systems; but it is a rare entrepreneur who comes naturally by process and system skills. That is why so few break through into the big time and develop into all-round business successes.

The transition provides a tough test of character and business intelligence. Many would-be entrepreneurs never even summon up the will to make the effort. But one group of businessmen got lucky. They were given a helping hand for the elevation required to achieve their ambitious target: to expand their sales nearly four times in three years, and to raise their business efficiency at the same time. In fact, you could hardly achieve the former without the latter – which is the whole point of the transition.

The Japanese group Sharp Electronics had selfish motives for its helpfulness. It could not meet its own target – the massive 285 percent, three-year rise in British sales just mentioned – without assisting its small company dealers to cross the management barrier. Sharp operate only through dealers, and they had to grow in step. So the company very sensibly offered them a course in advanced business techniques.

Their subsequent experience proves that any entrepreneur, in any business, could and should learn the same relatively cheap lesson. The deal was attractive enough to persuade over 80 percent of dealers selling Sharp photocopiers to sign up for a programme called 'Integrated Quality Standard'. The project actually aimed beyond quality in pursuit of total business development. Not only would sales soar four-fold over the three years, if IQS paid off, but profits would also multiply.

What did the dealers need to know? The programme forced them to concentrate on management matters which affect all smaller companies, but which most (shopkeepers and other traders in particular) never tackle with true professionalism. The needs cover every function, starting with top management itself. The boss of the business must define and document policies for the whole spectrum of operations. Nothing can be left out. That means covering finance (how the company raises and uses its cash); marketing (how it finds its customers and services their needs); sales (how the actual sales process is managed to achieve optimum profits); the administrative tasks of operations and services; the statutory needs of health and safety; the semi-voluntary but equally important issues of the environment; and (the key to everything else) human resources.

The reasons why human resources, otherwise known as people, hold the key begin at the top. Establishing a 'delegate, not abdicate' structure and culture is crucial. John Keith, whose Business Development Unit consultancy was hired by Sharp to run the IQS project, says: 'The biggest problem is changing from themselves to a management team.' The freebooting entrepreneur, in this case very likely a former copier salesman, must install both management disciplines and people skilled enough to apply them.

It is no easier for sales people to transform themselves into entrepreneurs than for a salesperson to make the notoriously difficult transition to effective manager. Sharp's dealers, though typically only employing between thirty and fifty staff, had several incentives to take their heads out of the usual small business sand. The industry had earned a bad name for the financial skulduggery that attracted the disapproval of the Office of Fair Trading. IQS guaranteed, among many other points vital to customers, that the finance and leasing arrangements would be honest and transparent.

Another compelling reason was that Sharp needed badly to break into the corporate market, selling bigger copiers to bigger companies. The dealers were just as hungry for the big time. But sophisticated customers buying more sophisticated products require higher standards from their suppliers. The upgrading, up-market technique, however, is one which the Japanese have used to great advantage.

Some variant of 'Pile 'em high and sell 'em cheap', Jack Cohen's famous starting-point for Tesco, is the way that many entrepreneurs begin: lacking other means of differentiation, they cut prices. Japanese invaders like Sharp, too, have customarily used low prices for high-class goods to crack Western markets where they had no presence.

Once a sizeable market has been attracted, however, the obvious move is upwards in price and, if necessary (as it almost certainly will be), in quality. If you want to upgrade your trade and your clientele, you have to upgrade your management. The necessary degree of uplift was made clear in the Sharp case by an initial, quick appraisal which showed each dealer, activity by activity, where he fell short, measured in precise percentages.

Inevitably, there is a long distance to travel between this starting-point and the objective. If the aim is to have a professional management system, however, your own final assessment is never enough. How do you rate by outside standards? In the Sharp case, the dealers aimed for external certification by an independent body, testifying that the company had satisfied six sets of quality standards, with annual checks to follow.

The sponsor claimed that this was the first time that anybody had integrated as many as half-a-dozen of these standards. They come complete with mysterious initials and numerals (like ISO 9000) and certification badges, to which the British Standards Institution will happily act as guide. While nice for letterheads, though, these decorations are not important in themselves.

What matters is that every single item in the business system has been examined. What's found wanting (or missing altogether) then gets submitted to planning, improvement and

testing – and testing is the word. Take finance. How many proprietors, hand on heart, can swear that the following are up to
snuff?

- financial planning
- budgeting
- margin control
- management accounting
- variance analysis
- costing systems
- cash management

Anybody who needs 'variance analysis' explained needs much
else besides, but there's no point in producing a timely and
accurate set of weekly or monthly figures without plotting them
against budget and quickly (a) finding out what caused any
variances, and then (b) correcting any revealed faults with equal
swiftness.

Figure-work is not just an accounting exercise. The power of
financial control and analysis was shown by William Morris,
Lord Nuffield, many times in his career. In the 1921 slump,
Morris cut the price of the Cowley saloon by nearly a quarter,
against all advice. In fact, he had a much better understanding
of the relationship between volume and cost than his advisers.
Cowley output quintupled from its low point, reaching 30 percent above pre-slump levels, and profit per car jumped to over
three times the £15 gloomily forecast by the advisers.

A red-hot modern manufacturer such as Compaq Computer
rests on precisely the same figure power. After plunging into
loss in 1991, Compaq changed its 'financial model'. Where it
had relied on high prices and relatively low volumes, Compaq
now aimed, just like Morris seventy years before, at much higher
volumes achieved by sharply lower prices. The result was a spectacular increase in sales and profits, and world leadership in PCs.
Given that so much, as in this case, rests on the financial model,
this is one responsibility that the entrepreneur cannot delegate.

Nobody pretends that learning to understand the construction
and dynamics of financial models, or modernizing management

in other ways, comes easily or cheaply. At the most, however, the IQS programme took thirty consultancy days; some of Sharp's dealers had already embarked on their own quality programmes, and needed less help. But the overall experience is a good guide to the cost of elevating management capability. The average dealer faced a bill for £7,000–£8,000, while the highest amounts paid were £10,000–£11,000.

The dealers were lucky to have a Japanese supplier picking up the other half of the tab. But even at £14,000 to £22,000, the total cost should be quickly recovered. At one small business of my acquaintance, the reigning entrepreneur found that just updating and computerizing the management accounting system was the critical factor in turning a £100,000 loss into a profit almost twice as high. This expenditure is not cost for its own sake, but the deliberate investment of money to earn high returns.

Money is by no means all of the cost, however. Relatively small entrepreneurs like these – fifty-five dealers with 130 outlets, mostly exclusive to Sharp – have only a few managers and supervisors. Management uplift demands that they all commit a great deal of time and effort to the pursuit of excellence. As Keith says: 'They have got businesses to run. How hard and fast can you push them?'

That's the snag that kills many efforts at self-improvement. The will may be there, but the over-stretched entrepreneur is far more comfortable selling than learning. Yet the real issue is not how hard and fast you are pushed, or push yourself, but how good a business you run, and how its performance compares with the competition.

That consideration emerged very significantly from the start of the Sharp programme. The dealers insisted that they should all plunge into IQS simultaneously, and not in stages, as their friendly supplier originally intended. The reason? Nobody wanted another dealer to steal a competitive advantage – and that's what the business of business is all about.

Realizing the Dream

'A dream come true' is how Soichiro Honda regarded his first true motorbike – and 'Dream' it was duly called.

This process of turning dreams into reality is the essence of being a successful entrepreneur. But how do you actually go about the conversion? It isn't a matter of wild hunches or inspired guesswork (though these may well have a place). Dream realization can be subjected to planned processes as usefully as anything else in human activity.

First, the dreamer must start from the right place with the right question: What is the problem? That is, what really is the dream, and what needs to be solved before it can be realized? The dream isn't usually something like, 'To continually enhance the ability to trade creatively, ethically and profitably', which happens to be the mission statement for the Body Shop. At the start Anita Roddick and her husband were inspired by a single strong idea: marketing cosmetics produced without torturing animals. That idea happened to be highly creative, genuinely ethical and exceedingly profitable. The Body Shop's hard success could later be justified by high-falutin', soft words.

Almost invariably, though, the entrepreneur's dream is very hard: a product or a service for which he sees a market. The dream may be inspired by technology or a perceived market need or both. For instance, Edwin Land's dream was to allow people to see their photographs almost immediately, rather than wait for the films to be developed and returned at a leisurely pace. If that objective of immediacy could be achieved, everything else – including the all-important matter of finding a market – would surely follow. Land's technological skills had been applied abortively to automotive headlights, but had burgeoned successfully (and unexpectedly) into Polaroid sunglasses.

The problem with the cameras lay within the range of optics where Land was at home. He still had to invent a basically new photographic technology, and this had to depart from the existing forms in every way except in the use of light, focused through a lens, to expose a film. In his case, as in every other, once the problem was known, the next stages followed with perfect logic.

1 What is the problem?
2 What solutions are possible?
3 Which solution is the best?

The three-stage process sounds like, and is, simple common sense. It applies to the smallest enterprise, which will benefit greatly by just going through the stages with methodical intelligence. You wouldn't think that large and sophisticated companies, as opposed to small and unversed entrepreneurs, would need instruction in this methodology. Yet one consultancy, Smith System Engineering, created its own entrepreneurial growth from applying the process to the problems of very large organizations, public and private.

In fact, the unversed entrepreneur may well apply the routine instinctively, while some of his largest brethren don't think either before or after dreaming. The NASA space agency, for instance, spent a fortune on developing a ballpoint that would work in zero-gravity. Their mistake was a wrong definition of the problem. By thinking 'ballpoint', NASA missed the true problem, which was simply how to write in space. The Russians solved that brilliantly. They used pencils.

NASA is where Dr Bruce Smith, one of many Britons on the Apollo moon programme, first got his idea of using bright young scientists, whose academic work teaches them how to solve problems, to work as independent consultants. The same principle can and should be applied by entrepreneurs. If it is applicable to your enterprise, hire the best academic talent while it is available, young and willing.

Entrepreneurial dreams thrive on ideas, and the best ideas come from the brightest brains; moreover, the younger they are, the more fertile the minds. In Smith's case, the dream wasn't to supply the client with final designs, but to work with him to produce the right specification. Anybody who has commissioned building work should know the principle: if you want to get a superb building, don't tell the architect what to design, tell him what you need and what you're prepared to spend.

R & D departments respond best to the same approach. Be clear about the dream and leave the technologists enough room for some dreaming of their own. Smith came back to Britain to realize his dream and to put his common-sense principles into practice, starting in 1971 with one man (himself) above a solicitor's office. Five years later, he hired his first two Cambridge PhDs.

The business, finding its main customers in the defence industry, promptly 'took off', says one of that original pair, Chris Elliott. In the early 1980s, it passed the customary threshold for a 'small' business, 100 employees; an important threshold in matters other than mere numbers. Somewhere around that level, the dream is liable to outgrow the dreamer's own reach.

The pragmatic, prosaic skills of the down-to-earth administrator and finance expert become essential to carry the business forward to the next stage. Honda, for instance, was extremely fortunate in having at his right hand Takeo Fujisawa; just as Bill Hewlett was very lucky to team up with Dave Packard. The two entrepreneurial dreamers produced the breakthroughs, while their partners provided the steadying hand of business management.

'Steady as she goes' was the experience of Smith Systems. Even when turnover was far from small, at £11 million, there were still only 130 employees, based in Guildford. That total had been reached by remarkably stable expansion, which carries its own lesson: growth of 15 percent per annum may not sound very exciting, but compound arithmetic is powerful stuff. That pace, for all its apparent modesty, doubles a business every five years.

'It wasn't planned', remembers Elliott, 'but that's the way it worked out.' Unplanned growth doesn't sound the right behaviour for a planning consultancy – but there's a very significant explanation for the way it happened. The company had a policy of doing everything from within, including developing the 'new, bright, but a bit nutty' young scientists. It takes about five years for these to mature fully.

That sets the limits to growth, which at a steady 15 percent generates enough cash to finance the next year's expansion. Every business has its own growth limits, and trying to exceed them is an excellent recipe for failure. MIT Professor Peter M. Senge has set out the process in brilliant fashion.

A high-tech entrepreneur, say, grows fast on the back of new products. The technologists grow in number accordingly, until the senior ones spend more and more time managing, and less time on products. Development times slow down and so does overall growth. The firm may never recover its momentum, and could slide into a downward spiral. Dreamers should hearken to Senge's advice: 'Don't push growth; remove the factors limiting growth.'

Smith avoided the growth limits trap, but found another highly reliable recipe for failure in the 1980s. The top management began to worry about whether the market for independent technological advice was big enough. 'Chaps', says Elliott, 'have to make products.' Being so bright, why shouldn't they develop high-tech wonders themselves and earn huge profits from licensing the results to manufacturers? They started the venture – and it taught them 'a very big lesson'.

First, they risked committing commercial suicide by going into business for themselves. It took away their claim to be independent and dispassionate – 'being neutral is a winner for us every time'. Second, 'the culture of a service company like Smith is fundamentally different' from that of a manufacturer. As a consultant, you can justify 'bending over backwards to please the customer', even at some economic (or uneconomic) cost, but that's a 'disaster if you try to do something for yourselves'.

The obvious question stared them in the face: 'What are we playing at?' The physician needed to heal himself. The question could be rephrased as the first one in their catechism for clients: What is the problem? By defining it wrongly, as the need to supplement consulting income, they had condemned themselves to getting the wrong answer and playing in the wrong game.

In other words, do as most successful dreamers do: stick to

the knitting, especially if the wool shows no signs of ever running out. Demand for independent technological advice turned
out to be 'virtually unlimited'. A lot of people wanted to buy
from Smith and his colleagues at prices at which they wanted
to sell. So don't have too many dreams; one good dream will
do very nicely.

Once Honda's dream had come true, he waited for many years
before dreaming of anything but motorbikes. By the time he
went into cars, his company had all the attributes that were
required for the new market: the technology, the marketing
skills, the world-wide distribution know-how. It could both
identify and solve the problems that lay between dream and
reality.

Note, however, that the original market in motorbikes did
not disappear, but continued to thrive. It is common for entrepreneurs (as at Smith) to become nervous about dependence
on a single product or market and to believe dismal forecasts
about their growth potential. The anxiety about one-product
companies is perfectly justifiable, but it often results in
unjustified leaps into unknown territory.

Worse still, it is also common for the leaper to neglect the
base business in consequence. That is a terrible mistake in any
circumstances, and it is compounded by diversification into
unfamiliar new activities. Smith's has learned both lessons. Its
market (with defence the most important customer category)
consists of 'problems where you can't ignore science and technology'.

While both Elliott and the founder, Bruce Smith, have moved
on to new horizons, their successors have a rich heritage of
coping with such problems, which naturally involve very exacting practical and theoretical work. That high-tech bias in no
way invalidates the Smith lessons for less scientifically oriented
realizers of dreams.

Indeed, you don't always need computers and PhDs for the
three-stage process. Instead, Elliott speaks very highly of 'the
back of an envelope'. That embodies 'the principle of maximum
laziness', doing just enough work to know whether the dream is
worthwhile. Back-of-envelope calculations would have stopped

many of the great and small fiascos of our time. And you can even do them in zero-gravity – with a pencil.

Building the Brand

Every business is a brand, however small. The entrepreneurs who win big and go on winning do so because of their success in building either brands for products and/or services, or the total brand of the company, or both. The brand game can reach levels of great complexity, but the basic principles are simple and clear: branding is all about attracting and retaining the customer.

Entrepreneurs are adept at exploiting any path to this end. Their energy helps to explain an apparently odd facet of the personal computer industry. At first glance, it seems to consist of only of a few mighty firms, led by Compaq and IBM, with perhaps half-a-dozen major contestants. In fact, many thousands of tiny PC makers have survived, taking a quarter of the world market. These so-called 'no-names' make no effort to match the massive brand spending of the leaders.

To the customer, the no-names are real names. They include a Manchester firm called Adams Technology which makes a positive virtue of its smallness. According to the *Wall Street Journal*, when PCs need upgrading, Adams doesn't charge for the installation, just for the hardware. It telephones customers to tell them when new developments, like the latest advance in microprocessor speed, are coming their way. It reckons to take computers in for repair within eight hours of notification: 'Many customers have their units up and running again the same day.' The no-names are small entrepreneurial businesses which sell largely to others in the same category. This ability to identify with the customer is their branding, which they sustain by their performance. They will send out technicians to the customer's site, for example, and won't rely on some high-tech answering system to deal with inquiries: the phone will be manned (or womanned) by a genuine human being.

Real people underlie the customer relationship and the strength of the brand. Both depend on the willing and intelligent

co-operation of the workforce. An ace retailer like Marks &
Spencer must master all four Ps of retailing: Product, Place, Processes, People. But M & S has always put most emphasis on the
last P. You may be selling the right things in the right places by
the right methods, but you also need to have the right people
managed in the right way.

This people-based approach to the four Ps has accomplished
a classic exercise in brand-building. Every element in the
business is geared towards the dual promotion of the exclusive
St Michael label and the chain itself: M & S is a genuine 'power
brand', defined by T. Bradley Gale as 'a name that means satisfaction, quality and value to the customer'. He argues correctly
that, to achieve power brand status, 'you have to manage both
the quality of the product itself and the system that helps customers to perceive that quality'.

Note that Gale says nothing about size or corporate wealth
or advertising spend. The principles of managing quality and
perception form a credo that will build any brand and any
business. Entrepreneurial brand-building demands that you . . .

- manage and lead the market
- put customers first
- achieve high returns
- seek competitive superiority
- optimize promotion, but always tell the truth
- defend the brand's integrity and strength at all times
- change continuously
- form strategic ambitions
- seize all opportunities.

The great store chain managed its market from the beginning
when its founding entrepreneur, Michael Marks, adopted the
slogan: 'Don't ask the price, it's a penny.' That limited the 'catalogue' of goods which M & S would sell. Ever since, the company
has stayed in full control of what it will offer and at what price.
Let yourself be managed by the market, and you end up with
commodity products sold at prices that yield no profit.

Market management rests on leadership. That isn't a matter

of size, but of excellent attributes valued as such by the customer. As Gale's power brand definition stresses, superior quality of product and service is essential. Sometimes entrepreneurs are tempted to take short cuts in the spirit of a magazine which once asked: 'Does it pay to build quality into a product if most customers don't notice?' The only safe assumption is that all the customers notice all the time.

They also notice what the academics call 'differentiated value propositions'; meaning that the customer thinks you offer outstanding value for money with a product or service that clearly differs from anything else on the market in ways that the customer perceives and appreciates. That in turn rests heavily on innovation, such as the High Street food-only stores which reversed the flight from the city centres and gave M & S margins beyond the fantasies of the supermarkets.

'Putting customers first' has many facets. One is exemplified by the long-standing M & S money-back guarantee: any goods returnable without question for whatever reason. How you deal with inquiries and especially with complaints has a profound effect on the customer relationship. Dealing well and swiftly with a complaint often achieves excellent results where perfect service might only have satisfied. For a start, respond after apologizing and always within five days, even if it is only to promise action – but then, of course, act.

That is one way of prejudicing the customer in the company's and the brand's favour. There is another – that is, if you can safely make promises like these. 'We will . . .'

- attend to you within five minutes
- always serve you politely
- have items from our standard stock list available at all times
- deliver as promised, in the morning or afternoon
- inform you before our truck sets off, if the delivery is incomplete
- respond to your quotation request within five working days
- reply to your invoice query within ten working days
- have goods not available in the branch today available for collection first thing the following working day.

The test isn't only whether you could make and keep such promises, but whether you believe that they are desirable. They constitute what's known as a 'service guarantee', a very powerful tool. This one comes from the Graham Group, a chain of builders' merchants which was successfully spun off from the BTR conglomerate. Part of the recipe for success is symbolized by the fact that all Graham employees carry a plastic card which reminds them of the obligations that the company has assumed in its 'Customer Care Pledges'.

The key is what happens 'if we don't meet our pledges'. The customer can immediately claim the sum of £20 in cash, because 'Graham is all about service and stock availability. Let our customers down, and they won't come back. If they don't come back we have no business! Make sure they keep on coming back. KEEP THE PLEDGES.' The eight pledges end with a further warning: 'If we don't get it right, our customers will not come back!'

Now, the £20 sum is not very great, but this service guarantee works effectively on both sides of the relationship. First, Graham establishes its brand in the customer's mind as that of a company that puts its money where its mouth is. Second, employees are constantly reminded of the service standards and their part in ensuring that the standards are achieved. And the expense is, of course, trivial. In three years, Graham had to pay out only £15,000, meaning that 750 failures had been pounced on by unhappy customers, who each became £20 happier as a result.

Employees cannot, however, deliver service promises without the back-up which only management can provide. The system within which operatives work is neither designed nor regulated by them. The Graham service guarantee forces the boss and other managers to match their own performance to the promise. If people feel the pain of service failures in their own pockets – because the payments for service failure are deducted from the profit-sharing pool – that will only intensify their eagerness to avoid failing.

Devices like service guarantees all help to establish what advertising agency Young and Rubicam names as the four pillars of the brand: familiarity, esteem, relevance and differentiation.

The first pair create the brand's 'stature'; the second pair establish 'brand vitality'. What are the key issues?

1 Is the business/brand distinct? Is it continuing to demonstrate its difference?
2 Is the business/brand proposition meaningful and right for the target audience?
3 How highly do customers think of and feel about the business? What is their perception of its quality and of its 'momentum' – its growth in popularity?
4 How many people know the business/brand and, more important, truly understand what it is about?

The temptation outside the big battalions is to think that you cannot compete with them because they can simply spend their way to brand awareness. 'Traditionally marketers have believed that increasing awareness was the steadfast route to building a brand.' But the Y & R findings – from a study of 6,000 brands and 30,000 users in nineteen countries – knocks this notion firmly on the head. They 'demonstrate that familiarity is the culmination of successful brand-building. Spending money against a weak idea will not buy familiarity. It has to be earned.'

In other words, the strength of the brand comes down to the strength of performance. That's why entrepreneurial 'no-names' like Adams and Graham can create all the brand power they require within their own environments. Remember that for decades M & S did little or no advertising and is still a parsimonious spender today. Its stores, and the goods and practices which they contain, are enormous and most effective ads. Build the business and you build the brand – and that builds the business still more.

3

The People in Power

How to be a Boss

The entrepreneur is the boss. How any boss behaves has a profound effect on how other managers perform, and thus on the
performance of the entire outfit. That's a self-evident truth. Few
bosses, however, acknowledge the corollary: that inferior
performance by others is partly the boss's fault, and that it is
always possible to improve others' performance by improving
the boss.

If you believe the late W. Edwards Deming, the American
management expert who was a genius in these matters, the
'partly' responsible comes close to wholly. He attributed 85 percent of all failure to failed management. As he stressed, people
work within the system established by the boss class. The
system's defects limit people's ability to perform, without their
having much chance to influence the faults or suggest new virtues, unless they have a truly good boss.

Being 'a good boss', though, is generally understood as being
humane, fair and understanding, rather than suggesting high
competence. Being a good boss in that sense is an art in itself,
and one which has changed over time. Today the best bosses aim
to get people performing more and more productively through
taking over their own bossing. Everybody shares responsibility
for achieving the object of the enterprise, which is success for
all hands; of course, the boss's share of success is the biggest.

It isn't just a matter of establishing a system which does not
get in people's way, but of creating one that helps them to

achieve their best. Nor does the system alone create success. The personal characteristics of the boss also affect the outcome. When the very successful and very entrepreneurial head of a high-technology business was asked to explain his achievement in pulling the company up from huge losses to rich profits, his recipe had five ingredients – none of which ranks high in the technology of management.

He started with nothing more complex than a lot of *common sense*. Much of good management, like most of the principles of entrepreneurial success, rests on sensible, balanced, fact-based reasoning – and that includes the next item on the list, *trust in people*, which should probably be placed first. 'The economic loss from fear', wrote Deming, 'is appalling'. In failing to trust, managers fear being let down, while those who aren't trusted are afraid of failing. That's a huge, self-imposed handicap on both sides.

Third, said the high-tech boss, *don't ask others to do anything you wouldn't do yourself*. That's the Patton Principle, named after the great, prideful American general who was never too proud to lead from the front, and by example. Fourth, you need the ability to *work with and through others*. Fifth, *total dedication to the task* is required; nothing less will do. Anything that *is* less will be reflected in a lower commitment from other people.

A top subordinate added three other important qualities to the list possessed by his boss (with an apology for what the Americans call 'apple-polishing' – the Brits have a ruder phrase). The extra three were a great deal of *energy*, *no office politics* and total *loyalty to colleagues*. These should be natural attributes of the entrepreneur, and their possession explains much of the ability of entrepreneurs to outrun, outwit and outdo corporate managers.

But none of the eight attributes should present any difficulty, even to the latter. Would any boss admit to the reverse charac- teristics? 'I haven't got much common sense, I distrust every- body, I play office politics like mad, I am disloyal to those who work for me, I'm not committed to the job.' No doubt, everybody has had the misfortune, at one time or another, to work for just such a creature. Very likely, the creatures are in the category who understand their responsibility for the performance of others, not in the sense of Deming's 85 percent rule, but solely in hire-and-fire terms. It does seem easier to fire under-performing failures. But I've come across Japanese examples that take a quite different line.

In one company, if nobody can understand why a manager has consistently under-performed, he is promoted; and in three-quarters of the cases, performance improves at once. In another company, management takes responsibility for people who prove wrong for the job, because management made the decision to hire them. Rather than firing, these Japanese firms try additional training, education, or a new job. This approach, too, usually succeeds.

Now, Japanese culture is very different from Western norms, and many people think that what works in Japan won't work here. Yet every manager can recall cases of sacked colleagues or subordinates who went on to achieve outstanding performance with a new employer. The self-evident lesson of these cases, alas, isn't absorbed. Part of the Japanese genius, though, is the ability to entertain apparently eccentric notions that challenge conventional behaviour.

If the unconventional works better, then they incorporate that approach into their way of corporate life. That's also a prime characteristic of the entrepreneurial boss. You don't start and build a terrific new business by slavish imitation of others. You do it your way, and never mind the conventional wisdom or established ways. Promoting a flop stands the hire-and-fire culture on its head, but standing on your head can sometimes work wonders.

For instance, what if the boss, instead of automatically being the head at all meetings, surrenders the chair and its powers to subordinates, who take the top spot in turns? That's equally offensive to normal Western practice, but this is a wholly Western example, from that same high-tech firm whose boss was quoted above.

What happened in one department provides a fascinating insight into the nature of modern bossing. An underboss surrendered the chair of a committee which he had set up to raise efficiency. He became just one of the boys (or girls), and found to his delight that people lost their fear of exposing problems. Being temporary boss, moreover, presented them with the necessity of taking and implementing decisions.

That was a lesson in both leadership and teamwork. But when a management thinker named Meredith Belbin classified team roles long ago, he found several, not one of which is clearly that of leader, let alone entrepreneur. The key seven are co-ordinator, critic, ideas person, implementer, external contact, inspector and team-builder. Study the history of most enter-prises, though, and you will find that the entrepreneurial leader has to play all these roles at different times.

The test of the good boss is to ensure that every single role is played; the team and the enterprise will not achieve peak performance if any of these functions are neglected or missing altogether. Nor will the boss achieve his or her personal peak. The Belbin roles provide a checklist for the individual perform-ance of those with ultimate responsibility for the success of the enterprise, whether the business has already grown to significant scale or still consists of half-a-dozen people or fewer working hopefully in a start-up.

The questions seldom get asked, but score yourself on a scale of 1 (minimal contribution) to 5 (total); 2 is inadequate; 3 adequate; 4 good enough, but room for improvement.

1 Do you ensure that everybody is working together towards agreed and shared objectives?
2 Do you criticize constructively – and praise merit as well as find fault?
3 Do you encourage and organize the generation of new ideas?
4 Do you insist on and organize the highest standards of execution?
5 Do you keep close and productive contact with customers (internal and/or external), suppliers and other parties outside the business?
6 Do you monitor activities continuously, with effective feedback?

7 Do you develop the individual and collective skills of the team
  and strengthen them as needed by training and recruitment?

If your score is 28 or over, the proof should lie in excellent
results – which, of course, means excellent performance by the
enterprise. The checklist enhances performance by reminding
you to keep a close eye on yourself. Under the pressure of
demanding work and conflicting relationships (not to mention
powerful egos), entrepreneurs easily settle into 'their' own
unchanging and unalterable style. By becoming self-conscious,
in the best sense of the word, you get better work from yourself
and thus from the team.

The Interpersonal Breakthrough

Any expert in 'human resources' or HR (once simply known as
'personnel') can explain the importance for business results of
'interpersonal problems'. In simple non-jargon, getting on badly
with others at work is a well-trodden path to business and personal failure.

An authoritarian atmosphere encourages bad behaviour
between people at all levels. On the other hand, set the people
free in a collaborative culture, and their performance will surprise you, and them. It is easy to activate the dreaded problems.
Just be 'insensitive, manipulative, critical, demanding, authoritarian, self-isolating, or aloof', according to two of those HR
experts.

Unfortunately, some of these characteristics are widely found
among entrepreneurs. They started the business, and probably
own it. Their word has been law from the beginning, and
their risks have been lonely. Their method is instinctively
critical, demanding and authoritarian, and it works – up to a
point.

What if you want to go beyond that point? Adopting the
opposite behaviour should achieve the magic aim: getting the
best from those who work with and for you. The key lies in
the word 'authoritarian', describing a fault which historically

has been the prevalent mode in all business management, great and small. True-blue authoritarians never explain orders, expect those who receive commands to do exactly as they are told, ruthlessly punish failure and capriciously reward success, again without explanation.

Some of these tough nuts make fortunes, like Linda Wachner, the Warnaco textile tycoon, who once ordered a manager to head office and kept him waiting three days for a two-minute interview. Tom Watson, the founder of IBM, was a marvel at motivating a sales force, but when it came to dealing with individuals, he displayed similar rude, unfeeling habits. ('They're well-paid,' he said when Tom Jr complained about the waiting minions.)

Watson's achievements were wondrous, but the awful, disastrous Robert Maxwell was also in the Wachner mould. Don't make the mistake of assuming that authoritarianism equates with success. Brutes might well do better with the anti-authoritarian methods of properly organized feedback, review and appraisal: that is, sitting down with an employee to discuss past and present and to plan a better future.

In fact, one study of 437 companies showed spectacular before-and-after results from introducing this so-called 'performance management'. Productivity soared by 94.2 percent, while the shareholders were better off by a quarter. The study's authors, though, report that the managers involved thought little of the procedures, rating them only 'slightly effective' or 'somewhat effective' in helping to achieve a company's ambitions.

So what produced the bumper results? The researchers, quoted in the *Harvard Business Review*, came up with obvious but powerful findings. People need to know clearly what is expected of them; to be told clearly how they have or have not lived up to expectations; and, in the latter case, they have a clear need to discuss how to improve.

Mismanaging subordinates by ignoring this trio of needs is not going to help them, the mismanagers, or the business. The entrepreneur who can do any task better than anybody else (or thinks so) tends to under-estimate rather than over-estimate the underlings' abilities. That contradicts a fascinating truth about such expectations: pitch them high. That doesn't mean setting impossible targets, but it does mean highly rating people's ability and potential.

Do that, and you will benefit from what Professor Dov Eden, who teaches at Tel Aviv University, calls 'the Pygmalion effect'. To turn Eliza Doolittles into stars, try regarding them as such. Working with the Israeli military, Eden found that soldiers whose potential was rated 'high', or so their instructors were told, received superior grades and got more out of their training than comrades whose rating was supposed to be only 'regular' or 'unknown'.

The catch was that the ratings were fictitious, entirely random. They plainly influenced the attitudes of the instructors, however – and that was the route to an otherwise inexplicable success. The same thing happens with bosses and the bossed. It's another proof of the old adage, 'Give a dog a bad name.' Give a dog a good name, though, and he becomes even better.

Eden had another clever ploy. He arranged for soldiers to be told, again at random, that they had high potential for success. The blessed ones 'considerably' outperformed course members who believed themselves to be only average. In other words, if somebody is under-performing, maybe it is because they are under-rated – by you and consequently by themselves.

That helps to explain the irritating phenomenon, mentioned in the previous section, of the man or woman who is sacked for under-performance but proceeds to work wonderfully well elsewhere. Review, feedback and appraisal will help avert such waste, but you need something extra: reward. One school of thought pays more for performance against clear targets. Another body of opinion advises paying extra only for super-performance. A third approach says that super-performance should be part of the expectation, and that bonus payments should only come from profit-sharing schemes.

Whatever the system, today's interpersonal success formula includes sharing the wealth. The flood of corporate entries to the now defunct Unlisted Securities Market during the Thatcher boom shared one notable common factor. The entrepreneurs

GOLDFINGER

How Entrepreneurs Get Rich by Starting Small

ROBERT HELLER

HarperCollinsBusiness
An Imprint of HarperCollinsPublishers

HarperCollinsBusiness
An imprint of HarperCollinsPublishers
77–85 Fulham Palace Road,
Hammersmith, London W6 8JB

Published by HarperCollinsPublishers 1998

1 3 5 7 9 8 6 4 2

A catalogue record for this book
is available from the British Library

ISBN 0 00 255846 7

Set in Meridien by
Rowland Phototypesetting Ltd,
Bury St Edmunds, Suffolk

Printed and bound in Great Britain by
Caledonian International Book Manufacturing Ltd, Glasgow

thus enriched also enriched their employees. This wasn't out of the goodness of their hearts; rather, they believed that sharing the wealth would encourage each individual co-worker to create still more loot.

In addition to wealth-sharing – which is, of course, highly symbolic of a new kind of interpersonal relationship – consider the similar virtues of another piece of HR jargon: 'empowerment'. One survey in the mid-1990s found that 56 percent of the British companies questioned were planning to empower their employees – meaning obviously that well over half those companies had not yet introduced whatever they meant by 'empowerment'.

They were far behind their times. It is a very old idea that individual employees work more effectively when allowed to use their brains, not just their hands. The problem lies in giving deeper practical meaning to the concept. The traditional bureaucrats, with their emphasis on control, standardization and obedience, cannot function in a climate of empowerment, which demands giving people the ability to run and improve their own performance.

Such an approach can thrive only in liberated surroundings where the climate isn't 'insensitive, manipulative, critical, demanding, authoritarian, self-isolating, or aloof', but sensitive, dead straight, praising, supportive, communal and friendly. It can be. But the unpleasant myth that capitalist success is inimical to niceness is widely held and the source of much discontent.

Thus, an East German quoted by guru Charles Handy bemoaned the passing of the four Fs ('family and friends, festivals and fun') in favour of the four Ps ('profit and performance, pay and productivity'). The name of the new entrepreneurial and interpersonal game, though, is to make 4P economic miracles with 4F humans. You won't do that without taking power out of the equation to a considerable degree.

At one highly entrepreneurial family company, the advanced and expensive IT system is crucial to competitive advantage. But it was not made exclusive to an all-powerful IT centre. The company used focus groups of future users to design what they wanted the system to do. And an evaluation mechanism was built in to allow staff to suggest enhancements while the program was actually in use.

If interpersonal relationships between departments can be placed on a common-sense and co-operative basis (and they can), so can those between individuals. At one large and immensely successful financial services company, for example, I was deeply impressed to find a young woman, working on systems in the finance department, whose boss, she said, would listen to any idea she put forward, adopt the idea if it was good, and always tell her why if the idea was rejected.

Should such natural, sensible behaviour really be regarded as impressive? The opposite, unnatural, conduct can only create remarkable nonsenses. The Forum Corporation found, astonishingly, that only 4 percent of all the problems and opportunities known collectively to the junior employees ever reached the ears of top management teams. This interpersonal waste on a vast scale can happen as easily in the small entrepreneurial company as in the large corporation, if power becomes decisive.

Relationships built largely on power and powerlessness will not serve either the self-interest of the boss or the economic interests of the business. The reality is that authoritarians, often unwittingly, sometimes deliberately, impede individuals' ability and even their efforts to improve their performance. The oldest impersonal adage is to do unto others as you would be done by. Senior people expect to be seen and heard, but so do their juniors.

Here another piece of HR jargon rears its head, providing bosses with perhaps the greatest interpersonal shock of all: 'upward appraisal'. Not only do subordinates get their performance reviewed by the bosses (something which most of the latter, incidentally, dislike doing), but the bosses (which they dislike far more) get compulsorily reviewed by the bossed.

That often chastening experience should finally scotch the belief of authoritarians that in all circumstances the entrepreneurial father-figure knows best. He doesn't, and the sooner he knows that, the better for everybody – including him.

Our Most Important Assets

No management cliché is pronounced with more fervour but less sincerity than 'People are our most important assets'. The chairmen of large companies love to chant this mantra, even when said assets are being downsized (i.e. fired) by the thousand. In many, maybe most, cases, the human assets are treated with a lack of care and maintenance that would incapacitate a piece of machinery in no time at all.

Yet that old chestnut happens to be true. It also happens to pay off, if you treat humans with the same care and attention that are devoted (or should be) to plant, equipment and premises. Many case histories show, however, that, whatever happens in big corporations, the best entrepreneurial companies find it much easier (and highly profitable) to turn lip-service into reality in ways that anyone can copy.

The one-on-one interpersonal relationships discussed in the previous section are an essential ingredient in the human assets formula, but people in groups act differently from individuals and require different treatment. The object is to narrow the gap between the intelligent, common-sense attitudes which come naturally to most individuals and the collective unreason which can take over when they associate.

My time as a journalist is a case in point. I've never worked with more co-operative, friendly and skilled people than the printers who put together newspapers in the old hot-metal days. Assemble them as a union chapel, though, and they would take ridiculous, ruinous decisions – ruinous to their own economic interests and those of the paper.

Every employer knows this phenomenon of collective resistance to what is manifestly right. Like any management problem, it can be handled properly and effectively. Given the will, there's always a way. For instance, if you want genuine teamwork, don't just say so, but use teams as a prime tool for running and improving the business.

One American entrepreneur does precisely that, tapping employee power wherever he can. 'Time teams' are set to 'scrutinize every procedure, process and program' used in the business to answer three burning questions:

1 Why do we do this?
2 Do we need to do it at all?
3 If so, how can we do it better?

Team tasks of this nature not only improve the business, but develop habits of working together constructively. The team approach, though, won't work unless it is underpinned by strong foundations. Several companies featured in this book have rightly laid great stress on their basic people policies. Edward Smith, formerly of John McGavigan Automotive Products (see next section), called his employees 'the experts' and treated them accordingly.

To 'exploit the potential' of these people, McGavigan invested heavily in 'training, teams and communication' – the Holy Trinity of effective human asset management. McGavigan is a manufacturer. But David Craven of NST (see Chapter 1), selling educational tours, is just as emphatic about the need to find and develop 'very highly motivated, skilled staff'.

'Only work with people you like, know and trust – and never under-estimate their abilities' is advice I picked up from the advertising business. There it comes naturally, because advertising thrives on the presence and full contribution of individual and collective talent, and is throttled by its absence. The need for high creativity, however, is by no means confined to companies whose output is stamped 'creative'.

More and more, the competitive wars, at all levels of corporate size, are being won by those businesses which generate the best ideas and execute them with the greatest ingenuity. That's one reason why people management necessarily provided a dominant theme for the Major government's drive to improve national competitiveness. A DTI study, carried out with the CBI, looked at 121 best-practice businesses, which claimed to 'unlock the potential of their people' by . . .

- creating a culture in which employees are genuinely empowered and focused on the customer
- investing in people through good communications, learning and training (the Holy Trinity again)
- flattening and inverting the organizational pyramid.

What those fine words mean in real life – and in smaller companies – is shown by three case histories. The first, Navico, makes navigational equipment and waterproof radios for the recreational market. Freeing its ninety employees, who were stuck in an old-fashioned, highly supervised, multi-layered hierarchy, required drastic action. It involved both courage and creativity; you must be brave enough to try bold ideas, breaking out from the habitual patterns into wholly new ground.

That's internal entrepreneurship. Navico's boss, Mike Bowerman, closed the factory for two days (an extraordinary act in itself), took everybody to a hotel and explained why they all had to change. Teams, note, were crucial to his approach, so he needed team leaders. They weren't appointed by the boss. Instead, Bowerman advertised for them: three out of four came from the shop floor, not from the supervisors. He did, however, nominate 'product champions', people 'who have a desire to drive and get things done'.

Leaders and champions alike went on a training course in the modern technique of cellular manufacturing: the assembly line is abandoned in favour of small groups which have all the interchangeable skills required to complete an entire product or component. The technical requirements are considerably more exacting, which means that every employee in the factory was retrained. All are now multi-skilled. In two years, Navico's turnover rose by 70 percent to £5.1 million and profits did even better, advancing over eight-fold to £0.5 million.

Teams were also the key at Dutton Engineering (Woodside), where twenty-five people were making precision stainless steel enclosures for the electronics industry. Turnover per direct employee duly rose by half in four years, following the introduction of team working – and trust. If you treat employees with suspicion and fear, they will repay you in kind. Treat them with trust, and the repayment will be invaluable. 'The men and women on the shop floor', says Dutton's Ken Lewis, 'are skilled enough and professional enough to make it right in the first place.'

That wasn't an easy idea for Lewis's managers to accept. Instead of giving orders, they had to learn to 'coach, facilitate, lead'. While that sounds straightforward, human and natural, some managers (and entrepreneurs) are so indoctrinated by years of command-and-obey that they simply cannot make the change. At Dutton, the teams themselves had inhibitions to overcome, too. Introducing a system of annual hours changed their thinking: 'Once the tasks for that week were finished, the team could go home. They worked a lot more effectively once they realized that.'

At Sunrise Medical, managing director Barrie Payne also used focused teams in his winning people formula. The 370 employees, making custom mobility products for the disabled, were encouraged to find their own ways to do things better. Like Bowerman at Navico, Payne was prepared to take creative initiatives, and even to put people before production in the interests of change: once a month the factory closed for half-an-hour to praise their achievements. That meant 'anything an individual has done, however small, over and above what they might be expected to do'. The achievers got entered in a prize draw, which adds some spice to the usual reward scheme.

It still doesn't sound like a big deal, but there's no need for the deal to be large, anyway. Small, low-cost, original ideas can have a wholly disproportionate impact: so can less original devices, like giving people presents rather than cash as rewards. These small gestures can help to produce major incentives and large results – such as Sunrise's eleven years of 20 percent compound growth.

Managing people imaginatively isn't the only winning way that you need, of course. The DTI–CBI studies also stress the importance of constantly innovating in products and services, and of really knowing your customers. Even here there's no escaping the need for effective people policies. The employee assets hold the keys to innovation and customer service, as they do to everything else. It has become a cliché that you only get satisfied customers through satisfied employees.

Just as you need not just satisfied customers, but very satisfied ones, so you need more from employees – their full involvement in the customer cause. The great entrepreneurs have an instinctive feel for what their customers want, and often share their tastes. Quite frequently, an enterprise is built by converting a personal hobby into a business; the entrepreneur is his or her own best customer.

That translates into a two-pronged strategy: to raise customer satisfaction by satisfying employees in order to create the widest possible lead over the competition. The two-pronged process never ends. Customer and employee satisfaction are both moving targets. The more you satisfy people, the more they want. As so often, though, virtue is more than its own reward. The more you satisfy people, the more all your measures of achievement will improve, including the monetary ones.

That is why effective people managers try to develop attitudes that are specific to the business and to the wants of its clientele. Thus, at Navico, everybody went sailing to get in the same boat (so to speak) as the customers. Every Sunrise manager has direct customer contact. So do Dutton's manufacturing cells. As the DTI publication, *Winning*, says, 'Winning companies know people make the difference.' That's the gospel truth.

What Quality Really Means

One apparent advantage of being an entrepreneur is that you needn't bother with the big nostrums that gurus and consultants love to sell to big corpocratic companies. Or is it an advantage? What if, say, TQM (Total Quality Management) is the right road to making money? Quality doesn't only mean products that work and service that satisfies; total quality requires aiming for perfect processes, and that means enlisting the total commitment of one and all.

In many businesses, this is no longer an option, for top-class quality is fast becoming the only road. If you are supplying giants (for example, in cars) they may well insist on quality certifications like ISO 9000. Getting these can be expensive and burdensome; they don't require plunging into TQM; but, if you're going to all that trouble, it makes sense to launch a total quality drive.

Companies taking that route are following in the footsteps of some highly enterprising Scottish engineers. Total quality made much sense to Jack McGavigan, who before retiring in his eighties was chairman of John McGavigan & Co., founded by his grandfather in 1860. The family firm was a traditional printer, but developed from the 1960s into specialists in 'graphics-related plastics technology'. Touch switches and backlit fascia panels in cars are examples of the uses.

McGavigan, rightly keen on innovation, has constantly expanded into new technologies and product lines. Consequently, the group's car parts won a 12 percent world market share. None of this might have been achieved if McGavigan hadn't reacted to impending crisis in mid-1987. Sometimes even a highly entrepreneurial firm needs a crisis to jolt the business into better performance, using methods that, shamingly enough, were always available.

At McGavigan, costs were rising, the company was being squeezed between strong suppliers and stronger customers, and competition was intensifying. The firm had been using quality circles for years, with employees banding together to tackle quality issues, Japanese-style, in a voluntary, bottom-up effort to improve. Much, much more was needed to avert disaster.

Total quality was the answer, passionately advocated by Edward Smith. The future managing director of John McGavigan Automotive Products had joined the company as a mere stripling in 1963. Now he wanted to exploit the expertise and potential of his people, which entailed not only the use of training, team-building and communication skills, but something else. That extra is the essence of the entrepreneurial drive – 'the will to win'.

Looking back at his experience, Smith stresses that 'You have to have that very clear in front of you. You're not nice guys.' Rather, you are tough, determined managers who don't let anything or anybody stand in the way of 'exceeding customer expectations'. In the automotive part of the business, which is where McGavigan's total quality drive started, those expectations have grown sky-high.

Once, motor industry customers would live with 1.5 to 2 percent rejects. The maximum became '500 parts per million – that's .005 percent'. The TQM methods which achieve this super-performance are basically bottom-up, like the quality circles: the ideas flow from the people in the front line, whether that's the counter in a shop or the factory floor or the warehouse. But in total quality, everybody in the firm becomes involved – otherwise the 'total' is meaningless.

The lofty aim is to produce only perfect goods by only perfect processes, and to deliver the goods only in perfect ways to customers who are only perfectly satisfied with the results. One of Germany's greatest entrepreneurs, the original Robert Bosch, whose firm is still Europe's king of car components, expressed the urge wonderfully: 'It has always been an intolerable thought to me that someone should inspect one of my products and find it inferior.'

If the quality ideal sounds impossible to you, you're right. It's the striving for impossible perfection – 'continuous improvement', in the jargon – throughout the business, from start to finish, that is the name of the game. The name of McGavigan's quality circles was thus changed to 'improvement circles' – and improvement is truly the word for what has been achieved.

The automotive company, accounting for 70 percent of the McGavigan business, was producing 1.6 million parts a month with 190 people in October 1993. Two years later, production had reached 2.3 million, with only 152 employees. That's a rise in productivity of 80 percent – which Smith attributed to 'employee involvement'. Don't think that change comes easily, though. Is it tremendously difficult to 'change the culture'? 'Let's say we found it very, very challenging.'

The exercise started in April 1988, with all employees, in groups of between ten and fifteen, listening to the managing director as he stressed key points: first, that TQM isn't a 'flavour of the month', but lasts for many years; second, as noted, it involves absolutely everybody. In fact, everybody left the meeting with a Corrective Action Form on which as many items as they liked could be noted: 150 forms were filled in.

TQM work, very detailed and demanding, never stopped thereafter. If you want quality to work for the enterprise, as it has for McGavigan, forget about quality of product alone, and start thinking about a new way of life as well. Whether or not you choose to meet the quality standards required for ISO 9000 certification (or are forced to meet them), the real pay-off comes from going beyond that to apply top-quality procedures and processes throughout the organization.

This is not a do-it-yourself enterprise, though. You need expert guidance through the forest of alternatives and acronyms, starting with SQC. That is easier to say than 'statistical quality control', and also easy to understand. What you do sounds dead simple. You stop the wasteful practice of inspecting everything at the end of the process, and rejecting anything that doesn't come up to scratch. Rejects and rework chew up profit margins like locusts. SQC aims to eliminate both entirely by working on the scientifically correct theory that a small proportion will teach you everything you need to know about the whole. So during any process, you take regular, statistically valid samples, measure their characteristics against allowable variations, and react immediately with analysis and correction if results stray outside the permitted range.

Do all that thoroughly, and costs will come down as quality leaps up. Profits, other things being equal (such as charging the right price), will join the leap. That was the key to the spectacular relaunch of Japanese industry after the Second World War, thanks to the preaching of W. Edwards Deming. That great American quality prophet was without honour in his own country until 1980, when a TV programme displayed the full horror of the quality gap between America and Japan.

As an entrepreneur today, you dare not wait around for some shock (or a crisis like McGavigan's) to awaken the quality impulse. Whether it is quality of service or product, or the processes that provide both, a gap between you and the best competitors simply hands them the game. The only difficulty is that adopting a new quality approach means throwing away established practice and learning to manage in a different and challenging way.

In one sense, that should come naturally to entrepreneurs, since they thrive on difference and challenge. Alas, it also comes unnaturally, for total quality comes into the area labelled 'professional management'. Here entrepreneurs notoriously feel uncomfortable, although the exceptions include Philip Crosby, author of a celebrated title: *Quality is Free*.

So it is, in the sense that the savings which flow from defect-free production, and from the more economic processes which achieve that result, should pay for the programme, with plenty to spare. That sounds like a sure-fire selling message – and in Crosby's hands, that's what it became.

A former employee of the huge telecoms-to-hotels conglomerate, ITT, Crosby wasn't content merely to publish a best-selling book or two and give highly paid talks. He saw that quality could be sold like hamburgers, which meant establishing a chain of outlets to provide the same content to the same standards. Crosby Colleges duly spread across the land, making their inventor a multi-millionaire and proving that quality pays in more senses than one. It is all too easy, however, to have a level of quality that is inadequate.

By any criterion, winning the prizes awarded by the European Foundation for Quality Management or the British Quality Foundation is a tough and intimidating task. All the same, the EFQM model boils down to nine very simple, basic questions:

1 Are our customers very satisfied?
2 And our people?
3 Are we good corporate citizens?
4 Do we have firm leadership?
5 Are policy and strategy effective and articulated?
6 Are people well managed?
7 And resources?
8 And processes?
9 Is all the above proved by excellence in business results?

Note the 'business results' which links with the McGavigan
insistence on 'the will to win'. This isn't an exercise, but a real-
life demonstration of the pillars of all-round entrepreneurial
success. Does it pay off? The Scottish company's management
is adamant that 'you've got to have continuous improvement
to give your customers what they want'. From that, all else
follows. For solid proof of the consequences, the McGavigans
were able to sell the business (which today employs over 350
people) to Pressac Holdings for the highly satisfactory sum of
£9.75 million.

Partnerships that Pay

Behind many great businesses lies a great entrepreneurial partnership that began small but always thought bigger. Some of
these meetings of minds have become legendary, first in their
native countries, then world-wide: Hewlett and Packard in the
USA, or Marks and Sieff (not Spencer, of course) in Britain, or
Morita and Ikuba (who named their company Sony) in Japan.

Behind many an apparently dominant entrepreneur, too,
there's often an *éminence grise* (a 'day-wife', in one tycoon's
description) lurking essentially in the background. It's not simply
that two minds are better than one; good partners provide essential checks and balances for each other. Important though the
checks are, the balances, with one partner providing missing
skills to the other, matter even more.

At Sony, Akio Morita was the marketing wizard, while Masaru Ikuba provided the technical genius. That's a natural division, since very few inspired techies have an equal facility for
finance and management. At M & S, though, the matching qualities were different: Simon Marks provided the entrepreneurial
retailing dynamic, while Israel Sieff, working in close harmony,
perfected the management system and the people policies.

Such relationships demonstrate that nothing stimulates ideas
better than the interplay of equals. But entrepreneurial couples
(or triples, or more) also have to know, and obey, the partnership code. And all partners have to know and love the business.

You've then made a flying start: take a partner, especially a person you know well, and the chances of turning start-up into take-off are substantially greater than for a soloist.

It's as well to recognize the missing abilities before starting up. Peter Kindersley, for example, had the idea of publishing a new kind of reference book while working as an art director for publishers Mitchell Beazley. That function determined his approach: 'Traditionally, the problem with this kind of book . . . is that the people who made them came from Oxbridge. And if you go there, the importance of pictures gets drummed out of you.'

Kindersley's big idea – 'Through the picture I see reality: through the word I understand it' – still had to be turned into actuality. For that purpose, he found a like-minded partner at Mitchell Beazley in Christopher Dorling, a cartographer who had been converted into a salesman: 'We used to meet secretly in a Chelsea restaurant, where nobody would recognize us, and plotted how to set up the company.'

In the typical division of powers mentioned above, Kindersley concentrated on the creative side, while Dorling handled the business. It published its first three titles (despite a disastrous fire at the printers) in time for Christmas 1975. A dozen years later, Dorling sold his half of the business and retired. He received £3 million for his share of Dorling Kindersley, no doubt a large sum at the time: at end-1996, though, half of DK was worth the best part of £150 million.

Partnerships may begin equal, but they don't always end that way. However, the beginning is essential in ensuring that there will be something worthwhile; by definition, every successful partnership starts with a successful idea. The DK genesis is a perfect illustration. Like that pair, the partners have to decide what they are, what they can be, what they should be.

This step, a very important one, often isn't taken, though 'it's more important', says one experienced partner, 'to get the brand right than to get the product out'. Most businesses throw all their energies into producing without deciding on their 'brand' – the reason for the customer to buy from them and not from somebody else. When they started Pret a Manger, chartered surveyors Julian Metcalfe and Sinclair Beecham actually got that wrong.

They saw that the typical sandwich bar was 'either incredibly expensive or incredibly bad', but didn't see clearly how to improve on this. The price of their error – after starting with a shop in Victoria – was 'four relatively miserable years' spent delivering croissants, running delicatessens and opening a sandwich factory. That all distracted from the core vision of providing a better lunchtime product at a better price in better surroundings.

Once the pair concentrated on that vision, the second shop, in Holborn, produced a fifteen-month payback: profits ran at some 10 percent of a turnover which burst through £25 million as the shops expanded to thirty-two and their ambitions aimed for 200.

Partners, like Metcalfe and Beecham, or Dorling and Kindersley, must have a shared vision of the business, but it helps to have something in writing. It needn't be a long document. It's a manifesto, a credo, something more than a business plan. The ideas must be compatible, even if the personalities are like chalk and cheese, which is perfectly possible: partners can run the gamut from dead opposites to blood brothers. While one partner's strengths should complement the other's weaknesses, role reversal is also very valuable: the intuitive partner starts calling for more data, while the fact-based thinker retaliates with 'gut feelings'.

It isn't necessary for the partnership to be cemented by friendship outside the business. Some partners deliberately choose to stay at arm's-length: at one British engineering company, the three original partners, right into old age, rotated the chairmanship every two years and never used each other's first names. That kind of behaviour sounds quaint and is less and less likely to be found as management becomes increasingly informal.

Too great a degree of personal and family intimacy, however, can become a major difficulty if tough decisions have to be taken. One such decision can arise when the suspicion dawns that something on which you've been working is fundamentally wrong – including even the basic business idea. Like Beecham and Metcalfe at Pret a Manger, you must go all the way back to the beginning. That has to be easier for partners who have a good personal relationship. In the end, and the beginning, human relationships hold the key not only to successful part-nering, but to all sustainable business success. The human side won't work unless some simple rules are followed:

1 The partners (whether two or three or more) must contribute equally to the success of the enterprise. Imbalance will quickly lead to discontent and departure.
2 You can criticize each other's ideas, but you can't just dismiss them. If any partner insists on getting his or her own way at all times, and is intolerant of ideas put forward by others, it isn't a partnership and it will probably fail.
3 Flexibility is vital in any enterprise, since events rarely follow the planned and predicted course. That demands flexibility from all partners, who otherwise won't be able to react to change (or crisis, like DK's fire) in a timely and effective manner.
4 Fair shares for all. Some promising businesses have foundered on arguments about the disposal of money that has still to be earned. Greed is the least satisfactory motivator, and the most disruptive element in a partnership.

There are, of course, problems in partnering. The main disad-vantage – an insuperable one for the archetypical entrepreneur – is that power has to be shared, and that compromises and disagreements are bound to arise. So long as the partners share common objectives for the business, and complementary ones for themselves, that price is worth paying. The differences can be minimized, too, if each sphere of major influence is clearly delineated: the techie doesn't try to run the business, and the businessman doesn't attempt to call the technological tune.

Sometimes crossover is essential. When the wonderful en-gineer Soichiro Honda obstinately refused to accept that cars (unlike his beloved motorbikes) had to have water-cooled engines, his long-term partner, Takeo Fujisawa, was sent into action by the techies. Although Honda grumbled that the issue was 'difficult for a man like you [a finance and organization whiz] to understand', he was forced to accept Fujisawa's logic: either Honda ran the company or the engineering – he couldn't do both.

The story is a superb illustration of the way in which the strengths of a good partnership outweigh the weaknesses. Interestingly, the two Japanese hadn't even seen each other for some time. As the business develops, so the intimate collaboration with which it began must be diluted by the advent of others and the delegation of authority. As many high-achieving entrepreneurs stress, all other factors are outweighed by the recruitment and motivation of talented, creative people.

None of the partnership requisites will work without adding other human talents in the same spirit. Partnership is an initial way of achieving that essential end. Sharing in the business attracts talent which would never have joined a struggling start-up as hired hands; and sharing in all decisions achieves that synthesis of minds which, as noted, is inevitably more powerful than the operation of any single brain.

Sooner or later more brains are going to be required, and the key is to treat non-partners like real partners. Optimize their contribution, entertain their ideas, treat them flexibly and share the wealth – and you may well end up with a mini Hewlett-Packard, or a modest M & S. That should do fine.

Excellence by Experiment

There's no one right way to manage a business. Finding the right way for yourself requires trust, trial and error, and heresy. Time and again, inspired eccentricity pays high dividends, which is one major advantage of owning your own business: you can mind that business any way you like. However eccentric the entrepreneur's ideas may be, nobody can stop him putting them into practice.

When the family owner of an engineering company acted on that freedom, it did more than make him successful – it made him famous. The business, Semco, is actually in Brazil, but

Ricardo Semler spends much of his time travelling, partly because of his fame as a way-out manager and best-selling author. His book *Maverick!* entertainingly expounds the way-out ideas, but you quickly see that becoming a rich oddball is a very serious business.

For example, Semco features twice-yearly evaluation of its managers by subordinates. If the boss is rated low, he can lose his job in consequence. The multiple-choice questionnaire refers to the boss as 'the subject'. The first question out of thirty-six is 'When an employee makes a small mistake, the subject is (a) Irritated and unwilling to discuss the mistake, (b) Irritated but willing to discuss it, (c) Realizes the mistake and discusses it in a constructive manner, (d) Ignores the mistake and only pays attention to more important matters.'

There are no prizes for knowing the right answer, or for seeing that Semler has an ideal of management behaviour. The orthodox purpose behind the unorthodox approach is to obtain effective management – and low-rated leaders cannot provide that. Semler expects bosses to be relaxed, secure, fair, friendly, participative, innovative, very trustworthy and highly competent. And so say all of us, no doubt. The issue is whether orthodox organization helps people to behave in those ideal ways. Or should you emulate Semco and look for unorthodox approaches?

In the film *Goodbye Columbus*, a college graduate, just starting in his father's building supplies business, decides to stagger the men's lunch hours, to provide continuous cover. The father countermands the reform: 'No fancy deals! We all eat at the same time!' That's the natural reaction of the conservative in all situations. The traditional way is the accepted way. Any change is regarded with deep suspicion – let alone fancy deals.

It may be understandable, but it is indefensible once you recognize that every process in every business is capable of being improved. That is, better results can always be won at lower cost and in faster time. If somebody comes up with a potentially good idea (even the owner's son), rejecting the notion out of hand makes no sense. Ask, rather, what are the benefits? What are the drawbacks? What are the costs?

Would you, for example, copy Semler in these other ways?

Would you shut down twice a year for an afternoon while everyone cleans out the places where they work? Useless files, scrap and old machinery get ruthlessly thrown away. Would you limit all memos and reports to one piece of A4 paper, always headed by an arresting tabloid headline that sums up the key message? ('New Toaster Will Sell 20,000 Units for $2 Million Profit.')

The point is that rules are there not only to be kept or broken, but to be tested. Jim McCann, who founded and runs a world-wide business called 1-800-FLOWERS, wrote an entertaining piece in the *Wall Street Journal* that listed some excellent business rules. They included:

1 Get a good business education.
2 Choose a business you know well.
3 Be creative.
4 Go where the labour is cheapest.
5 Aim for high profit margins.
6 Have a strategic business plan.

The only problem is that McCann broke all six rules (and some others as well). He sees no entrepreneurial advantage in having a degree from a business school (something which Semler, however, does possess). Before McCann bought a small Manhattan flower shop in 1976 for $10,000, he knew nothing of the business; he believes firmly that the 'skills set is the same for any business', and that everything hinges on the entrepreneur's personal brand management: 'The brand you're managing is you.'

As for being creative, McCann has unashamedly stolen valuable ideas and practices from admired companies, and argues that real creativity lies 'in leveraging absolutely everything of value, regardless of its source'. It's very foolish to reinvent somebody else's invention, and very sensible to adopt and adapt the brainwave for your own benefit. If one of Semler's ideas (or McCann's) appeals to you, try it. Very possibly, it will work just as well in a new context.

Generally, it is wiser not to follow conventional wisdom, as

McCann found out when he moved from a good lease, in an area brimming with cheap labour, to Long Island. There, business costs are exceptionally high but, more important, the throbbing New York marketplace is very close. If the quality of labour matters more than the costs (which is usually the case), go to areas of abundant intelligence: that's why Silicon Valley's entrepreneurs are crammed into a narrow, expensive space, inhabited by high-cost people, near the great West Coast universities.

As for high margins, McCann believes that if you look after your employees and customers properly and keep the overheads low, margins will look after themselves. That really counts as a strategy, which is something he claims not to have. On his account, first 'we built a small chain of retail shops. Then we had ourselves a little wholesale company. Then 1-800-FLOWERS [a freephone delivery service] came along, and we tacked that on to the rest, crafting it into a brand.'

Instead of having a strategic business plan, 'If it seemed like a good idea, we did it.' In other words, McCann specializes in organized opportunism, which is the entrepreneurial version of corporate planning. He had a clear overall objective, which was to optimize organic growth, and a clear philosophy for turning the opportunities into profit. He runs a $250 million business on the same principles that he discovered in a previous incarnation as a social worker – motivating the unmotivated, setting goals and managing purposefully. 'In so many ways, the job I do now . . . is the same job I did back then, only easier and the pay is better.'

If McCann's broken rules seem like good ideas, implementing them involves very little time or trouble. Semco is full of brainwaves of similar description. The issue isn't whether or not others borrow Semler's specific innovations; he doesn't want imitators or disciples, only fellow experimenters. The issue is whether, like him, they are prepared to embark on a similar exercise of challenge and change – to try to create a company where they are more comfortable managing, and others are more comfortable being managed.

The comfort, of course, will be illusory if the business results are bad. Semco's are good – and apostles of unorthodoxy argue that doing things differently will improve profits. That comes about, for example, by cutting down on unnecessary activities such as enforcing rules and regulations, paying for expensive perks, or having unneeded support staff: Semco has shrunk its head office jobs by more than three-quarters, and cut its management layers to only three.

You don't really need more than three layers even in a great and grand business. American guru James Champy argues for that number. The top layer consists of 'enterprise managers', people whose responsibilities run across the business. If the firm is small enough, that may mean just one man or woman. The enterprise managers look after the second tier, 'people/process managers', like the person in charge of the workshop or the shop. They in turn take care of the rest: a third line of 'self-managers'.

That's a concept dear to Semler's heart. He believes in giving workers the maximum autonomy, the greatest possible opportunity to control and improve their own efforts. The three layers need to be supplemented in many businesses by a fourth strand: 'expertise managers' – people such as technical experts, who are indispensable, but who don't have a place in the management chain. They are, however, subject to the same checks on empire-building.

Empires eat up money, which is why McCann demands: 'Are you trimming the fat from everything – most particularly the executive row?' Any competent management consultant, of course, could achieve similar one-off savings to Semco's by 're-engineering' the business processes: studying each process end-to-end and eliminating unnecessary stages and costs. But the savings of unorthodoxy are the by-product of creating a unique company which goes on generating powerful new ideas, such as 'self-set pay'.

As Semler writes: 'Paying people whatever they want seems a sure route to bankruptcy, but we've been doing this for eight years, and we've never done better.' Self-awarded rises of as much as 10 percent, it seems, are exceptional. That wouldn't have been easy to sell to the fat cats who manage Britain's utilities. But that's the nub of the issue. You don't want to emulate bureaucratic corporations in any way. And if it's your own business, you certainly don't have to.

4

Avoiding the Traps

Strength in Weakness

The true entrepreneur surely doesn't walk around fearing that nemesis may be about to strike. Surely, these confident people stride out into the future with absolute certainty. Yet the most successful entrepreneur of the late century – software tycoon Bill Gates – asserts that 'Microsoft is always just two years away from failure'.

This isn't self-deprecation but a sober analysis of his mega-company's Strengths, Weaknesses, Opportunities and Threats. The greatest trap for the unwary businessman is to ignore the master's example. The SWOT analysis is invaluable. You take a calm, cool look at the organization's SWOTs. Then you seek to capitalize on the Strengths, eliminate the Weaknesses, seize the best Opportunities and counter the Threats.

Could the magnificent success of Microsoft, with its 90 percent gross margins and $9 billion of cash, really be threatened? In a brilliant study in *Worldlink* magazine, Howard Anderson showed that the answer is Yes – a dozen times over. Some of the threats, moreover, could affect any firm:

1 Could newcomers (including breakaways from your own company) create damaging competition?
2 Could a rival technology or some similar challenge come out on top?
3 Is the market developing in ways that favour competitors more than you?

4 Could your customers become your competitors?
5 Is there a major area in the market where you lag rather than lead?
6 Could an unsuspected challenge arrive from outside the existing industry?

The seventh question, of course, is whether, if any of the above apply to your business, you are doing anything effective to counter the Threat or, better still, to convert Threat into true Opportunity. As Anderson points out, it's all too easy to miss the Threats when riding high. For instance, his company, the Yankee Group, had been deeply impressed by the Strengths deployed by IBM in 1982 – and not surprisingly. IBM led in every important market of the time: mainframes, communications, mainframe storage, mini-computers and personal computers. It earned more profit than the next nine computer firms generated in total *sales*, and it spent more on R & D than they *earned* in profits. The Yankee Group concluded that IBM was invulnerable.

Yet the giant was about to begin a prolonged slide that left its market value amazingly far behind Microsoft's – at $86 billion in mid-1997 compared to $149 billion. Supposedly a highly entrepreneurial company, IBM was severely damaged, not by large rivals but by much smaller, sometimes very small entrepreneurs. What enabled the minnows to eat away at the whale?

The conventional explanation offered when great firms stumble is that they suffer from 'incompetence, bureaucracy, arrogance, tired executive blood, poor planning, and short-term investment horizons'. The words are from Clayton M. Christensen, whose book *The Innovator's Dilemma* investigates why 'new technologies cause great firms to fail' – and finds conclusively that the conventional explanation is all wrong. Incompetence, bureaucracy, and so on aren't to blame.

The failures of integrated steel companies against mini-mills, mainframe computers against microprocessors, variety stores against discounters, were paradoxically the result not of mismanagement but of managerial excellence. The book gives example after example to show that the failures lost leadership because they did exactly, expensively and very well what any business school professor would be happy to recommend:

1 Listen to your customers.
2 Invest aggressively in new technologies that will meet those customers' rising demands for performance.
3 Carefully study and meet market trends.
4 Allocate resources to investments that promise the best returns from the largest sales.

These four carefully calculated Strengths showed up in large and rising profits and sales. But the Strengths turned into Weaknesses because in industry after industry – disk drives, computers, retailing, steel-making, earth-moving equipment and many more – there was never a sound argument for going into the 'disruptive technologies', which nobody (not even their entrepreneurial creators) expected to inherit the earth.

The makers of 14-inch disk drives, for instance, had no reason to combat the small entrepreneurs who produced 8-inch versions of much the same technology. Their sole customers, the big mainframe companies, all wanted 14-inch drives and nobody much was interested in 8-inch products. These eventually found their market with mini-computers, then a tiny segment. As it grew, so did sales – and so did the power and performance of the 8-inch drives.

Stage by stage, they took over the entire 14-inch market. Not a single maker of 14-inch drives survived, and that included those who tried – too late – to meet the disruptive competition. A disruptive technology appeals to a different category of customers. They're typically attracted by lower prices and by different functionality, which in combination enable the purchasers to generate new types of product.

This is the classic entrepreneurial pounce. The Weakness of the innovators – they can't compete with established firms for established customers, and have little or no idea of where their products will sell – becomes their Strength. Rubbing in the paradox, these disruptive entrepreneurs break all the four rules of good management cited above.

1 They don't listen to customers, because they have none.
2 They develop lower-performance products instead of higher.
3 They don't rely on market research, because it's useless in these circumstances.
4 They head off into tiny markets, with sales ranging from zero to insignificant.

Christensen's analysis explains how a shrewd outside observer like the Yankee Group could be so spectacularly wrong about IBM. So can anybody, including insiders. How do you avoid the trap? In the first place, never concentrate just on your own Strengths. That's highly dangerous, because they can so easily turn into Weaknesses.

Gates's domination in PC operating systems equated with dependence: that dominant position almost led Microsoft from Strength into Weakness as the Internet took off. Gates was much nearer than his 'two years away from failure' when, with a mighty effort, he reversed engines and poured billions into Net software, probably just in time. The key Strengths at Microsoft evidently include a decisive ability to take drastic, radical action at speed.

Success can kill this entrepreneurial ability to react, because the whole company is geared to serving existing customers better and better. That makes it more and more difficult to encompass disruptive change. What happened to the 14-inch disk-drive-makers was repeated again and again every time a new generation of entrepreneurs reduced disk sizes. The rich old boys proved incapable of resisting competition which used the identical approach that had made their own wealth.

Strength outside in the market, where the customers are, is rightly the prime aim of any business. But existing market share should not be seen as a Strength in itself. The issue is how the share, whether leading or not, has been achieved and sustained. Is the product or service perceived as superior? Is it cheaper? Is the distribution more effective? Is the cost level lower? Is speed-to-market faster? Are customer requirements met more accurately?

Beyond that, are there disruptive technologies around which

threaten to enlarge and upset the market? One of Britain's classic
entrepreneurial success stories, that of J. C. Bamford, came from
disruption. In 1947 Joe Bamford produced the very first hydraulic excavator – a little machine, designed to go on the back
of tractors, that was entirely unsuitable for major construction
jobs. These were dominated by cable-actuated systems.

Their makers studied the hydraulic newcomers but, to quote
Christensen, 'Hydraulics was a technology that their customers
didn't need – indeed, couldn't use.' When hydraulic machines
could finally match cable, it was too late for the cable champions
to react: JCB and the rest took most of the market. In the process,
Joe and his son Sir Anthony took sales to great heights: £700
million in 1995. Their combined fortunes, created by a company
that remained resolutely private, hit £800 million in 1996.

That wealth creation is typical of 'weak', disruptive entrepreneurs. Those in one industry studied by Christensen achieved
$62 billion in sales between 1976 and 1994, which was twenty
times the figures for rivals who stuck to established ways. If that
isn't convincing enough, sales per firm in the second group
averaged a cumulative $64.5 million; the successes – all entre-
preneurial newcomers – averaged $1.9 billion. What were the
Strengths that made their Weaknesses so powerful?

The answer basically lies in highly adaptive people. In these
disruptive businesses, with their uncertain markets, there was
no alternative but to learn as you went along; to make false
starts and mistakes, but to react swiftly until you found the
better path. That's why by far the best way for large companies
to avoid the 14-inch fate is to finance imitation start-ups themselves – independent outfits that can attack small emerging
markets in the style of small emerging companies.

That is also a good way to cope with a general Threat today.
The brightest and best employees are tempted by their personal
SWOT analyses to break away. They could stay with the company and develop their ideas within its embrace, but fragmented
markets and booming stock prices, coupled with increasingly
plentiful venture capital, offer a constant temptation to join the
entrepreneurial ranks themselves. Giving them internal disruptive start-ups to run keeps them at home.

The canny entrepreneur lets his mavericks challenge the organization and help it, not only to take today's abundant Opportunities in style, against multiplying Threats, but to defend Strengths against becoming Weaknesses. And, equally important, to demonstrate that Weakness can be turned into Strength.

Entrepreneurial bosses, however, dare not forget that they are also and always one-person teams. They have to look after the future while expertly eliciting top performances from a smoothly running organization whose members are encouraged to be as enterprising, innovative and full of initiative as the boss.

That's multi-functional, and all the functions hinge on the basic ability to handle human beings and to surrender some of the boss's prerogatives. In the example mentioned in Chapter 3, where the permanent boss rotated the chairmanship of the committee and excluded himself, there was another indispensable part of the deal: the team decision – reached by consensus – had to prevail.

For the naturally dictatorial, that's hard to accept. But the results in this case were a marvellous bargain. The same small number of people were able to handle a workload that had multiplied almost eight times in the past few years. And if people perform that productively by bossing themselves, they must have a marvellous boss.

The Expansion Business

The Business Expansion Scheme was near the very core of the Thatcherite drive in the 1980s to regenerate the British economy through the workings of free enterprise. It was intended to encourage the spirit of capitalist venture and to stimulate a rich stream of new entrepreneurs. So whatever happened to the BES?

The scheme itself, which allowed investors to offset their contributions against income tax, is dead and gone. So, alas, are many of the small companies into which investors sank their funds. Most BES companies failed, relatively or absolutely. Some of the failure is attributable to the government of the day. The scheme excluded family and limited the participation of the entrepreneurs themselves – the two most likely and lenient sources of funds.

Then, the rules were made more and more restrictive as officials tried to prevent abuse of the scheme by tax-avoidance artists. The enforced legal and other expenses, moreover, were high in relation to the limited sums that could be raised under the rules. The net result was that many BES companies, though they tapped investors for significant funds, emerged from the operation under-capitalized.

Alas, to many of the wannabees it didn't feel that way. They spent the funds fast, and the subsequent failures flash an important warning. Raising money is essential, but fund-raising achieves nothing of itself. The future of the business hinges on the use of the capital, and the warming sight of cash in hand can tempt entrepreneurs away from using that money wisely and well.

The Thatcherite formula was thus deeply flawed in application, both by its political authors and its business users. One professional participant in the BES bonanza-that-wasn't believes that the death rate of genuine traders, providing products and/ or services, was alarmingly high: nine out of ten. That's far greater than would be expected – higher even than the typical failure rate of new businesses. And many of the BES companies were already reasonably well established.

There's disagreement about the statistics. Charles Fry of Johnson Fry, the leading player in this game, reckons that the fall-out rate was actually far less: about half. That's hardly encouraging, either. Johnson Fry's own experience was a failure rate of 40 percent. Fry points out that this compares perfectly well with the normal experience of venture capital.

The business cycle also turned against the BES. Companies that raised their BES funds just before the 1990 recession did 'frightfully well' to achieve survival. The amount of money they could raise (with the upper limit progressively scaled down by the government to a patently inadequate £500,000) wasn't nearly enough to shelter them from the recessionary blasts, and very few were able to persuade shareholders to provide more.

That's where the forbidden family contributors might have been forthcoming. There was no hope of persuading institutions to put their money alongside that of the suffering shareholders. Small, under-capitalized and struggling businesses aren't the most attractive homes for institutional funds. The consequent failures make a general point about any business venture, and not just the kind that queued up for BES capital.

As Fry says, 'it never goes according to plan'. Venture capitalists seldom believe the business plans with which they are presented; they look for evidence of coherence and intelligence, but they know that events will diverge, sharply and probably soon, from design. So, when they take on an investment, the venture capitalists include provision for later injections of capital if required.

That's only wise. If you haven't lined up second-round finance at the beginning, the money won't be there if it is urgently needed – which will probably happen. Recession isn't the only threat: success itself can stretch the finances of a growing business to the limits and beyond. Without adequate working capital, expansion cannot be financed, and fast growth, as noted in Chapter 1, can be as fatal as declining sales.

Not that the BES firms which dodged the second Thatcher recession worked wonders. The experiences of Johnson Fry's own first five offerings were better than most. Two were wine companies, which in the end paid their investors respectively 82p and 124p in the £ (to which 40p tax relief can be added), and three were property firms. (Note that none of the quintet really fitted the hopes for enterprising economic regeneration with which the BES was launched.)

One property firm paid out £2.40, another £1.20, and a third could have yielded £2.50 – if you got out in time. The company went public and then went bust, a victim of the aforementioned recession. That claimed many victims up and down the land, including major groups. But small firms in their early days are especially vulnerable to deterioration in the economy or the market. If you are walking a tightrope, any severe oscillation is liable to make you lose your balance.

As Fry notes, such vulnerability was by no means confined

to BES enterprises. Nor are they the only victims of the other
weaknesses that laid them low, such as under-capitalization. He
recalls a six-shop chain which, to make economic sense, 'needed
to have twelve'. It couldn't raise any more money, and duly
went the way of all flesh. In other cases, people who coped
perfectly well with two pubs, say, were completely thrown when
confronted with six and the need for 'totally different skills'.

Northern pub group Café Inns did develop the necessary arts
and crafts, and joined the first of the few in the Alternative
Investment Market. As an investment, however, the company
did not match the huge success of others in its business. One
Hugh 'Sooty' Corbett made £4.5 million from his first two pub
chains, the Slug and Lettuce and Harvey Floorbangers, before
starting a third. David Bruce achieved the requisite number of
a dozen pubs in nine years and sold his Firkins for £6.5 million.

That's a mere tenth of the fortune created by Tim Martin's
110 pubs, gathered together under the J. D. Wetherspoon name.
And Martin is left far behind by David Cannon's sale of 270
Magic Pub outlets for £197 million; £70 million going to the
happy entrepreneur. The pub winners show that the BES failures and relative disappointments ultimately resulted not from
poor choice of market or recession, but from poor exploitation
of the opportunities, including failure to find enough capital
from sources other than the scheme.

Very few other BES entrepreneurs had the skills set of Britannia Marine, for example, a supplier of offshore support vessels
for North Sea oilrigs. Britannia prospered so well that it entered
the main stock market, and investors who got in at the bottom
trebled their money in fairly quick order. By and large, though,
the BES record, like that of the venture capitalists, shows that
investors in start-ups and like ventures have to be mentally
prepared for failure.

That mental preparedness doesn't always exist among entrepreneurs, says Fry, and that's another reason why they fail. They
are, rightly, hooked on success, which is the essence of the
entrepreneurial drive. Unfortunately, if they miss their targets,
the mind-set of success becomes mindless; instead of buckling
down to the task of renewing and redirecting their efforts, they

'throw their hands in the air' and are totally unable to cope.

'That's when we send in our own people to clear up the mess' – if it can be cleared up, that is. The would-be cleaners are liable to find too many skeletons jostling in the cupboards. However much care has been taken before the decision to invest, the surprises are often nasty. Sometimes entrepreneurs who seemed to be 'perfectly sensible people turn out to be complete idiots'. Others succumb to the personal problems and strains that often accompany the entrepreneurial existence – 'all human life is there'.

Nasty surprises are far less likely to arise if entrepreneurs obey a brief but powerful code of practice.

1 Answer to a solid board of outside directors, meeting regularly.
2 Establish an accurate monthly reporting system against budget which triggers corrective action if the numbers stray off line.
3 Build up strong staff with clear responsibilities.
4 Concentrate on building up strength in the marketplace.
5 Run the finances well enough to maintain good relations with the bank.

The BES failures fell down on some, if not all, of these simple but stern necessities. Yet all the businesses had passed fairly stern professional vetting before being allowed to solicit funds from the public. Too few, however, regarded the enforced improvements in their financial housekeeping as a foundation on which to build better procedures and better management. However much money you have raised, and however rapidly the business has grown, those improvements are more than valuable; they are imperative. The need for further improvement will never disappear.

The Virtues of Failure

When Thomas Watson, the founder of IBM, observed that success lies on the far side of failure, he was preaching a double sermon. The first lesson is to persevere through all setbacks, which will be numerous. The second is equally important. Unlike almost everybody else, learn from your mistakes – they will be plentiful, but they will teach you plenty.

Setbacks are inevitable in the history of any enterprise. Many great entrepreneurs looked like nothing better that stumblebums in their first stabs at business. Henry Ford, who eventually created the largest personal fortune of all time, went broke three times before making his breakthrough. Innumerable other venturers, big-thinking and small, can look back at similar flops. The important difference, however, is that they still looked forwards.

The entrepreneurs' attitude towards error, as opposed to complete failure, has the same forward-looking quality. They are far less interested in blame than in how to capitalize on the lessons of failure. Treated in this spirit, mistakes can yield far more reward than rejoicing in success. Moreover, such an approach avoids a common trap for entrepreneurs: to bask in their own glory, and to assume that success sanctifies their methods and proves their cleverness.

That is no way to learn, and without learning progress grinds to a halt. Another American entrepreneur, Royal D. Little, founder of the Textron conglomerate, was typically wise to entitle his book *How to Lose $100 Million and Other Useful Information*. The ability to analyse one's own mistakes, so that you will not repeat them, is indispensable to the entrepreneur; risk and opportunity always carry within them the seeds of potential error.

The greatest of errors, though, could be the self-fulfilling prophecy. Every time a business is closed, a project is cancelled, or a product is withdrawn from the market, those responsible have slammed the door on the possibility that, tackled differently, the business might have flourished, the project might have made a money-spinning breakthrough, or the product might have become a market leader. The far side of failure cannot now be reached.

The true entrepreneur instinctively seeks to make the best of what initially seems to be an impossibly bad job. A prime example of avoiding the self-fulfilling prophecy and crossing over to success comes from a company whose brand-new product, considered a certain winner, was losing money heavily, making no impact in the market and causing extreme stress and overwork. The disaster flowed from a common error: mindless extrapolation of the past into the future.

That can prove fatal even when the future is very recent. The company had experienced strong demand in this market segment in the preceding months, and saw an opportunity to cash in still more heavily. The new product was intelligently designed to cream off more boomtime sales. But even as it was launched, the market went dead. The company had been misled by looking only at its own sales. With the results of its competitors factored in, the chosen market was evidently far too weak to support another product.

How could the company escape from its devastating losses? The answer is to do what all true entrepreneurs do in such predicaments: their homework. The thorough analysis that had been wrongly and dangerously absent beforehand now revealed only three alternatives: battling on regardless, or closure, or 'tweaking' the product (altering its configuration to attack a different segment of the market).

Fighting on was futile and far too costly. Closure would also have been costly, not to mention embarrassing. Only the third course of action offered any real hope. The plans could be scaled down without loss of opportunity, simply because the originally chosen segment offered none. The heavily tweaked product duly surged on to expand and dominate its new segment as a highly profitable market leader.

Such triumphs do not, of course, mean that failure is always reversible. But that raises a fundamental and taxing problem. How do you decide when to persist, keeping the patient alive and seeking a radical cure, rather than letting nature take its course? That answer must lie, as in the case just cited, with dispassionate analysis. Here the management accountant came into his own. His sums showed that by scaling down production to serve the new segment, first-year losses would be kept to £50,000. Breakeven the next year would be followed by £100,000 profit in the third. So it transpired – almost to the penny.

Dispassionate analysis and sustained faith are both required to take new projects safely through their most dangerous moments: when they are taking far longer, costing far more, and earning far less than expected. The most careful business plan is liable to under-estimate the time and the cost by half, and to over-estimate revenues by the same amount. Do the sums and the plan all over again. If the numbers still make sense, and the faith still shines, carry on. This time, the chances are better because you are learning and applying the lessons of failure.

The main area of business failure, however, is not the one-off disaster, but day-to-day operational error, compounded month-by-month and year-by-year. That's far more likely than a single dud investment to bring a company to its knees. On that there's no sharper authority than Albert J. Dunlap, who boasts in his book, *Mean Business*: 'I save bad companies and make good companies great.'

A one-man entrepreneur, skilled in the business of reaching the far side of failure, Dunlap specializes in eliminating mistakes on the grand scale. He personally earned $100 million from a rapid turnaround of Scott Paper in which 11,200 jobs were lost as managers were sacked, offices closed, R & D cut, suppliers crushed and unwanted businesses sold off. As he says: 'A similar situation faces every company, every day.'

The business, or part of the business, is being wrongly managed at excessive cost; or products or services are wrong for the market and have the wrong cost and pricing structure; or (see above) a project is aiming for the wrong targets and missing them because of wrong tactics and strategies; or 'everything' is being 'done wrong' – as the future Lord Weinstock, who had joined GEC as a radio and TV entrepreneur, found on taking command of a rapidly failing electrical empire.

His turnaround was achieved by applying the entrepreneurial razor to a bloated corporate body. Like all other examples of failure turned into success, the 'real old mess' that Weinstock unearthed and cured raises a key question: Why does it so often need the threat of failure to stimulate a business to cross over to success? That need is a failure in itself. A crisis rarely happens overnight. It stems from a history of bungle laid upon bungle, in a system that stops people from taking action to prevent the build-up from becoming terminal.

The safest assumption is that gross failures – such as taking three times as long over manufacture as needed, requiring three girls to sell a customer six bottles of wine in a supermarket, or making parts for two-thirds more than the necessary cost – are symptoms of deeper malaise: of systemic failure. Never believe that if you improve parts of a system, you will necessarily improve the whole. The whole can only be improved as a whole.

If the business is suffering from systemic failure, though, that can also be the springboard for success. The opportunities for advance (as at Weinstock's GEC) are far greater than when a system is already operating at high efficiency. The better time to act, however, is before failure strikes, while the system still seems to be good. The good can become the enemy of the better, and will rapidly cease to be the best without continuous challenge.

The same approach that saves threatened manufacturing plants and businesses will work equal wonders at any time. Check everything – the products, the methods, the costs, the marketing, the ratios – against the best competitive benchmarks, and set targets which are much higher than the highest you can find. Matching the best may simply not be good enough. The entrepreneurial urge to outdo everybody in sight is the right way to progress.

By the same token, you cannot afford to tolerate systemic failure. The system is failing a manufacturing company, according to James P. Womack and Daniel T. Jones, the authors of *Lean Thinking*, if . . .

1 you do not know what the customer values most
2 you have not specified where to create customer value
3 you have not identified every step in the process, from design to production to final distribution
4 you have not eliminated waste by smoothing the flow between each step
5 you do not produce only to customer order

6 you do not strive for perfection, in which every action improves profitability.

These six failures, if reversed, adapt easily into a code of success for non-manufacturers and manufacturers alike. Success will follow from finding out what the customer wants, and supplying that value to order, through the most economical flow achievable. But the most important element in the philosophy is the striving for unattainable perfection.

The greatest entrepreneurs have never been able to satisfy themselves with anything less. They also knew – and know – that you can approach the ideal only through trial and much error. Perhaps old Tom Watson's saying needs modification. It's not only success that lies on the far side of failure, it's also perfection.

When the Plug is Pulled

Going bust is the fate which businessmen most fear. Paradoxically, though, you can be too fearful. Avoiding financial risk altogether can also mean missing opportunities. Risk in this context does not mean gambling. True entrepreneurs only bet on sure things – or so they believe. They don't back long shots, which are no more likely to win in business than on racetracks.

This truth was marked indelibly on my mind at one of a series of dinners given by Edward de Bono. The object was to think about the subject he has made his own – thinking. At this particular dinner, the specific item on the agenda was risk. Why didn't British managers show more enthusiasm for ventures involving risk? Why did they prefer the safety of the *status quo* to taking chances?

The answers seem obvious enough. If the risk proves too risky, the project and your career may blow up in your face. Sticking to the *status quo* looks inherently safe; taking a chance is by definition dangerous. I noticed, however, that three self-made multi-millionaires sat opposite me. When I asked whether they had ever taken a risk, the answer was unanimous: No. Yet all three had turned unproven business ideas (like making commercial vehicle kits for assembly in the Middle East) into proven fortunes.

What explained their answer was the confidence mentioned above. They wholly believed in the strength of their ideas, and were totally convinced that their plans would work. They were running risks, of course, but these risks are common to any enterprise – indeed, to almost any human activity – and are completely unavoidable.

First, you may be wrong. Second, you may be right, but your execution may be wrong. Third, you may be outdone by somebody else. If any of these three 'risks' invariably put people off, no enterprise, from matrimony to medicine, would ever get off the ground. The terrible trio, however, can cause a paralysing degree of fear. There is no such thing as a frightened entrepreneur. Enterprise means having the courage to back yourself. So its greatest enemy is the anxiety that stops most people from ever taking the entrepreneurial road, or stops them short after the journey has actually began.

Entrepreneurs face specific difficulties, however. One is that opportunists have big imaginative ideas – and their reach can easily exceed their practical grasp. They sink into the financial mire, not because the venture is wrong-headed or their management inept, but because they lack the capital resources to finance success and to bridge the long and usually unplanned wait (two years is the norm) before project turns into profit.

For that reason, many of today's rich and respected businesses once teetered on the financial brink over which far more firms toppled. Going bust in this way, simply running out of money, is a horrible experience, but it isn't the end of the world; nor need it end the entrepreneurial dream. That is what two entrepreneurs, Christopher Ward and Michael Potter, happily discovered when their venture capitalists decided to pull the plug.

At the start, the partners were fully aware of the risks of over-reaching. They knew that one way to avoid that fate is to launch a 'bootstrap' operation; you then grow organically only as fast as resources will allow. They considered and rejected that safer option. Instead they decided in 1983 to set up Redwood Publishing on a distinctly more ambitious programme.

As experienced professionals, Ward, ex-editor of the *Daily Express*, and Potter, ex-Haymarket Publishing, thought it better to raise what capital they could and run as hard and fast as possible. Many entrepreneurs make the mistake of hanging on to the whole equity, but the pair argued (rightly) that it is better to seek 40 percent of a mountain than 100 percent of a molehill. They duly brought in outside investors.

The pair proceeded to execute their intentions well, and quickly established a reputation for publishing high-quality magazines under contract for customers like American Express and Marks & Spencer. That delighted the venture capital financiers, but the money men were far less enthralled by large early losses. The hard-and-fast approach always runs that risk: as expenditure piles up more rapidly than income, the business starts building towards financial crisis.

At Redwood, crisis duly arrived just before Christmas (the traditional season of good cheer and sackings). The financiers had their fingers on the plug; no more money would be provided unless the bank first guaranteed the overdraft. The bank was happy to do so, but only, of course, if the financiers first provided more finance. Catch 22.

At the last gasp, Ward remembered meeting a more amiable and amenable banker on a courtesy trip to a champagne house. ('I often wonder what would have happened if I had not visited Veuve Cliquot'). After agreeing to see the partners at very short notice, the friendly banker broke the vicious circle by giving the necessary guarantee. Redwood was still in trouble, though.

Characteristically, the strength of the projects was uneven. The idea behind one magazine, *Airport*, distributed free at airports to all those passengers milling about, and theoretically eager to read the magazine and its advertisements, sounded great. But the project was losing money heavily. Ward was miserably contemplating *Airport*'s inevitable demise when the super-rich American entrepreneur Chuck Feeney, founder of Duty Free Shoppers, passing time between flights, rang from Heathrow for a chat.

Hearing the news, he told Ward to hold everything, rang again after having touched down on Concorde in New York, bought the ailing magazine and pumped some extra finance into Redwood for good measure. Because the basic business was sound, and because Ward and Potter provided the apposite blend of commercial and creative talent, the wind was now set fair – though even the partners were joyfully surprised by what followed.

Redwood passed into the hands of the BBC, which wanted a magazine arm to exploit some of its programmes. When that eventually proved politically embarrassing (it was stigmatized as unfair competition), the Corporation sold the company back to the partners, minus the programme-linked titles. In the process, Ward and Potter were turned into millionaires. Far more important, they had a saleable asset which could take them into the multi-millionaire bracket.

Redwood was bought by the advertising agency Abbott Mead Vickers in 1993 for £12.5 million. That's a tribute to the consistently high quality of the partners' products in an expanding market, their ability to win and sustain lucrative publishing contracts, and their persistence. But without proper, permanent financing, Redwood would still have been felled long before this splendid coming-of-age.

Over-reaching your resources is the classic cause of bankruptcy. Whether it takes the form of under-capitalization (you haven't obtained enough equity or loan capital) or over-trading (you're taking on more business than you can finance), the result is the same. You simply run out of cash.

Most over-reachers, however, compound their troubles by errors on other fronts (like *Airport*). Direct mail consultant Drayton Bird, who retired from running a world-wide direct mail empire to win individual success with his own business (see Chapter 5), remembers in excruciating detail why his first business flight plunged to earth. The first cause was over-reaching: he was in seven different businesses at once. Worse still, nobody had told him to keep his various interests separate so he lumped them together and the most addled business, over-trading vigorously, pulled the whole lot down. That disaster was

predictable, given that Bird had failed to plan for anything at
all, let alone the worst. Like many entrepreneurs (and not just
in their first forays), he and his partner were seriously over-
optimistic. That's an occupational hazard. No entrepreneur plans
for failure, and high hopes are easily converted into excessive
targets.

Bird had not played the simple, essential game known as 'Best
World, Worst World'. You put down on paper your estimate of
the worst that could possibly happen, and of the best that you
have envisaged in your wildest dreams. Either the worst case or
the best could stretch finances beyond breaking point – the worst
because you lack the revenue to sustain your expenditure, the
best because you lack the funds to finance your success.

The analysis establishes what risks you are running, and what
crises you need to forestall, if you can. Analysis should be backed
by attitudes. The entrepreneur greatly reduces the risks of failure
by following eight powerful principles:

1 Update: stay in the forefront of knowledge about your
  business.
2 Newthink: never stop looking for new ideas and adopting the
  best.
3 Aim: always have clear, written objectives.
4 Fire: when you have to act, act fast.
5 Revise: look for continuous improvement in everything.
6 Assess: get quick, accurate measurements of everything that
  matters.
7 Inform: tell your people all you can all the time, and listen
  to what they say in return.
8 Decide: when a decision must be made, make it.

By no coincidence those eight principles spell a vital word:
UNAFRAID. Their proper application will sustain confidence and
reduce risk, even in the darkest days, helping to avert a Red-
wood-type crunch and to avoid a Bird-like crash. Today, the
Redwood partners, very understandably, with a market-leading
twenty-two magazines printing 120 million copies annually, are
absolutely sure that their chosen risk was right. That's hindsight;

but their fearless confidence was always correct. As good poker players know, scared money never wins.

How to Diversify

If you sell an unvarying, unaccompanied product and service, sooner or later the well is likely to run dry. The technology may be overtaken, like mechanical typewriters, zapped first by the electric and electronic versions and then by the PC. Or competition may drive down margins to so-called 'commodity' levels, so that profits become harder and harder to earn. Or whole markets may vanish.

To protect yourself against such fates, you have to open the windows of opportunity – to diversify. That can be done safely by following intelligent processes. It can't be done only on hunch and hope, though hope has to loom very large if you are buying into, or starting up, a business of which you know nothing. The failure rate in such circumstances is intimidatingly high.

For all that, at any given time, entrepreneurs are happily buying other unrelated businesses to diversify their risks and raise their growth rates – while other businessmen are unhappily offloading the disappointments that have resulted from following the same strategy in the past. Probably the numbers of buyers and sellers are about equal. The success rate will never improve, because of the inherent difficulties of mastering a business of which you are ignorant.

The first step in intelligent diversifying must therefore be to ensure that you are fully exploiting the opportunities under your own nose. Even highly successful firms with a history of developing winning products can slide gradually into a rut. Thus one company which had raised its earnings to new records for thirty-eight consecutive years suddenly found that its emphasis had shifted to reducing costs – and that was not enough: 'We were cutting, cutting, cutting. But you can only go so far.'

The solution was to go back to the drawing-board. The boss inaugurated two-day sessions devoted entirely to the search for internal growth opportunities. Many entrepreneurs would find this approach too formal. But if you neglect the formalities, you may miss the chance for a Double Whammy. In a business with 10 percent margins, if sales and costs rise in step by 50 percent, that is also the percentage rise in profit. Cut 5 percent from costs at the same time, or boost sales by an extra 5 percent without raising costs, and your profits double.

The search for the Double Whammy effect must take precedence over diversification. In strategies designed to boost sales from existing product lines, a company is playing from strength. In contrast, unfamiliarity with a new business must mean that you're playing from weakness – and that you will be lucky to get away merely with weak results. Firms that propose to make a complete break from their present abilities are asking for trouble; and that is generally what they receive.

That isn't true only of acquisitions, it also applies to organic diversifications that the company has started itself. Listen to an expert like Fred Buggie of Strategic Innovations International (SII), and the first lesson to be learned is the one above: that successful diversification is far more likely to spring from your existing strengths, and not from the supposed strengths that you acquire.

The lesson is almost always learned the hard way – as in the miserable case of a young company which made several costly purchases. All were unsuccessful save one; the only one, of course, which was in exactly the same business. The other, unrelated buys were so misguided, and lost so many millions, that the whole company almost went under. The reasons why ventures into strange areas are so unlikely to succeed were made perfectly clear by one of Sir John Harvey-Jones's celebrated troubleshooting visits (see Chapter 1).

The company concerned was a small sub-contractor, Velden Engineering, which decided to indulge itself in golf carts and adjustable beds. These could not have been much further removed from its main activity, making small components to order for other engineers.

The golf carts looked quite nifty, but not the firm. First, it had no experience or capacity in marketing. Second, it had no experience or facility in efficient series production of assembled products. Third, it already made far too many products far too inefficiently. As the troubleshooter pointed out with some force, it was using obsolete, slow and labour-intensive machines on the argument that they are cheap – a big mistake. Poorly performing machines will destroy productivity and damage quality.

Despite (or because of) buying cheap machinery, Velden's profits were exiguous. You cannot hope to diversify successfully from a weak base. Any new enterprise will divert time, attention and money from the main business. The first step in diversifying, therefore, is paradoxical: Look at the base activities and make sure that they are being run as efficiently, productively and profitably as possible.

This is the first stage of a Buggie investigation. SII begins by assessing the existing strengths of the would-be diversifier (an exercise which in Velden's case would have been deeply depressing). What if your inventory of strengths, honestly compiled, comes up with a more encouraging platform? The world is full of possibilities, which is a problem in itself. It is not just a question of making a random choice.

Going into a market because it seemed to be booming led some of the world's greatest companies into computing; they were nearly all forced to exit after heavy losses. Before reaching the stage of making a more intelligent choice, management must establish a list of alternatives; that is, potentially valuable uses and extensions of the firm's true talents. If you're publishing a newsletter, for example, you know about using direct mail to tap targeted audiences. What other lines of business does that suggest?

The answer will go beyond the extension of your existing product line which I cited above as the logical first step to growth. Such extensions account for most so-called 'new' products, very few of which are truly new. Even when Mercedes-Benz moved down in size and price to compete against BMW's executive saloons, it wasn't truly diversifying, but broadening its market. Its later venture into micro-cars with the Swatch watch company, though, has taken the company into genuinely new territory, because both the product concept (a tiny two-seater) and the market are unproven. Mercedes' deep know-

ledge of cars and engineering (and its equally deep purse) remain
key strengths. The fact that the micro-car market is so different
explains why Merc was sensible to ally itself with Swatch, which
knows far more about low-cost production, miniaturization,
fashion and mass marketing.

But if the mighty Merc needs outside help, true diversifiers
of any size must be in the same boat. If you can't afford to
hire consultants, however, the next best thing is to adopt their
techniques. Buggie's formula is easy to follow, but (like most
things in the entrepreneurial life) harder to execute:

1 You have already established with total honesty what the firm
   does well (and badly).
2 You now set down the criteria (product characteristics, return
   on investment, sales volume, share of market) that the new
   line of business should satisfy.
3 You look inside the company, forming a group with mixed
   backgrounds and talents, and asking the team to assemble a
   list of hopeful projects that suit the firm's abilities and promise
   to meet the criteria.
4 You look outside for expertise as well as inside.

Beecham would not now be part of SmithKline Beecham, a
global health-care giant, if its boss hadn't turned to Ernst Chain,
the great penicillin pioneer, for advice on where to direct its
research. That counsel led to fermentation chemistry and the
money-spinning synthetic penicillins (which, according to
legend, reached the market just in time – a matter of weeks
ahead of the closest contender).

Buggie calls his equivalent use of outsider expertise a 'brain
bank'. The internal team starts the process by brainstorming as
many ideas as possible in a highly organized session, preferably
held away from the firm's premises, using a leader from inside
and a facilitator (preferably from outside). The session needs
from five to seven people, drawn from different backgrounds.

You then import 'brain bank' experts, recruited from universities, the trade press or wherever, to help the insiders to screen
ideas and to test their technical and economic feasibility. Unlike

consultants, incidentally, experts used in this way come extremely cheap. The insiders and the brain bank together will
generate a short-list. Then you go through the same process all
over again, until you arrive at the single diversification which
best satisfies your original criteria.

The procedure sounds painstaking and time-consuming. So it
is. That's why most diversifiers (see Velden) instead operate on
hunch and hope. That is one good reason why they fail. Another,
however, is that diversifications are like any other business. It is
not enough to plant them; they have to be watered, nurtured and
pruned – in a word, managed. The business requires the same key
attributes that *Fortune* magazine identified from a study of fast-
growth companies. Its guinea-pigs had five traits in common:

1 Stable, experienced management teams.
2 Heavy spending on research and development.
3 Intensive training of all employees.
4 First-class recruitment.
5 Effective systems for planning, developing people and
markets, measurement and reward.

In theory, the five apply whether the diversified business is an
acquisition or a start-up. The latter is extremely unlikely to have
a stable, experienced management team, or the financial
capacity to afford major investment in R & D, or the time and
spare management capacity to develop systems. Those three
capabilities come only with success. Any firm can afford top-class
recruitment and training. To put that another way, no diversification can succeed without them. Many diversifiers try to prove
this wrong. They don't succeed in that; and that is why they
don't succeed.

What You Want is What You Get

When GUI (the graphical user interface) came along, users of
PCs quickly came to appreciate the associated initials WYSIWYG:
What You See Is What You Get. The words and images on the

screen reappear exactly on the print-out. For entrepreneurs, WYWIWYG are the magic initials: What You Want Is What You Get. The ambitions set the bounds for the success.

One basic question that faces every firm establishes the key desire. Do you want your business to grow, or are you broadly content with what you have? In the first, expansionist case, according to a study by Michael Hay and Kimya Kamshad of the London Business School, you could be either a 'value-builder' or an 'empire-builder'. If growth doesn't appeal, however, your type might be 'controller' or (more likely) 'life-styler'.

Life-stylers agree with this statement: 'I am not very keen to grow the business much beyond its current size since to do so I would need to change the ownership structure and/or control of the firm.' If that is your style, which is, perhaps, the traditional image of the smaller firm, it is out-of-date. You are in a small minority, and you are certainly no great shakes as an entrepreneur.

Nor is anybody who echoes this statement: 'I am not very keen to grow the business much beyond its current size since to do so would make it too difficult for me to keep track of the firm's operations.' These are the no-growth controllers. But, even if you throw in the life-stylers and other reluctant heroes, the growth-averse accounted for well under half the small firms (in printing, software and instruments) that were the subjects of the study.

The growth-minded majority included those (a quarter of the subjects) who wanted to build value rather than empires: 'I am very keen to expand the business and then find a buyer to buy me out.' The biggest group, however, are the idols of all those Thatcherites and post-Thatcherites who hold that the dynamism of smaller businesses is the lifeblood of free enterprise: 'I am very keen to expand the business and continue to run it myself.'

The big question, though, is whether the dynamic attitudes of these entrepreneurs had dynamic results. Apparently not: in the year studied, 11 percent of the firms grew not an inch, while 35 percent suffered a drop in sales. Since a great British recession was still in full swing, that's not too dismal a result; economic gloom must have contributed to the largest confessed restraint on growth – 'intensity of competition'.

A less obvious factor is that the firms paid more lip-service than service to innovation. Without innovation, you cannot expect to grow in a climate of intense competition. That is a permanent feature of the new economy. Innovation, however, involves risk, to which both growers and non-growers seem averse, especially proprietors; 30 percent were 'unwilling to pursue any risky growth strategies'.

That compared with 18 percent of the non-proprietorial managers, a more thrusting bunch altogether. All the same, only a fifth even of the managerial types agreed that 'Growth is everything: we cannot survive in this business unless we grow. Success only comes from taking big chances, and I would risk a lot for a strategy which promised to deliver strong long-term growth.'

Those rather intimidating words may help to explain why some three-fifths of the firms replied in favour of relative safety, taking a 'medium-risk option' – if growth prospects are 'reasonably good'. But growth isn't their leading objective, anyway. In all three industries, more firms ranked profit as 'very important', with growth second (though quite close), followed by market share, steady employment and value for sale.

Looking at all these responses, the LBS *Business Strategy Review* argued that 'a key reason' why many smaller owner-managed firms don't grow is simple. WYWIWYG: their owner-managers have other, lesser objectives, and that is what they get.

Move on to 1996, with the British economy booming again, and you might expect a stronger showing from the growth addicts. The LBS was again involved in much wider research by Pulse, along with the two linked accountancy firms, Binder Hamlyn and Arthur Andersen. The research looked at a sample of 3,000 private companies, supplemented by analysis of the financial performance of nearly 14,000 private firms. The conclusion was much the same: 'it is the directors' attitude towards growth that is crucially important.'

Binder Hamlyn's Mary Reilly adds: 'Without the right attitude, a business with everything going for it will fail.' The later study differs somewhat in its nomenclature: it still uses 'life-stylers' and 'value-builders', but has as its third category 'value har-vesters'. The latter 'seek to extract cash out of their business, perhaps prior to the owner's retirement or to reduce debt in highly geared companies'.

You cannot trust directors to put themselves in the right one of these classifications. In fact, 'despite what many directors say when asked, analysis of their company records shows that they are clearly going for the comfortable option of maintaining their lifestyle.' These people account for over two-fifths of the Pulse sample. Their businesses grew or shrank by no more than 25 percent over the four years 1990 to 1994. In contrast, 17 percent of the sample, obviously value-builders, more than doubled, while another 16 percent grew by 50 percent to 100 percent – and you won't achieve that kind of growth without real entre-preneurial zing. That zing, in turn, is most likely to be found among the young. The Pulse survey showed firms whose direc-tors were under thirty easily outstripping other age brackets in growth of pre-tax profits.

The profit out-performance was won even though the four-year turnover expansion of the younger group was identical to that of the thirty- to forty-four-year-olds. One explanation is immediately obvious. The companies in the latter group added proportionately more employees – the entrepreneurial motiv-ation to maximize profit by minimizing costs dwindles with age.

How greatly the motivation has been preserved can be tested against half-a-dozen factors derived from Professor J. W. Hunt's *Managing People at Work*. Using a scale of one to five, rank them in rising order of their importance to you:

• Recognition of your achievements by others.
• Power to influence others.
• The ability to do what you want.
• A comfortable life-style.
• A well-ordered life, in work and at home.
• Agreeable relationships with others.

If the score for the first three factors is outweighed by that for the others, you are opting for comfort over growth. As the drive for profit optimization lessens with age, so the longing for comfort rises, and the entrepreneurial urge flows into the sand. Ageism plays into the hands of internal factors 'hostile to growth', including lack of innovation. And these appear to dominate external factors – even 'lack of market growth' – in determining the business outcome.

The response is equally obvious. If you're no longer young personally, always surround yourself with very able, younger people, and then sustain their motivation with share incentive schemes. According to the study, such schemes are much more effective in boosting profits than bonus plans, but any incentive is substantially better than none. Youth and incentives do not work in a vacuum, however.

As Reilly says: 'There has to be an active growth strategy in place to plan for growth and the best way to achieve it.' In other words, you need a formal written business plan. Some 70 percent of the respondents to the Pulse inquiries duly had such a thing. However, since only half of those replying said that the plan was actually used to manage the business, the whole point had been sadly missed.

WYWIWYG, remember. Those who had set out to hit objectives for growth in capital and income tended to grow faster – they got what they wanted. Almost certainly, too, they were less likely to be among the 25 percent-plus whose firms had found problem areas in finance, operations and personnel. That commonly happens when the entrepreneur-in-chief, as the company grows, loses contact with its base activities.

Many people are so frightened by this prospective loss of control that they fail altogether to cross the entrepreneurial barrier – the one that separates a life-styler from a value-builder. They shy away from the key questions posed by Dr Steven Abbott and Dr Michael Hay of the LBS:

1 Why do you want the company to grow?
2 What are your motivations?
3 If desire for growth is driven by an aspiration to become richer, are you prepared to accept the higher level of risk required?

If that risk is unacceptable, you are not an entrepreneur. An entrepreneur is essentially a taker of calculated risks including, above all, the risk of misjudging one's own abilities. Risk also arises, of course, in judging the abilities of others. As the LBS pair made clear, if your entrepreneurial goals are not shared by senior colleagues, they may get in the way. Moreover, the success of that business plan (which, to repeat, you must have) hinges on the quality and numbers of those who must help in its composition and execution.

Don't just harness their brains. Emotional commitment is vital. Anybody who doesn't recognize the emotional nature of the entrepreneurial drive has never met an entrepreneur. Although their psychological types vary from cold fish to hot cat, these are people who all know never to ignore a positive hunch. The out-of-the-blue idea, properly studied and effectively executed, can outdo the best laid of rational plans in creating a better, richer business result.

As Reilly says, businesses will also sometimes 'succeed against all the odds due to sheer determination'. That's emotion again. WYWIWYG, indeed. Wanting something brings it within reach. By bringing everything to bear to win the profitable growth which they want, entrepreneurs can best assure continuity and a winning life-style. Nothing else does.

5

Service with Several Smiles

Closeness to Customers

Every firm these days is supposed to get close to its customers. *In Search of Excellence* discussed eight attributes of supposedly excellent companies, when seeking that closeness was the only one of the octet that looked outside the firm. But what do you do once you are close?

The 'excellent' companies mostly failed to produce answers that satisfied either the customers or – eventually – co-author Tom Peters. Over the intervening years (*Excellence* was published in 1983), Peters has promoted customer satisfaction from member of the backing group to lead singer. With evangelical fervour, he preaches 'service with soul' as the key to growth and profit.

Since soulfulness (dedicated personal commitment) is hard, if not impossible, to achieve in large corporations, Peters now finds his heroes among small- to medium-sized entrepreneurial firms – some of which can, and do, achieve prodigies of perform-ance (see 'Plumbing the Heights', below). These winning entre-preneurs go beyond customer satisfaction into the highest possible realms of customer service.

Total perfection will rarely, if ever, be achieved. But you can, like one firm whose market lies in serving anglers, reach the extraordinary height of 98 percent satisfaction. Once close enough to understand completely what the customers want, a star company like the anglers' friend (House of Hardy) doesn't just seek to satisfy them; rather, to quote another star, 'We aim to delight our customers'.

The speaker is Edward Wilson, chairman of the family-owned Ulster Carpets in Portadown. One of its delightful methods is to give domestic customers a sixty-day product guarantee. That is a powerful incentive to perform to standards of perfection and delight. But can you measure the latter? Both 'satisfaction' and 'delight' are vague terms. As one consultant points out, moreover, they are not words that customers readily use themselves.

Asked how the service was, would you reply 'Satisfactory, thank you'? Or, asked for your reaction to the service experience, would you answer, 'I was delighted'? One manufacturer regards satisfaction as no complaints and delight as a letter of praise. But neither aggrieved nor thrilled customers necessarily respond, so that won't do, either.

Market researchers try to achieve differentiation more scientifically. Their often elaborate customer surveys will show what proportion of customers are 'very satisfied', as opposed to merely 'satisfied'; or think your product and service quality 'excellent', as opposed to plain 'good'. That difference is enormous when it comes to one truly vital statistic: the percentage who will buy again. When Xerox examined the relationship, it found that the 'very satisfied' customer bought again six times more than the 'satisfied'.

That's money in the bank. Entrepreneurs know instinctively that it costs far more (fourteen times as much, in fact) to find a new customer as to retain an existing client. They hang on to customers for all they are worth – which is plenty. According to an expert from Bain & Co.: 'Raising customer retention rates by five percentage points increases the value of an average customer by 25 percent to 100 percent.'

Those companies that link executive pay to customer satisfaction, however, don't usually employ retention rates as their yardstick. They use what one consultant calls 'the Big Brother customer survey' – and they don't make the vital distinction between 'good' and 'excellent'. Moreover, their measures are not reliable; a professor of accounting at Wharton, David Larcker, says rightly that 'customer satisfaction is too complicated to measure by means of an unsatisfactory sample giving you a knee-jerk rating on a scale of one to five'.

Certain crude conclusions can be drawn from this imperfect number, however. American statistics (the nation-wide Customer Satisfaction Index) suggest that, unless your numbers are over 75 percent satisfaction, you have no competitive advantage. Also, what are the sector ratings? In an industry where customers are prone to unhappiness, more possibility exists of achieving competitive breakthroughs through customer closeness. But you won't discover the correct strategy from an index. Anecdotal surveys are essential to enable you to answer these vital questions:

1 How are we presently rated by customers?
2 What improvements will increase their satisfaction and retention?
3 What changes in people policies do these improvements demand?

Once the specifics of dissatisfaction are laid out clearly, it is very hard to ignore the evidence and to avoid the necessity of improving. The effort will certainly pay off. At one company, lambasted in front of the entire management for its failings, to the visible fury of the chairman, the information about the faults that needed correction proved so valuable that the firm later won a vital touch-and-go contract from the critic.

When the customers vote with their feet, though, you can be sure that they mean it and that you have failed in some serious respect. Even if the customers claim to be satisfied, or call your service and quality good, they may still walk out. The figure for customer retention is a more valuable guide to your service quality than the satisfaction numbers alone, especially if you lump together 'satisfactory' and 'very satisfactory' to produce a high overall figure.

That provides no help – given that (see above) good is not good enough, and excellence is the only worthwhile objective. Achieving excellence depends on what aspects of the product and/or service matter most to the customer. To spray-gun manufacturer De Vilbiss Ransburg, that includes providing 'a better,

easier paint finish, more information about how to get the best
from the product and quick and reliable delivery'. Its average
lead-time has consequently been lowered from four to six weeks
to two days. Delivery performance has improved from a miserable 40 percent to near-perfection: 98 percent.

Such figures look and are marvellous, but beware. First, unless
you are right about customers' requirements, it is easy to waste
time, trouble and money on satisfying a requirement that
doesn't matter to them – or matters less than something else.
Second, excellence is always relative. If your high standards are
bettered by a competitor, your standards are too low. Third,
the goalposts are always being moved, and not only because
competitors seek to up the ante; the more customers receive in
service quality, the more demanding they become.

On the first point – what the customers put first – companies
can all too easily throw out the baby with the bathwater. Two
firms speeded up their performance, one via its telephone staff,
the other via its delivery drivers, only for market share to slump
in both cases, for the same reason; customers wanted time to
chat and resented being hustled. J. Sainsbury found the same
resentment when it tried to speed customers through the supermarket checkouts.

Likewise, Federal Express jacked up its delivery speed, only
to find that misdirection of consignments soared as well, and at
inordinate expense. Getting close to the customers thus has one
clear meaning: make sure that you really understand their needs
and meet them.

House of Hardy, which every angler knows for its tackle and
fly reels, achieved its 98 percent performance by some spectacular improvements. They included a huge speed-up. Delivery time
in the UK, once four to five weeks, fell to almost invariably
twenty-four hours. The firm is sure that this truly matters
because 'We have worked very hard to find out all we can
about our customers and what they want'. The key, in a diverse
marketplace, was to slash distributorships from 1,000 to 50
specialist dealers. Just as you can have too many customers, the
bulk of whom make the firm no money, so you can have too
many outlets.

Not only does concentration provide better control and stock-ing; the dealers provide manageable, knowledgeable sources of customer feedback. You can't get close to customers without having good channels of communication – and using them to obtain a continuous customer health-check. A model example is MSL Advertising's 'client service appraisal' system. It checks every aspect of the relationship from personal and telephone contacts to individual assignments and the general understand-ing of the client's business.

Filling in a form isn't satisfactory on its own, however. It's the discussion of the appraisal between MSL and its client that creates the closeness. That is the key to getting really close to customers – the face-to-face meeting in which you learn their individual likes and dislikes. True entrepreneurs know that, and they are not impressed by unadorned, unexplained statistics.

Customer surveys lump many different standpoints and reac-tions together. They may say *what* is happening overall with fair accuracy. They won't say *why*, or tell you precisely *how* cus-tomers rate their experience of your service. Nor will they tell you how to advance from satisfaction (or dissatisfaction) to delight, from goodness to excellence.

That's why entrepreneurs habitually do the rounds, visiting their customers or prowling the shops, talking and listening. The criticisms and unsatisfied wants that they pick up, and react to, will have repercussions throughout the firm. For one thing is absolutely certain. Excellence of service cannot be achieved through acting on a single dimension of the business.

The service chain requires many links: starting with customer research and continuing with employee training, continuous improvement of processes, innovation in product and service alike, monitoring and feedback, in a cycle which never ends. It's a winning cycle. Companies whose customers rank their quality and service highly tend to have higher returns on capital, faster expansion and (so research suggests) faster stock market growth.

According to Larcker, in one six-month period the Top Ten satisfiers in the US easily outpaced other shares, rising by six times the average. By absolutely no coincidence, Ulster Carpets,

De Vilbiss Ransburg and House of Hardy are all firms picked out
by the DTI as 'winning companies'. To turn customer closeness
into success, all three did far more than improve their service.
They had to modernize their businesses from top to bottom.
That's very demanding: but there is no other way.

Corralling the Clientele

The sternest challenge for the start-up (and the started-up) is to
find customers. The cold call and the cold letter are often essential and mostly disappointing. But the cold can be made hot if
you learn the rules from the masters. That was the approach
taken by a brand-new firm of consultants, whose cold phone
calls were getting nowhere. At my suggestion, they took instruction from an expert in telephone selling.

The maestro started by listening to them making a pitch, and
then sadly shook his head. 'You're no good as consultants, are
you?' he asked. The partners indignantly denied the charge.
'Then', he went on remorselessly, 'why did you keep on apologizing for taking his time? Can't you do him any good?' The
consultants proudly said that their advice would save and make
the client a great deal of money.

'Then', said the sales expert, 'sound like that. Instead of you
apologizing to him, he should be thanking you' – and that was
only one piece of excellent advice. Listen to any top sales trainer,
and you will quickly find that this is one area of business management which is singularly short on humbug and long on
detailed and effective know-how. Using their methods, for
example, the cold caller should *always* be able to get an
appointment.

Moreover, if that produces five dates a day, one on average
will yield a sale (which means that any blank day is liable to be
followed by a double hit). Other rules of thumb are that twice
the activity yields 2.3 times the sales. Halve the activity, however, and sales will drop by two-thirds. The born entrepreneur
comes by and uses this salespower instinctively, calling on customers personally anywhere in the world.

Whatever the country or the tongue, the entrepreneur masters a language which is transnational: the lingo of persuasion. Persuasive patter may sound corny and meretricious, but is always founded on sound psychology. A smiling voice, for instance, sells more effectively, so when phoning, put a mirror before you, and smile at it while you talk. 'Please' and 'thank you' are powerful weapons. The three hot buttons to press are time, money and efficiency. You always tell the customer that you would be happy to drop by and give him the opportunity to ... You *never* (see above) say, 'I'd like to take some of your time.'

Unlike the consultants mentioned above, the entrepreneur does not need reminding that his offering is marvellous – that he takes for granted. You can't, however, always rely on meeting customers face-to-face. Most business people have tried getting customers by mail order, by letters soliciting their custom, and most of the writers have had the galling experience of receiving little or no response.

Very few have succeeded as well as one three-partner start-up. As one of the trio, Drayton Bird, fondly recalls:

A four-page letter helped *me* succeed more than I ever expected. It was to persuade people they ought to employ the services of myself and my partners in a new business ... As you can imagine, I laboured long and hard on it. We only sent out twenty-five copies. My partner rang up the recipients afterwards. We got twelve jobs.

That success ratio itself testified to the value of the partners' services. They had founded a direct marketing agency, specializing in helping clients to win (and keep) customers through the post by composing the right letters and other material and selecting the correct targets. 'Within three years', writes Bird, 'we were the leaders in our field in Britain. Seven years and eight months later ... I sold that company, at which point I could, if I had so wished, have retired.'

After the sale, Bird stayed with the purchaser, the giant

advertising group Ogilvy & Mather, as creative director of its very large direct marketing network. On eventual retirement from that post, Bird (very unusually) launched into a second start-up. In contrast to the O & M set-up, Drayton Bird Direct is very small: with just three staff he operates from Westbourne Grove, London, on the lowest possible fixed costs.

Since the business should generate nearly £2 million in fees in its fifth year, small looks beautiful indeed to Bird. The low overhead is one lesson gleaned from past experience (which includes a previous business that, Bird says, 'soared to volatile success before plunging into liquidation'.) He keeps costs down by 'having a lot of others coming in and out as required, mostly working from home'.

This outsourcing of key staff is among the newer weapons easing the task of the entrepreneurial start-ups. Bird could not have afforded the full-time services of such high-calibre help, all people he has worked with before, and all thoroughly imbued with Bird's direct marketing philosophy. It is set out cogently in his *How to Write Sales Letters that Sell*. The passage on his earlier start-up's sales letter is one of many striking anecdotes in this invaluable £25 opus.

Two powerful tips spring from that very story. First, in this type of small, personalized mailing, *always* try follow-up by phone, and as soon as possible (usually you get at least five times more sales than from mailing alone). Second, the letter occupied a full four pages: this may go against your every instinct, and against the rational enough belief that people have very limited reading time, but long letters consistently outsell short ones.

Hearken to Bird: 'In thirty-seven years of writing, I have never known a short letter *making the same proposition* do better than a long letter. The last time I tested it, a four-page letter making the same offer as a two-page letter got 52 percent more replies.' That anecdote contains a third very hot tip: direct mail offers the opportunity to test the percentage response of one sales pitch against another.

That ability to measure is not always easy to come by, but is an invaluable entrepreneurial aid. With the comparisons made, you can concentrate your marketing money on the winner. A fourth tip is that you shouldn't concentrate on response rates alone. Again, for his own business purposes, Bird sent one mailing – much larger than the one in the anecdote, going to 1,000 people – without telephone follow-up.

The total cost, even including his own creative services, would not have exceeded £5,000. The response rate looked awful (1 percent said Yes and 7 percent Perhaps), but the lesson here is that return on investment is what counts. First-year business obtained from the mailing will total £200,000, and that is likely to continue over the next four years.

Using direct mail, however, is not Bird's first and foremost route to business success. He 'determined early on that the most important thing is to motivate the people involved'. Finding good people and training them loomed so large that, for his first business, Bird always wrote the recruitment ads himself. That was the cornerstone of the business, though Bird also had to endure serious mistakes: having three equal partners (one always ends up in the minority) and 'stupidly' landing on the wrong side of the 'narrow borderline between worry and concern'.

Every piece of advice in Bird's book is worth much fine gold, starting with its quotation from *The Inner Side of Advertising* (1920) by Cyril Freer. I've adapted Freer's words on sales letters to apply to the whole vital need of the entrepreneur: to put himself or herself and the business across to the prospect.

1 Attract the prospect's full *attention* by the arresting way you begin your pitch.
2 Hold his *interest* by a description and explanation that create a mental picture of the proposition.
3 Create *desire* for the proposition by the arguments you put forward.
4 You get the prospect to share your *conviction* about the value of the offer by persuading him that it meets his specific needs (and perhaps by offering another inducement to buy).
5 You aim to achieve *action*, at once, by the climax of the presentation.

AIDCA – Attention, Interest, Desire, Conviction and Action – is usually abbreviated to the more easily remembered, and highly operatic, acronym AIDA. You will not, however, get any response from people who are basically not interested; selling central heating in Central Africa, or booze to teetotallers, makes no fortunes. I found this out the hard way when trying to sell seminars, using the same principles that worked well with newsletters.

Send out 10,000 sales pitches, and you can reasonably hope to sell at least 200 subscriptions. Since the seminars broke even at thirty, the target seemed easy, but the letters mostly went to people who never attended seminars, and the business flopped. Bird's figures comparing best and worst results of a test mailing show that list quality made a six-fold difference, followed by the offer (three-fold) and timing (double). Different creative work and response mechanisms had very little effect.

The lesson applies with equal force outside direct response advertising. Aiming at the right market, with as little waste as possible, is axiomatic for entrepreneurial success. Much of Bird's other advice has equally general application, including the boiling down of great letter-writing to seven strong and simple *business* principles:

1 Know your product.
2 Know your customers.
3 Know how to begin the letter.
4 Know exactly what you want the customers to do.
5 Give them an incentive.
6 Get excited ('enthusiasm comes over so strongly'), but stay objective.
7 Know your competitors.

Bird had the advantage, in his second start-up, of knowing his product, customers and competitors backwards. He was still surprised by success. He targets each year with a percentage sales rise – 'If we can do that, we're doing well' – and each year the target has been overshot by large amounts. But that's the result of another business virtue: caution in word and deed.

He thus reports that a 'very modest investment of time, effort and money' in South-East Asia 'looks as though it is going to turn out quite profitably'. As that shows, for all his enthusiasm and ambition, Bird is like many entrepreneurs in approaching his business: 'I'm terribly pessimistic.'

The Fabric of Growth

How the business is regarded by the owners – its 'focus' – has a profound impact on how it performs. If a camera is poorly focused, the image will be blurred and the results disappointing. A business is no different, whatever its size. In fact, many of the world's greatest companies have recently sold off, or 'divested', enormous operations in order to focus on the businesses which (they fondly hope) will yield the greatest returns.

SmithKline Beecham, for instance, exited from animal health care and consumer products, dropping marvellous brands, such as Macleans toothpaste and Brylcreem, which had been the pride and joy of previous managements. The highly entrepreneurial Sir Alexander Maclean, a New Zealander of legendary drive, would not have understood. He simply believed in launching products on the market, and only dropped them if they failed. If they performed, he backed them for keeps.

You need a simple world to follow simple strategies. Maclean's successors felt that, unless they concentrated all their managerial and financial efforts on the complex and highly profitable markets for healthcare products, the company would not gain maximum advantage from its strengths. For smaller companies, Maclean's formula will still work – up to a point. But that point is reached much more rapidly these days; if, that is, the entrepreneur has big and bold ambitions.

That wasn't the original case with Camborne Fabrics, once a suffering fabric manufacturer in Huddersfield. This firm, however, went on to 'reinvent' itself with spectacular, world-wide results. Reinvention is a relatively new piece of management jargon. It means stepping back from the business, looking at what it sells, how that is provided, and to whom – and changing as needed in order to increase returns and enhance growth potential.

That may mean standing everything on its head, including the conventional wisdom, which isn't always wise. One thing that terrifies most businesses is a high and mounting level of stock. Very few managements would deliberately create a stock mountain on the factory floor, but this West Yorkshire business did precisely that. Camborne Fabrics proceeded to grow from £200,000 of sales to £25 million in nine years.

There was deep method in its apparent madness. Reinvention meant changing Camborne's focus from manufacture to something rare; it now regards itself as a 'customer service business'. The service standards that Camborne imposed on itself included next-day delivery, for which high stocks are essential. Camborne pressed on until it could meet the next-day requirement on 97 percent of 2,000 daily orders for furniture fabric.

Sensibly, at that point managing director Nigel Roberts was less impressed with the 97 percent than 'with what happened to the 3 percent. That's an awful lot of upset customers'. The cost of their dissatisfaction is unacceptable, and Camborne therefore poured great effort into striving to cut 'the cost of failure' by a quarter.

At the beginning, Camborne showed little sign of this future sophistication. Roberts, a disillusioned accountant who had been driving lorries, joined the firm and founder David Hill in 1980. Hill had started his own business when his boss refused to accept the stockpiling theory. So Hill became a 'manufacturer without machines', buying yarn, having it converted and getting it finished miles away.

That was a throwback to the textile trade before the Industrial Revolution, which integrated processes that had been divided between a whole chain of firms. Hill's fabric was eventually delivered to a garage in Camborne Road – hence the name. Despite its sound anti-conventional principles, the business only pottered along until 1980, when Hill's brother, Robert, and Roberts created a triumvirate that took radical decisions.

The lack of focus was obvious. Hill was running a toy importing business in parallel with the textiles. Toys were abandoned.

Now they would focus on fabrics; but the focus would be far tighter still – not just on fabrics for furniture, but specifically for office furniture. There were good reasons for that selection. This market, unlike most of the fabrics industry, has no fashion element: 'charcoal' and 'peat' have been the top colours for twenty years.

That's one important factor in the stockpiling policy: the stock stays readily saleable. Conventionally, says Roberts, people 'move stock from the asset side to the liability side'. But Camborne turns over its stock assets six-and-a-half times a year, generating over £1 million of cash annually in the process.

Every business passes certain watersheds. One arrived after rapid expansion took sales to £4–5 million in 1985. The pre-Industrial Revolution principles began to break down. 'Too many goods were flying around the Yorkshire valleys on commission. It was very hard to control.' The problems were solved by buying Hopton Mills from a supplier. That took Camborne into manufacture, which didn't change its customer service focus. But serious complications still followed.

The business lost sight of its core and the focus became blurred again. In addition to office furniture, the company started supplying leisure fabrics, wall-coverings, vertical blinds and carpet tiles. The top team felt that they could do anything. 'We began to believe our own bullshit. When you do that, you're in deep trouble.' Healthy disbelief took over in the nick of time. In 1989, they refocused – twelve months before recession hit Britain.

As Roberts says, that was 'pure good luck'. They had already cut overheads, reduced the cost base, concentrated on cash and profit as well as turnover, and, with considerable courage, dropped all the extraneous businesses. 'To actually admit you were wrong and let turnover go is not always easy' – especially when recession is shrinking the core business as well. Sales slumped from £19 million to £15 million in those 'extremely tough' times.

The business, backed by Lloyds Bank's venture capital arm, stayed profitable and, more important, kept generating cash: 'You can lose money a few times, but you only run out of cash once.' Equally important, Camborne diversified away from the

UK market – and by the mid-1990s half its business came from abroad. The rapid response service, made possible by those large stocks and by efficient forecasting (which was improved from thrice weekly to twice daily), explains how Hong Kong, Singapore and Thailand became Camborne's strongest markets.

Quality is also crucial, especially consistency of colour and the unblemished texture needed for screens in offices on the open plan – a principle which David Hill and Roberts strongly support. Roberts, who bought out Robert Hill in 1989, explains that the four-man top team have offices separated only by sliding patio doors to encourage 'a very open and communicative management style'.

Having started by challenging the conventional wisdom on stocks, they've continued in that vein: 'We're never frightened to try new ideas.' That's the way to make big new money from old, tired trades. The key to Camborne, however, is its highly intelligent three-stage tightening of the focus: from fabric, to furniture fabric, to office furniture fabrics – and thus to profits of £2.2 million on 1995's £27 million turnover.

Julian Metcalfe of Pret a Manger (see Chapter 1) understands the purpose and benefits of focus very clearly. As he told the Royal Society of Arts:

> It's important to find out what you want to do and stick to it. We have a mission statement on the windows of all our shops. I do that not as a marketing thing, but to discipline everyone who works in our company not to waver from what it is we're trying to do.

Single-minded purpose provides great impetus. The other way round, diffusion of purpose will almost certainly slow down progress, maybe to a standstill. It's true, however, that some enormously successful companies have no apparent focus. One of the fastest-growing major groups in the USA, the little-known Illinois Tool Works, Inc., makes adhesives, door handles for cars and other humdrum items through no less than 365 operations.

Between them, the 365 generated $486 million of profits from

$5 billion of sales in 1995, together with dramatic returns to shareholders. The chief executive, W. James Farrell, asks rhetorically: 'Is 365 operations too many? Will we lose contact? Our division managers say don't screw around with it.' Their attitude is explained by a sentence from *Business Week* about the secret of the company's success: 'Intense decentralization that gives managers the freedom usually reserved for entrepreneurs.'

Their freedom, though, doesn't include the power to create a fuzzy company. You can bet that the 365 are tightly focused – along the same lines as Johnson & Johnson, the great healthcare business (with 165–170 decentralized operating companies). When J & J 'launches a particularly hot product it 'may build what amounts to a new company around it, even giving the outfit a distinct name'.

The typical entrepreneur can't run more than one business, let alone 365 or 170, and shouldn't even try. But the same principle of tight focus that makes Illinois Tool or Johnson & Johnson viable will apply as powerfully to other, smaller businesses as it does to Camborne. Too many focuses spoil the broth. One can be plenty.

Plumbing the Heights

The paradox of splendid small businesses is that they soon cease to be small. Winning and satisfying customers rapidly takes them into a larger league. The challenge here is to retain the entrepreneurial zest, drive and personal touch, while mastering the corpocratic skills of control and organization.

The all-time classic example of the little grown vast must be the US retail chain, Wal-Mart. Not only did its founder, Sam Walton, start small, but he started in small towns, reckoning rightly that they could support sizeable discount stores.

In personal terms, he also started late. That was in 1962, when he was in his fifties. Despite the late start, Walton was running the world's largest retailer long before his death thirty years later. He resolved the paradox of the good small business by sticking to his small-firm, small-town principles, no matter how large the chain grew. (Its 1996 sales totalled an awe-inspiring $106.1 billion, yielding $3.1 billion of profits.)

'Listen to everyone in your company', he wrote in *Sam Walton: Made in America*, 'and figure out ways to get them talking.' He argued correctly that 'to push responsibility down in your organization, and to force good ideas to bubble up within it, you MUST listen to what your associates are trying to tell you.'

Flying his own plane around a group of stores every day, Walton managed to maintain personal contact in his gigantic and growing empire, chatting to his people, visiting their local competitors, learning as well as teaching. There are signs that this personal magic may have died with the magician, for Wal-Mart has slowed down significantly of late. Indeed, the challenge mentioned above, managing big companies in small-company style, is inherently difficult.

There's another way to resolve the problem: don't get too big. 'Getting big by staying small' is among the numerous slogans of a plumbing business called De Mar. Another is: 'Not the biggest but the best.' That's the decisive slogan for small companies seeking large prosperity, even in humdrum businesses like De Mar's. You aim to preserve the virtues of smallness while still growing – and this company is living proof that professional management pays handsomely anywhere.

The boss, Larry Harmon, used the familiar weaknesses of the plumbing trade as his springboard. You can work out what customers want in two ways, the positive and the negative. Harmon chose to focus on a negative aspect. Customer complaints about plumbing are as familiar in the USA as in Britain: high and erratic prices, delays, bad work, mess, and so on. To eliminate the negatives, Harmon devised a formula that earned De Mar a leading role in the Video Arts film *Service with Soul*, starring American guru Tom Peters.

Once a consultant to mega-companies with McKinsey, and an enthusiast for mega-company managements in the mega-seller *In Search of Excellence*, Peters makes De Mar an examplar of his new heroes, who are entrepreneurs rather than managers and work in smaller firms rather than large. That makes commercial sense for Peters – there are so many more small firms.

Any big business, however, might benefit from De Mar's basic offering:

1 Standardize prices and list them.
2 Provide service round-the-clock, seven days a week, on the day of the inquiry.
3 Guarantee all work for one year.

Standardized and listed prices apart, many British plumbers would claim to offer all, or most, of this list. But the Yellow Pages are full of tiny, often unreliable operators, among whom it is impossible to differentiate. Very few companies in the building and repair sector exploit small-company virtues vigorously to achieve advantage over the competition and build large profits.

In any business with a multitude of poor performers, though, the Walton magic will make a huge difference to the proprietorial fortunes. De Mar's philosophy and practice bear a striking resemblance to Walton's. It isn't just that Harmon knows all his people personally; that's true of any modest-sized business. His attitude to the staff is the vital factor that pulls De Mar clear of the pack.

Like Walton (who set the fashion for calling employees 'associates' or 'partners'), Harmon is very particular about how he describes his key staff. They are not plumbers, not even technicians, but 'customer service advisers' – and they are smartly uniformed to make the point. Their pay depends in part, moreover, on points earned from customer satisfaction.

Any management guru would applaud this practice, which enlightened large companies are now applying all the way up to senior managers. Fitting rewards to business objectives – such as getting high service ratings from customers – is the surest way of achieving the aims. By the same token, separating rewards from objectives is an excellent way of missing targets. That seems obvious, yet many companies still pay salespeople commission solely on turnover, which will never work well if the aim is profits.

Harmon argues that it is his own job to 'get the phone to

ring'. He has a full-scale marketing programme, which means spending real money on TV commercials and tele-marketing (3,000 calls a week). The role of the 'advisers' is to satisfy and thus retain the customers. Again, Harmon believes that a rose by another name smells sweeter. In his vocabulary, the customer service advisers are businessmen with 'a rolling franchise'.

The 'rolling franchise' refers to vans, loudly painted and covered with promotional messages, that are mobile ads on the Californian highways. Here, as elsewhere, Harmon doesn't miss a single professional trick. Entrepreneurs too often jib at professional techniques, but these mostly consist of exploiting your assets to the full. Since you have to use delivery vans anyway, why not exploit their potential?

People like Harmon, who constantly seek areas of opportunity, must win over those who operate in blinkers. The combination of professional management and small company virtues took De Mar from a mere $4,000 a week in 1985 to $70,000 – and rising. The business exemplifies several of the policies I recommend most warmly, including heavy emphasis on training (2 percent of turnover) and sustained effort to create a Unique Selling Proposition.

The Holy Grail of this effort is achieved when the customers don't think of phoning a plumber, but of ringing De Mar. Look again at the twenty-odd pages of indistinguishable ads for plumbers in the London Yellow Pages, and you'll see why uniqueness must pay. True, the Yellow Pages are a very different world from California, so are there elements of Harmon's formula that would not translate into British practice?

The evangelistic aspects, with 6 a.m. assemblies yelling 'Amen' to Harmon's invocations, might go down badly, although British workers will put up with more razzmatazz than conservatives might expect. In any event, everything else in the De Mar mix would work the same way: elevating a business out of the rut and into riches.

The most important ingredient is to treat both staff and customers with respect. You can't have one without the other. Harmon's use of 'advisers' serves this purpose of conveying respect just as strongly as Walton's insistence on 'associates'.

SERVICE WITH SEVERAL SMILES 133

The word is unimportant compared to the attitude which the more dignified name implies. For example, on Walton's store-to-store visits, he would talk mostly not to the managers but to the people who staffed the departments.

Like De Mar's plumber-advisers with their vans, Walton's associates were encouraged to regard their departments as franchises, as businesses which they ran themselves. They often responded by developing detailed knowledge and know-how about the customers and the market, and by motivating themselves to beat the local competition and to achieve high returns from their part of the business.

At De Mar, Harmon gets his team to study examples of the best in customer service from operations like Disneyland – and that, too, boosts people's morale and their performance. Mobilizing the full, unstinting contribution of those who work with and for you is the unifying force behind the first seven of Walton's ten principles for entrepreneurial success:

1 Sharing
2 Communicating
3 Celebrating success
4 Motivating
5 Appreciating
6 Listening
7 Commitment
8 Control of expenses
9 Exceeding customer expectations
10 'Break all the rules'.

Large groups cannot emulate the seven-point personal touch if top managers prefer huddling in head office to leading from the front. True entrepreneurs never make that error. Simon Marks, later Lord Marks, built the formidable ethos of Marks & Spencer by highly personal management. He would appear in front of a counter and demand to know details such as how much of a perishable foodstuff would be left at the end of the day, or where the missing sock sizes were.

Those two examples came from the career of a future successful management consultant. He has never forgotten the object lessons that the master taught. The food was cream buns: Marks came back as the store was closing and insisted on loading them into a wheelbarrow and tipping them out. Moral: never leave perishable food overnight (especially on a Saturday).

As for the socks, Marks personally led the assistant into the stockroom to find the missing sizes. Moral: you can't sell things that are not on sale. The two object lessons were separated by hundreds of miles (the young man had moved stores) and a couple of years. But on the sock visit, Mark's first words were 'Aren't you the young man with the cream buns?' That's the small-firm magic, but you don't have to be a magician to make it work.

Serving the People

These days, most major companies are striving, sometimes desperately, to achieve something which comes much easier to smaller firms – the excellence of customer service stressed throughout this book. Not that such excellence is easy for customers to find; everywhere, lip-service is more common than superb service.

That's a godsend to the ambitious entrepreneur who is always looking for an edge, something you have that the competitor doesn't. Plumbing entrepreneur Larry Harmon of De Mar won that edge by exploiting the areas where customers found other plumbers wanting. If everybody else's service is falling well below customer expectations, delighting the customers (by exceeding those expectations) is certain to succeed.

Even manufacturers are now finding that service, and only service, can provide the vital edge. Some businesses, however, are either all service, or vitally dependent on its quality. Catering is, very obviously, a business where service can make all the difference. So the experience of catering firms that have achieved superior standards of service is an important guide to the essence of service excellence at large.

The catering gurus emphasize at the start that excellence does not hinge on slick systems. You must have those, anyway, but the right systems will not achieve the desired impact on service standards without the right approach: the spirit of service and the desire to please. The words are easy, but the execution is difficult and takes time. Trying to develop that culture at speed will fail; it cannot be done overnight.

Nor can seekers after service excellence ever relax. The experts warn that if you ease up on service programmes, even after as long as nine years, standards will start to fall. After ten years of sustained effort, service enters the soul of the company. In this long-haul process, of course, you have to monitor the operations continuously to ensure that what the customers perceive about the service is what they, and you, want.

Certain elements are needed immediately, starting not with the customers, but the people. According to Hal F. Rosenbluth: 'People are the only sustainable competitive advantage.' His company, Rosenbluth International, is in another business – overwhelmingly, corporate travel – which depends utterly on service standards. The title of his book on service, *The Customer Comes Second*, expresses a profound truth. By serving its employees much better, management takes a giant stride towards doing the best by customers.

As an earlier chapter stressed (see Chapter 3), 'service' and 'culture' are functions of the use of human resources. You cannot expect employees to put themselves in the customer's shoes (the essence of a customer-focused culture), unless management can don the employees' footwear. The prime objective of both exercises is caring. Customers will quickly notice if you do not really care and do not get pleasure from serving them – and that won't happen unless the staff themselves get caring treatment.

Study the best caterers, and the intensive effort put into looking after their staff is obvious. Just as customer retention is the best guide to quality of service, so employee retention tells you most about your people management. You don't need expensive employee attitude surveys (though these have their uses) to check morale and motivation; the figures for staff turnover are not only a barometer of health, but a prime, direct factor in service levels.

If the loss rate rises too high (it reaches 100 percent or more annually in some businesses I know), grievous faults must exist. Also, inordinate costs must arise in under-performance, endless recruitment and wasted training. Worse of all, the constant turn-over gives customers a perception of poor service, which is probably what they receive. Just as a culture of service takes time to develop, so do the attitude and skill of a server.

To have any chance of achieving super-service, turnover should be so low that the company need hardly bother to measure it. Every personnel policy has a bearing on employee retention, but a general rule is that belonging to teams with specific service roles helps substantially to raise standards and maintain retention if the teams are (a) well-run and (b) not too large (no bigger than a dozen people and some numbering perhaps only three).

An average figure (in a well-run catering business, say) is seven, each with a team leader. Think of the teams as individual 'families' within the overall family of the business. In a typical set-up, team-leaders come under a departmental manager, who in turn reports to a general manager. The next level up is that of the directors – which in a genuine family firm might well be husband and wife.

Following these principles, the company ends up with five layers, which does not quite fit today's fashionable emphasis on 'flat, flat, flat' structures. But that is the inevitable result of adopting a justifiable preference for small work groups with a leader who has time for each of its members. Making time for people inside the company, like making time to talk to the customers, is indispensable for excellence of service.

Highly accessible management, other things being equal, means highly motivated people. At one prize-winning catering firm, new recruits have an induction day which starts and ends by meeting with the boss. In between they tour the entire business and play customer for lunch in one of the cafés. Rosenbluth makes the same point and adopts a similar policy: 'A lot of people never get to see their company's headquarters. They may never meet the top officers of the company. Here, they do both on day one.'

Rosenbluth is also very big on recruitment. His prime criterion in hiring is that the appointee must be 'nice'. The word sounds vague, but it is one which everybody understands. He uses it to mean a person who is pleasant to talk to, good to have around, friendly and co-operative, somebody you would enjoy meeting outside the office. A profiling study of reservation clerks supported Rosenbluth's view that even in a hard-driving environment like his, 'niceness' is a great virtue.

The study showed that the correlation between excellence in tasks and people skills was 'incredibly high'. Since 'nice people do a better job', they are clearly the only ones you should hire. You can see how niceness must affect service standards, especially among those who have direct contact with the customer. By the same token, since service is now so decisive a business factor, niceness must have much to do with running a successful company.

Alas, it bears little relation to how most companies are run, to judge by some surveys. Gallup once interviewed 200 chief executives and financial directors, finding that they appeared to take the Rosenbluth line: 'Britain's bosses believe that happy employees mean bigger profits.' The sting was in the tail: 'Yet when asked to state their most important future business strategies, motivating staff was mentioned by only 12 percent.'

Their error is emphasized by another study, this time by PIMS Associates, involving over 5,000 managers. The PIMS people knew already that '70 percent of profit performance derives from established measures of competitive strength, market attractiveness and productivity'. They then discovered that a further 15 percent of said profits is driven by how you manage people.

While that's impressive enough on its own, it also appears that people management is more important still, because it 'drives the achievement of competitive strength and productivity'. That explains why, when service aces explain their success, the so-called soft elements that dominate human resources management predominate in their formulas – which makes it tempting to think that having fun, caring and so on are all that matters.

They do matter enormously, but the hard issues – in catering, matters such as portion control, equipment, lay-out – are also critical. You need hard education, too: rigorous training on and off the job, especially of front-of-house staff. The job (waiting on table is an example) must be treated not as work that any amateur can handle, but as a real profession; mastery of the basics and product knowledge are *sine qua non*.

No one succeeds in service without an equally hard, meticulous attention to detail, or without insistence that everything be 'just right'. That won't work if detail is regarded as the business of the staff alone. Detail starts with the proprietor and the management. The PIMS research mentioned above found that the critical people in achieving outstanding service success were not the usual heroes of quality improvement success stories (counter-clerks, stewardesses and so on) but the people who manage the front-line performers. If you really want service and profitability to blossom, make sure that you and your managers can say Amen to all of the following statements:

1 I am completely trusted by everybody to do an excellent job.
2 We all work as a genuine team, with every member co-operating and contributing to the full.
3 I am comfortable with the company culture and I am sure that the culture explains its success.
4 I and the company have clear objectives which everybody knows.
5 Communications are full and clear from top to bottom – and back again.
6 I am confident in my ability to do my job, and in that of colleagues and subordinates to do theirs.
7 I have all the authority and resources I need to do an excellent job – and so do other managers.
8 I insist on and get excellent performance on agreed criteria – and that's what I achieve myself.
9 I genuinely care for my people.
10 I know what business results we must achieve against the competition – and we constantly seek to improve our competitive prowess and performance.

That last word, performance, is what a hard-nosed entrepreneur like Rosenbluth would always expect. Without hardness, he couldn't have developed a century-old family company into a $2 billion business with 3,000 employees and handsome profits. His formula, quoted in *Fortune*, is universal. If you want to succeed in service: 'Hire nice people, treat them well, encourage them to bind emotionally with the company, train them continuously, and equip them with the best technology. Then the customers and the profits will follow.' That they will.

How to Take Stock

One man's poison is another man's meat. To put that another way, one management's poison is an entrepreneur's banquet. If a job must be done, there's a market; and, if people particularly dislike the job, there's a demand for somebody else to take over the task. Hence the increasingly popular practice of 'outsourcing'. There is hardly a company now that does not employ outsiders for services formerly undertaken internally, or which hasn't considered doing so.

Outsourcing is the ultimate in service and customer relationships. The supplier takes over part of the customer's vital operations, which makes perfect apparent sense. Specialists in office cleaning, pension administration, legal services, running vehicle fleets, information technology, and anything else the company can separate from its main activity, should be able to perform to excellent standards at lower cost. The BBC has even outsourced its accountancy services.

Why do more expensively what others can supply more cheaply? Especially since letting them take over the task should also relax the pressure on scarce management resources. Stocktaking is a prime example of one of those chores which everybody hates but which must be done, and must be done right. One of the easiest ways to mismanage a business is through its inventories, and, according to one estimate, inventory management has not improved in the past decade.

Get stocks wrong on the upside, and you run into possibly

lethal financial difficulties (like one failed textile company whose excess stock so stuffed the warehouse that the new management could not open the doors). Get stocks wrong on the downside, and you lose customers and sales. If you get stock right, though, at one stroke you give customers better service and improve the key financial ratios.

Getting it right is what provides the Orridge Group with its outsourcing profits. Nick Holland-Brown didn't join Orridge because he had spotted the outsourcing trend and wanted to climb aboard, nor even because he realized the key importance of stock control to potential customers. Accident led to opportunity, as it so often does. He came in at the tender age of twenty-two through family connections.

The company was founded by Benjamin Orridge, Queen Victoria's pharmacist, who reckoned it was a good idea to act as agent for the sale of pharmacies. The first stock-taking work was for pharmacists, still considerable Orridge customers. For all its boredom, counting stock accurately is a foundation of good business – and the more modern the business, paradoxically, the greater the need. Holland-Brown says that with electronic point of sale (EPOS – now used by all up-to-date retailers), 'it starts going wrong from the day you get it right'.

In theory, the EPOS system accurately records every sale and subtracts the item from the inventory, but that's just theory. In practice, there's 'shrinkage', 'leakage' and just plain error, when the wrong entry is made. That produces 'all sorts of ripples down the whole chain of management functions'. You haven't got enough of the right stock, you have too much of the wrong stock, and your reordering goes haywire.

Errors can reach frightening proportions. About 1 percent of total UK retail turnover 'disappears' from inventory by various means. That's a gigantic sum, but you can do much worse than 1 percent. Many of Orridge's customers are far less able than Woolworth, Iceland, New Look and so on to bear the financial pain. But these small multiples or single stores also need an annual stock count, whose accuracy is just as vital for protecting their businesses.

Holland-Brown recalls one client with a large warehouse

whose stock proved wrongly valued by half-a-million pounds. The error was in the company's favour – but don't count on being so fortunate. Since accurate stock counts done by a specialist outsider can cost 10 to 15 percent less, they are doubly attractive.

As with all businesses today, however, there is more to success in outsourcing than meets the eye. It is not enough to spot the latent or existing demand for a job that people are prepared to let out to others, or to run through the menu of outsourcing advantages, although it does sound beautifully tempting. It makes a great selling pitch. Who can refuse a chance like this? You're enabled to . . .

1 reduce risk by buying experience
2 improve margins by economies of scale
3 achieve time targets by tying them to contractual payments
4 maintain focus on the core business by relying on expert partners
5 heighten flexibility by buying a service and not a collection of immutable technologies.

This list comes from a specialist in information systems (IS), the Sema Group, which adds that, in achieving the above results, the client 'can raise standards throughout the IS organization'. No doubt that is so. Given the complexity of information technology, and the multiplicity of choices, this is one area where companies are ill-advised to adopt do-it-yourself policies. The danger of relying on in-house computer experts is that they may become wedded to what exists rather than what is wanted.

Yet the annals are full of companies and organizations whose IT outsourcing has produced nothing but horror stories. Whatever the outsourcing service, it has to be developed and managed brilliantly to fulfil its potential. In stock-taking, some ten years ago, Holland-Brown formed the necessary 'vision' of what Orridge could become. 'We could see what could be achieved' by using the latest electronic technology. Unfortunately, the key hardware – hand-held computers – could not then be had at 'a sensible price'.

Once prices fell, Holland-Brown was able to transform the operation. Today he can supply as many as 500 people, full-timers and part-timers, all armed with their hand-held electronic marvels, for a big stock-count. He's also on the third generation of software, developed by Orridge itself and highly sophisticated; it must have state-of-the-art excellence to cope with the great variety of computer systems used by clients. The sophisticated approach wasn't adopted for fun, but from sheer necessity.

Service entrepreneurs have a particular bugbear, though. The nature of their business often produces what has become a familiar form of competition these days. You are not competing with like companies, but with single-handed operators, working from home with zero overheads, and selling on cut prices. This was especially galling for Holland-Brown because many of the under-cutting one-man bands were former employees: 'We've probably trained most of the stock-takers in the country.'

Try to compete with this kind of competition and you end up dead: the low prices won't support the overheads of a properly established company (Orridge has six UK offices and others in Dublin, Brussels and New Zealand). The answer must be to compete not on price but on quality. You can then hope to absorb the extra costs by winning far higher volume and much fatter margins. This strategy 'led us into a different, and more satisfactory market, and gave us a viable, good, modern business that will last into the next century'.

Thanks to the steady acquisition of shares, starting in 1971 ('I gradually bought people out'), that business came wholly into Holland-Brown's control. The key end-1987 share purchase, using borrowed money, was 'somewhat of a gamble', but it 'concentrated the mind' on matters like having 'good people and training them. It's nice being able to control all that'. Otherwise, you can't pursue a 'mission for quality' and, without quality, 'you can't survive in any service'. This is Orridge's key lesson.

The quality dimension is vital on the other side of the equation – the customer side. The entrepreneur who farms out all activities to outsiders, even crucial operations such as distribution and service, can get a flying start. The suppliers become extensions of the enterprise, operating much like internal operations: except

that the entrepreneur is protected from the three most problem-
atic areas. The enterprise invests no capital, employs no people
and takes no risk.

Or does it? What if the outsourcing partner fails to deliver? Or
if the promised savings fail to materialize? Or if the outsourced
activity turns out to be so crucial that it should have been kept
inside? One protection is to beware of grandiose promises. If
you are promised gains of 20 to 40 percent from outsourcing,
remember that one study found the average savings to be only
9 percent or so. Make sure, too, that you are not critically dependent on an outsider whose failure to perform would have deadly
results.

Also, beware of being locked into long-term, fixed-price contracts and locked out of the benefits when falls in prices lower
the cost of the outsourced product or service. More serious still,
however, is the risk involved in turning key operations over to
armies of mercenaries rather than your own dedicated troops.

The outsourcing danger isn't solely one of promised benefits
that fail to appear. At issue is the entire identity of the business.
What activities contribute to the culture and your Unique Selling
Proposition – the reason for customers to buy from your business
and nobody else's? What constitutes your Unique Employment
Proposition – the reason for your best recruits to perform their
best work for your company?

An entrepreneurial business like Orridge, outsourcing for
others, depends on its own integrity as an organization to provide the levels of service that create its success. That integrity is
vital to all outsourcing customers as well. By all means throw
out the bathwater of services better provided by others. But at
all costs keep the baby.

6

The Learning Curve

The School of Hard Knocks

Entrepreneurs come from every imaginable educational background, from high academic rank to near-illiteracy. Many are barely numerate and some are Masters of Business Administration; many more, though, have never read a management book or magazine, never attended a seminar, never met a management teacher or guru, and never felt the need to learn anything about managing, marketing, finance, strategy, planning, or any other aspect of business.

The academically unenlightened can actually perform all these activities, of course, and often brilliantly. However great their innate genius at spotting and seizing opportunities, though, the probability remains that their performance could be improved by study. After all, wonderfully accurate goal-kickers, established international rugby stars, go to a coach for kicking lessons. World-beating golfers, athletes and tennis stars all have coaches. There is no human activity that will not benefit from further instruction.

Truly modern entrepreneurs are increasingly interested in the preaching of gurus, not least because the wise ones are a potential source of new and profitable ideas. The business of management education has grown handsomely over the years, largely through courses for hired hands rather than their bosses. But that doesn't make education less of an entrepreneurial opportunity in its own right.

Indeed, starting a new centre for management education

taught two harassed entrepreneurs some hard extramural lessons on business start-ups. The executive job shop, otherwise known as the Labour Exchange, isn't the likeliest birthplace for a new business enterprise but that's where, in 1992, the Harrogate Management Centre set out on its mission: to prove that every business needs a strategy, which should apply especially to one whose business is teaching strategy.

Physicians are notoriously bad at healing themselves, of course. Michael Johnston and Tim Hurren, two unemployed executives who renewed their acquaintance at the job shop, duly made some costly blunders during the first, very slow months of trading. 'I was in despair', says Johnston. So was Hurren, but they hid their anxieties from each other and soldiered on. That illustrates one important strategic principle: stick with your ambition, so long as it's basically sound.

Their idea was to establish a business that would 'bring more people into Harrogate', and management development particularly appealed to Johnston. 'Something of a course junkie' himself, he had kept note of the more impressive lecturers heard during his time with the International Wool Secretariat (his job fell victim to a catastrophic drop in wool prices).

In setting up shop in Harrogate, he wanted to challenge 'the perennial belief that you couldn't organize anything meaningful North of Watford – you couldn't get the audience'. At first, the attempt to disprove this theory went swimmingly enough. The partners raised money initially from friends, one of whom suggested contacting Sir Thomas Ingilby, owner of the splendid Ripley Castle and the neighbouring Boar's Head Hotel.

Ingilby promptly offered 'a purpose-built Georgian management centre' and contributed to the original £60,000 of equity. The partners had meanwhile learned another strategic principle: focus. They would offer to corporate clients courses designed for 'room-sized groups', which could really get to grips with strategy and strategic management. Outside advisers to whom Johnston wisely turned had identified this as the key area. Now all he needed was clients.

As with most start-ups, 'our biggest competitor was ignorance of our existence'. Enter the biggest blunder: 'We spent too much on publicity.' It's a common enough fault. Starters-up go in for wide publicity, which amounts to using buckshot instead of aiming at specific targets. The cash drain was insupportable, and the partners (reinforced financially by doubling the original investment) were forced to learn the high value of the direct approach.

Marketing strategy evolved into building up 'a very sound database of contacts' – properly identified prospects who had a recognized need for management education. Johnston has been called a 'ferret' for his tenacity in following up these contacts. He sought to give a clear impression that the Centre was passionately interested in working for and with potential clients. Information technology enabled the partners to follow this plan – they became wholly dependent on their database software.

However excellent the systems, though, the results can only be as good as the demand for the product. And, like most initial strategic plans, the Centre's contained an erroneous assumption about the marketplace. Open courses for managers from different firms were supposed to be the major product, with in-house seminars for companies as a useful second string. The in-house business duly proceeded to swell, until it accounted for two-thirds of turnover.

Open courses still formed a separate line, along with seminars for public sector executives and 'master-classes', in which leading gurus like arch-strategist Igor Ansoff and another American, Richard Pascale, work with forty-five or so people for two days. The cost of £1,000 to £1,200 per participant may look high, but only if you don't know the far greater rates charged elsewhere. All the same, if the course is useless, it is too dear at any price. Personally speaking, however, I've never listened to top management gurus (and I have heard a great many) without learning plenty and being stimulated to learn and do more. That lesson at least has certainly sunk into HMC's customers: the July 1997 master-class given by a third American guru, Robert Kaplan, was so heavily over-subscribed that a second had to be arranged for September.

It is what you do after the learning and stimulus that counts, though. And for the Centre, winning through was built on the principle of making management development pay by linking it to the practical development of the client's whole business. For example, one in-house course, staged for bankers National Australia Group, ran at intervals over a full year and included real-life strategic projects which, says Johnston, added up to 'reinventing banking'.

Johnston is rightly a great believer in learning, not from academic case studies but, as happened on the NAG course, from confronting managers with 'real projects of strategic consequence for the business' – the one in which they actually work. As he says: 'They learn, and the company gets a return on its investment.' This kind of education is designed to benefit both the individual and the firm.

Two other skilled players in the education game, partners Jo Denby and Joanna Kozubuska, who are associated with the HMC, note that the dual-benefit course is at the opposite end of the spectrum from listening to Pascale, say. His seminar is aimed only at the individual. As with the conferences on a broad theme (such as quality, or creativity, or trading with the Pacific Basin, or whatever), people come from several organizations – which is another reason for attending.

You can benefit from the experience of others in different companies and businesses. And (who knows?) the new contacts may pay off in direct business terms. Otherwise, the benefits will be indirect. But the boss, or anybody he sends along, will only gain to the extent that the individual derives new ideas and knowledge from the experience: and, further, to the extent that the company is willing to accept the ideas. More often than not, the inspired individual comes rushing back, only to hit a brick wall. The inspiration soon dies.

Once, the boss of a famous family-owned hire company told me, with some irritation, that a senior manager had asked to be sent on a course. 'Should I let him go?' was the question, obviously hoping for a No. I argued strongly in favour: somebody so strongly motivated should be encouraged.

There was plenty for him to learn, and the experience of being taught was useful in itself. But the boss's attitude made it very unlikely that any benefit would be allowed to come from the course. The manager would only be frustrated – and that would do nobody any good. The natural reaction of that type of entre-preneur, somebody who has flourished without formal teaching, is to assume that nobody else needs educating, either.

That reminds me of the man who refused to buy an adding machine when his bookkeeper, a mathematical whiz, easily beat the machine to the count. The whiz rightly told the boss that he had made a bad mistake: 'How many people can add up as fast as me?' You may be a natural genius at business, but those who work for you will require help to come up to the standards that you need. On-the-job experience isn't everything.

Naturally, Harrogate provided both off- and on-the-job learn-ing experiences for the partners themselves. After the ugly first-year losses, they broke even in Year 2. The first return ('a very useful profit') arrived in Year 3. So their strategy has passed muster – the verdict is 'extremely successful'. Again practising what they preach, the Harrogate pioneers have moved on, though; literally in Johnston's case. The co-founder departed, as he had promised himself and his colleagues, at sixty.

The business he left behind has switched its emphasis some-what towards more strategic management training and develop-ment, based on a strengthened in-house team. Harrogate's 'never-ending problem', says Johnston, 'is the need to stay focused and to resist the temptation to dabble'. That's also a never-ending potential curse of most small companies. But can small firms – like HMC itself – really benefit from strategy? 'Wholly indispensable,' says Johnston. 'If you don't know where you're going, any direction will do. The small business that knows where it's going can compete with anybody.'

Train, Train, Train

Entrepreneurs often hate the idea of spending real money on training – and that is often their biggest mistake. Self-made, self-taught men are especially averse to spending on training in the first place; and, even more, averse to finding that, after their good money has trained an employee, he or she disappears into the arms of a rival.

The aversions are wholly misplaced. It's heads you lose, tails you don't win. If you don't train, train, train, your employees will be less valuable to you. Yet, if you ask most businesses how much they spend on training their people, you won't, unless the answer is nothing, get many exact replies. Ask how much they should be spending, and the answers will be even fewer.

Yet it's a vital issue. If a business isn't laying out at least 1.5 percent of turnover on training, its future is at risk, say the experts. Too few businesses shape up on this measure. But there's a mega-trend in progress from manual workers to know-ledge workers, from brawn and effort to brains and skill. That shift makes the training investment indispensable.

You can't buy much training, though, for £17,780, which is the average spend by companies with annual turnovers of less than £5 million a year. According to a survey from RRC Business Training, published in 1997, the largest organizations among the 420 companies examined spend more than £500,000 annually. And the trend is upwards – average training budgets had risen by 39 percent over the previous year, while three-fifths of the firms planned to spend still more in the two years ahead.

That encouraged RRC's managing director, Gary Fallaize, to conclude: 'It seems that UK businesses now realize there is a clear link between good training and improved bottom line results.' That link is certain but, more likely, the numbers reflected emergence from recession into relative boom. In recessions, firms automatically and foolishly cut back on training (even though that is when more time is available for the pur-pose); and it takes a considerable period of economic recovery to return the market to true buoyancy.

All the same, enthusiasts for training are clearly doing more and doing it better. BET's purchase of Style Conferences for £70 million in 1995 was one consequence. Style operates twenty-four training centres in various locales in Southern England – and itself has to spend heavily on training. Otherwise its 1,700 employees could never maintain the excellence of service that

satisfies blue-chip customers such as accountants Coopers &
Lybrands, Rank Xerox and the Prudential.

The training takes place in surroundings such as Latimer
House, Bucks; Wakefield Park, Berks; or Harber House, Beds. As
the names indicate, the centres are mostly fairly grand country
houses of the kind which, in a previous era, major companies
might have owned and run as training establishments themselves. That has become far less common as companies have
realized the folly (and the cost) of maintaining large operations
solely for internal use.

So training and training sites are among the major business
opportunities that arise today from doing for others what they
are no longer prepared to do for themselves – and may be ill-
equipped to do, anyway. So-called 'outsourcing' (see Chapter
5) spread like a bush fire during the recession. The business
attractions for the supplier are obvious. Taking on a training
site from a major company, and then running it, combines a
ready-made customer base with the chance to build a profitable
niche business on that foundation.

Style's founders are not the only training entrepreneurs to
have benefited from this outsourcing trend. Major companies
used to organize all the actual training in-house, too. Now most
rely heavily on outside trainers and lecturers, ranging from
American gurus to home-grow motivational firms, like Will
Carling's Insights.

The former England rugby captain's company, which uses
athletes and others to teach managers leadership, motivation
and teamwork, has been employed by blue-chips such as Royal
Bank of Scotland, Oracle and IBM, and is only one of an entrepreneurial legion of training firms. They have one obvious objective in common: to persuade more companies to train more –
and, Style would add, to use purpose-built centres away from
home.

Much training will, of course, be done in-house and on site,
and that provided the opportunity for an unlikely pair of entrepreneurs to make training's most famous fortunes. Comedian
John Cleese teamed up with TV director Antony Jay (now Sir
Antony, and famed as the co-writer of *Yes Minister*) in 1972.

Their company, Video Arts, broke away from the mould by using intelligent scripts and brilliant performers, notably Cleese himself, to put across the training message.

Leaving the old-fashioned, stodgy competition far behind, Video Arts prospered to the point where the partners could sell out for £43 million. The buyers, backed by three City institutions, were the management. They had taken on too much debt, however, and the business was worth considerably less when brought into a new multimedia group in 1996 – possibly the story shows how well Cleese and Jay had mastered the art of selling from their own videos.

The potential market remains enormous. Datamonitor forecasts that the European business and education market is due for an extraordinary boom: from $186 million to $7.7 billion in the decade ending in 2005. With new formats like CD-ROM and video-on-demand, the ability to stage effective and economic training sessions on site (and to profit by servicing the on-site trainers) is going to be greatly enhanced.

Off-site away-days, weekends and weeks are also powerful training devices. They necessarily involve hiring facilities *à la* Style. If giants can't sensibly afford to run their own establishments, how can smaller firms? Yet for these the value of training is just as great. It pays off doubly: first, the company gets new and enhanced skills; second, good training of itself gives a boost to morale – and a continuing one, if you carry on with the training.

According to the survey quoted above, you also get a better class of recruit, improve employee effectiveness and win better staff retention. That gives the lie to the big fear, mentioned earlier, that training will also give a boost to premature departures, as other employers, not having spent a penny on developing their staff, poach valued and trained employees from the spenders.

The fear is unworthy and unnecessary. Good staff will be loath to leave a good employer, and training is part of the goodness, as Style knows full well. The company, now a subsidiary of Rentokil, plans to have thirty centres by the year 2000. Managing director Toby Ward doesn't see the market ever being exhausted:

'The basic need to get people together is unlikely to change.'

Style's own offices are at one of the sites, Wakefield Park near Reading. This is one of its centres dedicated to a single blue-chip client, meaning that mid-week availability is limited or imposs- ible; the rest are 'open market centres'. But is it worth going away to smart premises like Latimer, with a 200-seat theatre, nineteen syndicate rooms, golf and croquet? If you can afford it, the answer is an unequivocal Yes.

Makeshift lecture rooms with inadequate equipment – the usual provision, alas – don't deliver the right message. Making training and education look and feel important gives pro- grammes a flying start. To achieve takeoff, though, make abso- lutely sure that you have clear business objectives, concrete and measurable benefits that you intend to achieve from the expen- diture.

A surprising number of companies which do spend money on training don't relate their programmes to business needs – so they can hardly complain if no business results are achieved. I learned this lesson from the most successful training programme with which I have been involved. The purpose was crystal clear. The company was desperately short of quality creative em- ployees. Could it grow its own?

This was the time of the Conservative government's levy scheme, when companies were forced to spend on training if they wanted to recover the levy. That persuaded the entrepre- neurs involved in this company (much against their personal instincts) to invest in recruiting graduates and training them to fill the vacancies. A dozen bright young men and women were duly recruited from the universities.

They were set to work in a six-month sandwich programme, one month in the classroom alternating with a month on the job. No final placement was guaranteed; the trainees had to find a unit which wanted to employ them and which they wanted to join. In the event, only one woman was left unplaced. The others included some notable future successes. The scheme was repeated with non-creatives, in a function also in short supply, and again it worked fine.

Typically, the chairman was later heard to grumble about the

£60,000 cost. But the expenditure not only filled the gaps, it raised the general standard of the staff, improved morale among the non-trainees (when they saw the company taking an interest in employee skills), and launched a continuing commitment to training that provided a platform for further highly profitable growth. In 1997 the company was named as one of Britain's most attractive employers.

Yet it's not only entrepreneurs who grumble about training; companies in general mostly feel that top management doesn't show the commitment to training that is merited by its contribution to profit. According to RRC, the return on the training investment does take time, but the time is a mere fifteen months. As any entrepreneur should know, that's no time at all.

What Consultants Can Teach

If entrepreneurs are commonly suspicious of training, they are often even more sceptical, if not seriously phobic, about management consultants. What can an outsider, however intelligent and well-educated, contribute to a practical creator who has shown, by self-evident success, how to build a business? People who turn to consultants for help, from this viewpoint, demonstrate by that act alone that they lack the right stuff.

This scornful approach is flawed in several respects. For a start, forget the familiar gibe about the consultants' credentials. It's a version of the old crack, if you're so smart, why aren't you rich? If consultants are so brilliant at business management, all the way from improving operations on the shop floor to devising a master strategy for surpassing the competition, why aren't they doing it for themselves instead of merely advising?

First, good advice isn't mere, it's invaluable. Second, they actually are running businesses, often with high success. Many management consultancies are rich and entrepreneurial businesses in their own right. Britain's larger members of the breed have handsome and growing revenues: collectively, they topped the billion-pound annual fee mark in the mid-1990s.

You can be sure that it's the big customers which cough up

all those hundreds of millions. But could a first-class consultant give any useful advice to smaller firms – if they could afford the fees? The answer is certainly yes: brains pay, for customer and consultant alike, at any level. Many of these experts draw not only on their knowledge, but on their experience. Some of the ablest and most energetic have proved their energy by breaking away from their employing consultancy to create start-ups. Here the trials and tribulations differ little from those of any other new business. Cold-calling to get clients is no easier for having an MBA or experience at consultancies like McKinsey and Bain.

Like any new-born business, too, the breakaway consultancy needs to establish credibility, and that is especially hard to grasp when you have left an employer of high reputation. Impressed by their own business backgrounds and qualifications, many starters-up fondly imagine that their professional or commercial ability and hungry willingness to work harder will outweigh their lack of established reputation.

Start-up entrepreneurs often feel the same in other businesses, too. One top consultant, however, found – and warns – that it isn't that simple. Many potential customers want the comfort of a known brand. That lands infant businesses in a Catch-22 situation. It's like the job that demands two years' experience, which you cannot get because nobody will give you a job. There's no alternative to building your own brand, using every possible method.

I observed at close hand what this approach involved for one start-up consultancy, the Kalchas Group. Their chosen method was to form a small board of top business advisers, including me, to provide counsel, contacts and that vital credibility. Another good strategy (which they also adopted for similar reasons) is to take in an established partner, who is given a minority equity stake.

After the initial association with an advertising and marketing group came to an end, Kalchas joined hands with the accountancy giant Ernst Young. Finding partners in this fashion has other advantages. Their money will also help to ease the growing pains. The entrepreneur's besetting temptation, which is to hang on to all the equity for dear life, may slow growth, cause cash problems and prevent essential long-term development.

Note the importance of the long term. Michael de Kare Silver of Kalchas advises that some things, like it or not, have to be taken slowly. Be enthusiastic, by all means, but don't be impatient. Every start-up hungers for the breakthrough into the big, or bigger, league. The breakthroughs may well be made eventually, but first the ground has to be prepared. That takes time.

As a general rule, waiting for breakthroughs requires a patience that entrepreneurs find difficult to muster. De Kare Silver's advice is to approach the build-up to breakthrough methodically. Target the key business you want to win, say, every year – perhaps a list of desired clients. Hitting the target is another matter, but you must learn, when nothing happens immediately, to stick with the targets. Don't get so disappointed that you abandon them for others.

Even if you are turned down, find a way of getting and staying in touch; never give up. Mike Ovitz, who became the biggest agent in Hollywood before getting $50 million for being fired by Disney, started on his way by persuading a key New York entertainment lawyer to accept one phone call a month. After many such calls, the lawyer let Ovitz handle a small film property. He did it brilliantly, and was on his way to super-riches.

Obey the Ovitz Principle. Whatever the lack of results, persist with dinners, lunches or breakfasts, mailshots, other kinds of communication – anything that fits your business and its potential clientele. Keep sowing seeds, and you will eventually get some sort of harvest. Self-belief and a genuine commitment to a long-term future demand nothing less.

Yet the big-time clients for whom the large consultants work often make the short-termist mistake: they start something, throw money at it and, if it doesn't work, move on – too soon. Good strategic consultants like Kalchas earn their costly keep by helping clients to form intelligent plans and to persevere with turning plans into effective action.

They can also act as the conscience of the king: the detached, informed friend and observer who holds the boss's hand, criticizes when criticism is due, acts as a sounding board and fills any gaps in thought or execution. That mentoring role is as valuable to the entrepreneur as it is to any chief executive.

This high-level contribution (which some entrepreneurs would wrongly dismiss as high-falutin') by no means exhausts the potential value of consultants. They and their specialisms have sprouted on every side. There's nothing a company may need, from recruitment to redundancy, from factory floor to cyberspace, from training to high technology, which isn't covered by some band of often brilliant experts.

If the company has a need in any key area – and that's bound to be so – buy in the outside advice, fast. True, that injunction is only good if the advice is. And that's another stumbling block. How do you know that this persuasive fellow who is sitting in your office will provide what you want, when you want it, and at a price that will be covered many times over by the results of his contribution?

There is no hard-and-fast answer. You can take references from previous clients, but that won't guarantee a similarly happy experience for your firm. Mike Bloomberg, the billionaire provider of financial information, knows the business of outsourcing computer technology from both sides of the fence.

Very few companies have the talent to answer their own IT needs internally. Very few of their bosses have the knowledge to second-guess any IT consultant. Bloomberg believes this doesn't have to be decisive. In *Bloomberg by Bloomberg*, he writes:

> Buyers who 'outsource' should find a way to try products they'll actually use before they pay the bill and even, if possible, before giving a firm order ... If you remember one thing from this book, make it 'Buy what's deliverable, not what could be!'

Start with a limited project, with a short time-scale and clearly defined objectives. See how your chosen consultant (in any field) performs under these conditions. If you're truly happy, widen the brief. But don't be like some vast companies (Guinness before the scandal was a famous example) which widen the brief so far that the consultants are practically running the group.

That's not the only big-time trap to avoid. Consultants see how big companies work, and don't work, and apply the lessons to themselves. Their prescription for effectively avoiding four organizational traps is universal and easy to follow:

1 Stay free of hierarchy.
2 Keep communication flowing easily – across, upwards and downwards.
3 Ensure that everybody knows what's happening.
4 Decide and respond at speed.

Many consultants find that open-plan offices greatly help in achieving all four aims; they don't want people hiding away behind closed doors. Another of their sound principles is to add overhead (including new members of staff) behind revenue. That means imposing some extra stretch on the business, especially its people. But having no spare resources is better for a growing firm than sustaining a costly surplus – particularly since you obviously want to avoid redundancies.

Achieving credibility will enhance the success rate with potential customers. But growth doesn't save the principals in any firm from the vital burden of winning new business. For people like consultants, who love doing their jobs, that requirement is onerous. You need to spend perhaps 30 to 50 percent of your time seeking new clients, however much you prefer working on existing business – another lesson that smaller companies often neglect, and at their peril.

Kalchas's credibility was amply proved after half-a-dozen years of independence, when an American consultancy, CSC Index, paid a goodly sum for the business. But credibility also has its dangers. Satisfying blue-chip clients doesn't make you a blue-chip yourself, any more than one successful shop makes you a Marks & Spencer. When you've only just completed the first lap, the best piece of consultancy advice you can have is a reminder that the race is going to be long. Then, stay in there – and stay to win.

The Intelligence Quotient

This is the Age of Information. That being so, you would expect people who peddle information, and who supply its means of acquisition and distribution, to be riding the entrepreneurial wave – and you would be right. The world's richest entrepreneur, Bill Gates of Microsoft, owes his tens of billions to the information explosion. But he is only the leader of a super-rich pack.

Larry Ellison of Oracle, a company worth over $30 billion in mid-1997, sells 'relational databases' which bring together data from different sources to tell a company all it needs in order to conduct its trade. Germany's stock market star, SAP, valued at $18 billion, has made four separate founding fortunes from supplying software that binds a big company's information processing together.

The Internet, which is to information what the telephone is to conversation, has also created hundreds of Midas-like entrepreneurs; or, rather, they have created the Internet. As it develops, further fortunes will be made, not only by the electronic pioneers but also by those who lead in trading over the Net, whether they are dealing in goods or information itself. Both Net uses are growing very fast.

No company can have an excess of accurate information about its markets and its business. That's obviously true in the financial sector, where speed, accuracy and depth of information can make the difference between vast losses and mighty fortunes – and where Michael Bloomberg, exploiting advanced technology, has built a private $1.5 billion empire.

Information can also be sold successfully without high tech: two start-ups by British journalists, of all people, have demonstrated that by exploiting the thirst for facts with old-fashioned print. In the case of Business Monitor International, a pair of reporters, Richard Londesborough and Jonathan Ferzoe, were inspired by their experiences in Mexico to launch six newsletters on Latin America. That only required capital of £24,000, of which all but £4,000 came from a government-guaranteed loan.

A dozen years on, 20,000 customers in 120 countries were contributing to a turnover of £3.5 million involving many more publications. To acquire the customers, BMI is a heavy user of direct mail (see Chapter 5), which costs a thumping two-fifths of turnover.

While BMI prospered from the surge of interest in new overseas markets, the other journalistic start-up waxed strong by demonstrating that it is the good companies which not only seek out the best information, but are not too proud to seek improvements as a result. *Business Intelligence* itself should in theory be among the best-managed smaller companies in Britain since it makes its living from publicizing and investigating best (and worst) practice on many of the key issues concerning management. Founded ten years ago, the company has certainly turned theory into successful practice. Ranking among the fastest-growing private companies, it has reached a turnover of £2.25 million and a staff of sixteen.

BI was founded in Wimbledon by two journalists, David Harvey and Ian Meiklejohn, for whom redundancy came in handy. They had been planning to leave *Business Computing* magazine anyway, and were debating, says Harvey, 'who should go first'. Their employer solved that problem by letting both go, and redundancy money largely funded the enterprise.

The pair planned to combine publishing with public conferences, bringing in paying delegates from a variety of companies. With a combination of luck and good judgement they settled on a hot topic – executive information systems – that brought early success. These systems, which provide key data at the touch of a button, were the early fruits of the electronic revolution in business information.

Blue-chip companies queued up for a conference which still sells out every year, with attendances of 450 people paying up to £800 for the two-day event. So, given its exposure to so much useful information, how does *Business Intelligence*'s own intelligence rate? 'On a scale of nought to ten, we're about eight,' says Harvey. In some respects, though, the company is in the same boat as the physicians who cannot heal themselves. For example, Harvey pays staff bonuses linked to company and individual results – so-called performance-related pay (PRP). Here's where information comes in. As a business manager, you need to know whether PRP works. According to one BI report, though, it was found ineffective 'in supporting change' by a quarter of the surveyed companies. Only a trifling 2.6 percent thought it 'very effective'. Yet, amazingly enough, 70 percent of the companies used this method of reward.

Firms frequently do stick to tried, trusted and useless methods while shunning new ones. Once you know the new facts, though, the entrepreneurial response is to act accordingly. In payment, the new star is 'competency-related pay' (CRP). Only 12 percent of surveyed companies reward people for their demonstrated levels of skill and capability, rather than perform-ance. The approach scored 80 to 100 percent for effectiveness among over half of the companies using it, and cases in the report confirm that CRP really does work.

Pay isn't the only area in which companies persist in using methods now proved to be outdated; appraisal of people's per-formance is another example. What really works? BI rates get-ting customers to appraise performance, and subordinates to assess superiors, as 'front-runners for effectiveness', with strong backing from the experience of firms such as building society Birmingham Midshires and Holiday Inns Worldwide.

Yet only a small minority of companies use either customer appraisal or 'upward assessment' by subordinates. In contrast, a huge majority are stuck with top-down appraisal by managers, even though only a third find that it actually works. All very deplorable, of course, but also all grist to BI's mill. The change in management styles from hierarchic ways has demanded many new methods, and 'very few people have a sound idea of how to make these things work'.

That gives Harvey and Meiklejohn's company the opportunity to tell them, and in as many ways as possible. In addition to financially weighty reports (*Pay, Performance and Career Develop-ment* cost £445), the partners have started subscription clubs and newsletters in a deliberate policy to 'proliferate media' – which has led them into electronic publishing.

The rationale is that each medium requires its different

approach and thus offers a further means of exploiting the 'areas of interest' to customers, who are mostly drawn from the top 1,000 companies. The strategy is eminently sound: cultivate your business garden intensively, and build around that core. Thus, information systems led BI to 'the role of IT in corporate transformation'. From there, it wasn't a long step to events and publications about business re-engineering.

Re-engineering means taking apart business processes with the help of the people involved and putting the processes together again, usually with far fewer of the said people. That very negative fact makes Harvey's current interest in the positive aspects of people management very understandable. The rewards report was a result. It contained some depressing news.

For instance, 80 percent of companies reported a decline in employee motivation: taking out management layers, often by re-engineering, cuts promotion opportunities. Good managers, though, don't rest there. As noted above, the correct reaction is action. Learning what is right implies that you are currently in the wrong, but that is no sin, unless you ignore the reality.

At BI, says Harvey, 'We're very aware of our defects', so they promptly re-examined their own reward system. That action embodies Harvey's main, optimistic thrust and the key to his firm's success: show companies the best way to proceed, and the good get better; at the same time, the organization that is the best at showing them how becomes richer.

Whether British information-sellers will ever approach Mike Bloomberg's super-richness is quite another matter, since he feeds off the goldmines of financial traffic. While his technological mastery is basic, it was his entrepreneurial get-up-and-go that led him to tackle Dow Jones and Reuters, the industry leaders, and to steal his fortune from their hides.

Bloomberg's first customer was the huge investment house Merrill Lynch. The client's in-house computer staff couldn't start on a new system for six months, so Bloomberg promised to complete the project before the six months were up, 'and if you don't like it, you don't have to pay for it'. The gamble paid off – just: 'The software bug that had befuddled us all weekend had

been fixed – *while we were in the taxi'*, on the way to deliver the
machine.

In moving on from providing other people with IT to building
his own information business, Bloomberg tied the customers to
his proprietary terminals and supplied them with material on
companies and markets that they could not obtain from the two
giants. The latter were beaten by speed off the mark – and
something else. As the hero recounts in *Bloomberg by Bloomberg*:
'I used to write all the cheques myself. I signed every contract.
I did the hiring and firing. I bought the coffee, sodas, cookies
and chips we nibbled on. I emptied the wastebaskets and dusted
the window sills.'

That 'something else' is the power of personal ownership.
Even in the Age of Information, supplying that information isn't
an automatic gateway to success. You still have to harness the
powers of the entrepreneur to make information pay. That
applies to both suppliers and users of information – and it is
vital information to both.

Triumphing Through Trends

Business strategies mostly founder on the same rock: man cannot foretell the future. But you don't need a crystal ball to
make more accurate predictions. The most important step is to
understand what is actually happening right now. Every
business that wins success does so by exploiting a profitable
trend that was right under everybody's nose.

In vast companies, the greatest strategic blunders arise from
refusing to look beyond that nose – such as Detroit's car companies resolutely failing to spot, as the Japanese did, the powerful trend towards smaller cars; or IBM lagging years behind
almost every trend towards smaller computers. Expert predictors
and entrepreneurs base their insights on careful observation of
the present, and never (as most businesses do) on extrapolating
from the past. In that way the aces avoid making wild guesses
about the future and still beat others to the punch, sometimes
by many years.

Can you really spot the winning trends in advance? One enterprising woman is absolutely certain that you can, and trend-spotting has proved to be a winning trend for herself. The trend that Faith Popcorn spotted was that businesses were increasingly trying to spot those winning trends. She proceeded to reinvent market research. Her company, BrainReserve, pooled expertise from many fields to forecast what consumers would buy in the years ahead. Note that the reinvention was crucial. By turning established industries upside down, you can create your own trend – as did former university don David Landau. His business is classified advertising. The reinventing idea was to publish a small ads magazine that sold copies, but published the ads for free.

Purely as a spectator, I was in on the ground floor of this upside-down enterprise. It was explained to me by Landau's associate, Dominic Gill, a friend who was then an excellent music critic on the *Financial Times*. A music critic? Naturally, I didn't take the plan as seriously as I should have done. By 1995, *Loot* had a £12 million turnover in London alone, a decade after starting up.

In a sense, Landau and Gill were copyists. Similar titles existed in other countries and Landau's inspiration came from seeing the Italian equivalent on a trip to Milan. Imitation may well be the sincerest way of making money: Ray Kroc, for example, stumbled across his fortune by enjoying his meal at a hamburger joint named McDonald's, and using the inspiration of that single establishment as the base for the world-wide chain.

The *Loot* pioneers needed courageous intelligence to see that the classified ads business could be stood on its head. Earlier breakthroughs had been made by 'controlled circulation'. The publisher gave the magazine away free to all interested parties: accountants, say. Magazines like *Accountancy Age* then attracted large revenues from recruitment advertisers willing to pay handsomely to reach the total market.

Selling enough copies of *Loot*, though, meant finding enough people willing to place free ads. That chicken-and-egg problem almost sank the infant venture, but the enterprise won through, largely because Landau and Gill were riding a trend. In markets as diverse as secondhand PCs and single people seeking dates, advertising needs were booming in response to trends and beyond them to what Popcorn describes as 'mega-trends'.

Her book, *The Popcorn Report*, lists ten mega-trends that are very hard to gainsay – because (remember the point about correctly observing the present) they are already strongly at work. An excellent test of your entrepreneurial ability is to go through her ten mega-trends, and think of ideas that promise to exploit them successfully.

1 'Cocooning' means people retreating into their homes for many things that are traditionally done outside: e.g. home shopping, which will be a major force in Britain by the millennium, thanks in large measure to the Internet.
2 'Fantasy adventure' can be enjoyed at home (all those video games and CD-ROM romps) or outside (e.g. virtual reality arcades in which customers can escape into three-dimensional fantasy).
3 'Small indulgences' offer innumerable opportunities. They are part of Body Shop's formula: attractive, affordable ways of pampering yourself.
4 'Egonomics' is the growing rage in marketing – fitting products to the individual customer's wants. From one aspect, this is a high-tech operation, depending on computer software which identifies specific customer groups and their wants, or which allows the customers to specify exactly what features they require.

   Note that the same objective can be accomplished with low technology. In so-called Mongolian barbecues you select your own ingredients and sauces for fast hotplate cooking. I spotted this succulent idea in Hong Kong, where it was packing in the thirty-somethings; and before long Mongolia had even reached Godalming.
5 'Cashing out' is what teleworkers do when they quit the office for home. Popcorn defines this trend as 'Working men and women, questioning personal/career satisfaction and goals, opt for simpler living'. They also opt for sophisticated machines: e.g. multiple-use PCs – a third of UK homes will have these by 1998.

That alone represents a huge market. There's even wider opportunity from two of Popcorn's last five trends. The first two are linked:

6 'Downaging' (the refusal of people to get old) and . . .
7 'Staying alive' (the health kick). You can already see the commercial results in quite different ways – nostalgia marketing on one hand and alternative medicine on the other. The major drug companies have concluded that, as treatment in hospitals and clinics gets more expensive, people will take increasingly to self-medication.

Retail chemists look set for a prolonged bonanza, and so do purveyors of Eastern magic and medicine, from Chinese herb shops (already appearing widely on the retail scene) to Shiatsu massage. I met one redundant executive whose hopeful (no doubt, too hopeful) business venture offered this therapy to uptight executives in the privacy and convenience of their own offices. Note how the mega-trends come together, offering people in self-employment, whether voluntary or not, new ways of achieving economic independence.

8 'The vigilante consumer'. Shell, with its hapless attempt to sink the Brent Spar drilling platform, felt the full force of this mega-trend. 'Green' products carry a cachet, just like expensive ones. Again, Body Shop is an example: it couldn't have grown so fast without the animal protection angle. The punctureless, environmentally friendly bicycle tyres of the Green Tyre Company (see Chapter 7) provide a similar model.
9 '99 lives'. There's no missing the force of this mega-trend, which means fast, convenient everything, not just food; in every market, speed and convenience today carry a premium. Popcorn found a 99-lives business in Seattle that combines a dentist's office, an espresso bar and a massage parlour, believe it or not. It's called Espresso Dental.
10 'Save our society' (anything from charities to recycling). One man's good cause is another man's entrepreneurial opportunity: for instance, the printing of charity Christmas cards.

All ten mega-trends are already making money for entrepreneurs. If you have come up with ten ideas, one for every mega-trend, you plainly have the entrepreneurial instinct. But there's a further stage – can you spot any more mega-trends? Popcorn's list is by no means exclusive. Nor are the trends necessarily difficult to spot.

Plainly, one is dining out. From their own experience, every potential entrepreneur in the land must have known that the number of people going to restaurants, and their number of visits, were increasing, while tastes were becoming more sophisticated. Some businessmen have ridden this trend near the top of the market, like Neville Abraham and Laurence Isaacson, whose Group Chez Gerard has nine up-market establishments and turns over £20 million annually.

Other entrepreneurs have brought an up-market gloss to a middle-market audience with carefully themed and readily replicated cafés, like Café Rouge, part of the Pelican group, which brewers Whitbread bought for £133.1 million. A little further down the market is Pizza Express, with yet another formula. Observe that every mega-trend can be divided into sub-trends, and that each division is perfectly capable of supporting a major enterprise.

The winners, though, invariably bring their own twist to the trend. To join the ranks of the victorious, emulate Popcorn and the *Loot* partners. Keep your eyes and ears open, understand the trends you spot, and seek to be different. Perhaps the broadest mega-trend of all is the desire of customers for differentiated goods and services.

An excellent way to find that winning difference is to look at what big, established firms are doing – and don't do likewise. They usually get it wrong. The best idea isn't to jump on somebody else's bandwagon. It's to create your own.

The Lasting Temporary Fix

Some people choose to be entrepreneurs; others have it thrust upon them. Their number is increasing, and will go on rising as companies close down whole layers of management, merge operations, seek economies and generally play mayhem with managerial security. The risk of an executive career crashing to a full stop is greater than ever before.

In these unwanted circumstances, entrepreneurial independence may look a better bet than the two alternatives: idleness or the daily grind round the appointments pages. Calling yourself a 'consultant' sounds better than admitting to redundancy or unemployment, even though the consultancy is only the odd day's work for a friend's business.

Some of the displaced have gone far beyond that level. They proudly belong to a new, successful and rising breed of entrepreneur: the one-man or one-woman management band. Success hinges on two variables: the amount you can charge for a day's work, and the number of days you can sell in a year – but that can add up to plenty. For those who can command £1,000 a day or more, incomes of £200,000 are achievable.

Given that overheads and other expenses should be very low, that generates profits well beyond those of many small entrepreneurs. The financial prospect looks good enough to entice executives who are in no danger of displacement, which explains a steady stream of managers opting for entrepreneurial self-employment. Such a move has become easier to contemplate, given increased specialization within large companies and the rise of quasi-independent project teams.

Once you have tasted full responsibility, and have achieved mastery of a highly saleable skill, the idea of going it alone looks more and more attractive. Moreover, real wealth can be won by the really successful, for there's always the chance that, from a base of selling only yourself, you can add other people and multiply the business. Thus quality guru Philip Crosby, as reported earlier (see Chapter 3), built a small empire on his own back.

Crosby also sold his business to a badly advised British consultancy group for £34 million, and in 1997 bought it back again for only $1 million. That's nice work if you can get it, but growing yourself into a genuine company is harder work than exploiting the market for individual freelance management skills. Demand here is expanding generally – and, as with any expanding market, it is providing entrepreneurial openings for those able to seize them.

The supply of displaced managers is a potential business resource, and a large one. Some idea of the numbers can be gauged from those on the books of Dunstable-based GMS Interim Management: 3,000 qualified executives ready and eager to make it on their own. As managing director Charles Russam says, working as an independent consultant is 'not that different from a small business'.

The independents have only one product to sell – themselves. But they, too, need skills in the sales, marketing, personnel and finance functions; and, like the small business, they won't have anybody else to supply these necessities. So one obvious response is to match the two needs: the independent consultant brings his skill to bear on the small firm's missing requirements.

Russam knows whereof he speaks. A former big company man, he worked on the Beefeater Steakhouse side of Whitbreads, which was the birthplace of at least two other executive breakaways. A personnel manager who had been counselling redundant brewery workers realized that this was a general entrepreneurial opportunity – and with the brewer's help, set up on her own. Eight years later her business was turning over £2 million annually. The brewer was equally obliging to its group training manager. Whitbreads became his first client, buying American courses in communication skills which the manager-turned-entrepreneur had found successful in his work for the company.

Russam himself followed a different route. After leaving Whitbreads, he filled in time as a consultant and temporary finance director. He then saw an opening for management consultancy linked to Accountancy Task Force, London, which supplies high-class financial temps. That worked well for a while. When he wanted to expand, though, his ally was unwilling, so Russam bought himself out in 1985, and promptly hit a snag. The clients wanted his consultancy less than they wanted the people he recruited for the necessary work.

So in 1987 Russam switched to what was then called 'executive leasing', and is now known, more loftily, as 'interim management'. Companies in need of executives for specific purposes for a while, maybe a long while, hire them from Russam and his competitors for a typical £300 to £500 a day. That gives some idea of the relatively high status of the work – and of the money that people entrepreneurs like Russam can make.

Russam cites one case where a competitor placed an executive at £700 daily, of which the supplier pocketed half. Margins are rarely that fat. But the client probably got a far better quality of manager than a full-time hiring would have obtained. The typical successful independent (and the easiest to place) is aged forty-five to fifty-five, 'a safe pair of hands', who has completed the cultural change from the employee mentality to the entrepreneurial one – and is a bit of a 'hustler'.

Hustling – pursuing the main chance wherever you can, even at parties – is one vital distinction between the big and small company person, between the hired hand and the entrepreneur. So is the ability to survive without any certainty of when the next cheque will arrive, or where from. Russam advises anybody to set time aside, no matter how heavy the pressure of current business, to work on generating future income.

That means forgetting the eternal bleat, 'When I'm working, I'm not selling: when I'm selling, I'm not earning.' The greatest entrepreneurial issue, 'the basic question', is in fact marketing yourself. Small businesses often plunge into a market unthinkingly, and so do independent consultants. Ask first, says Russam, what is my trade? What am I actually selling?

You quickly arrive at the importance of having a Unique Selling Proposition, a specialization where you're the expert; and it makes no difference to the principle whether the expertise lies in metallurgy, original cast albums or business planning. Whatever it is, the trade must be clearly defined, clearly recognizable and effectively communicated.

The second important message is to keep skills up-to-date. That's obvious enough for somebody who is acting as a temporary finance director; but running your own one-person business is equally demanding, and covers the wide range of functions mentioned above. Training improves performance every time, and another common bleat ('I haven't got time to go on courses') can prove very expensive.

Apart from its direct value, course attendance is a wonderful way of making contacts. The coffee-cups can be more valuable than the podium. To turn the contact into a contract, the one-person entrepreneur needs a set of general skills. To demonstrate that this really is your line of work, you must be able to . . .

1 approach business prospects effectively
2 sell face-to-face
3 deploy good presentation techniques
4 work continuously at developing all three of the previous skills
5 cope with the fact that the work is essentially lonely, and makes big demands on emotional stability – especially when business comes in slowly or not at all.

What the interim people are selling is of high potential value to other entrepreneurs, whose common problem is that their growth outstrips the management abilities of the firm. They can't justify employing a full-time, six-figure finance director with big company experience and top expertise, but they can more than justify hiring someone of that calibre for a few days.

Two or three days every month were all that one senior finance man needed, for instance, to complete a lock manufac-turer's management accounts and costing reports, and to advise on what the numbers showed. Sometimes the task can be much larger, nothing less than turning a company upside down – like the sawmill machinery maker that had wrongly allowed its emphasis to shift away from designing and producing finished equipment. The company knew what it wanted to do, but also needed the job to be handled by somebody with previous experi-ence of radical change. The interim manager chosen had to do everything from selecting suppliers to changing the flow of parts, cutting back from nine machine shops to one in the process, while shrinking the workforce by two-thirds.

Because of the proven effectiveness of such interim heroes, Russam's own business has been sufficiently successful, despite the stiff recessions of the Thatcher era, to make him glad that he took the independent plunge. He now handles his industry-leading database – 3,000 interim managers – from four offices.

Bringing the wheel full circle, he also bought himself an equity stake in Accountancy Task Force, the firm where it all started.

But he wouldn't launch his business on the world in the same way. His mistake, he says, was exactly the one he now warns the new, involuntary one-person entrepreneurs to avoid. 'When I started I tried to do too many things all at once.' The best advice you can follow (and Russam wishes he had from the start) is very simple: focus and specialize.

7

The Magic of Marketing

The Quartet of Success

Inside every successful business, there must be excellent marketing. If you are selling the right goods or services to the right customers at the right price in the right way, you must win; get the marketing quartet wrong, and the results will also be deeply erroneous. Super-salesmen, true, can sell (to cite the traditional example) refrigerators to Eskimos. The difference is that super-marketeers find an irresistible use for fridges to create a lasting Eskimo market.

Yet many businesses, great and small, rely on the brute force of selling and never think in marketing terms. The terms are as simple as the above quartet. For a start, 'don't go into a market to underprice. There will always be someone equally innumerate along in a month. Go for the profit.' This sage advice comes from Dave Patten, author of *Successful Marketing for the Small Business*. He lays down three basic principles:

1 *Differentiate your product* – the famous Unique Success Proposition, or USP. Why should customers buy from you and nobody else? The difference can lie in the goods or services (Post-It pads are a perfect example) or in, say, delivery (computers by mail order, which became a goldmine for Dell). But without the USP you'll be a mere, much less promising me-too.
2 *Identify your market segment.* There's no better example than Camborne Fabrics (see Chapter 5), with its identification not

just of furnishing fabrics, but of those supplied for office furniture. Patten adds an important rider: 'keep looking for something else you can supply to your devoted audience.'

3 *Promote with purpose*. The key question is implicitly asked by the customer: 'What's in it for me?' The USP gives only part of the answer. Patten says: 'Nobody buys things unless they need them.' These days, 'want' is a better word. Promotion must tell people why they desire the offering and how they can buy – and must deliver that message incessantly and consistently.

How does this three-part platform translate into practice? Tony and Maureen Wheeler found their USP the hard way. He had an MBA from the London Business School and a Ford Motor job offer; but the pair decided to travel the world by minivan on £4 a day. The money ran out in Sydney, where people's curiosity about the great, cheap trek prompted the Wheelers to write a book based on their experiences.

They didn't know whether a market existed – but sometimes the hard way is the only way to find out. Market researchers will object to this proposition. Frame the questions correctly, and in theory you should be able to establish, either from sample polling or focus groups, whether a market exists and what would satisfy that market. But many a business plan has crashed over this fence.

What people say they want is a hypothesis: would you buy this book *if* it were available? Reaching into your pocket for the purchase money is not hypothetical at all. Researchers try to overcome this difficulty by using mock-ups of the product and various other clever devices to simulate or anticipate the actual buying experience. Often the forecasts are brilliantly accurate; but again, you never know until the hypothetical market becomes reality.

At that point the entrepreneur must be prepared to abandon the plan or to modify it in the cold light of reality: or to reinforce success in the warm glow of initial takeoff – which is what the Wheelers won. Printing 1,500 copies of *Across Asia on the Cheap* in 1973 cost £625. When sales, built by personally going round bookstores, reached 8,500, Wheeler knew that he had found an exploitable segment.

To quote *Forbes* magazine, his market, plainly one with large potential, consisted of 'young seekers after adventure on the cheap'. Shoestring guides for South-East Asia and other areas followed – until India generated a 100,000-copy first edition hit in 1980. The couple had found the perfect marketing combination: a multi-product company built around a single theme.

The single-product company is notoriously vulnerable to the vagaries of its single market. The diverse multi-product company, on the other hand, risks losing vital concentration on each separate business. The themed multi-product company, however, builds up expertise that applies equally to all the products; it can concentrate its resources on what is in effect one market.

That build-up is especially important because of the 'learning curve'. In factories, costs halve with every cumulative doubling of production. A similar benevolent process applies generally. In other words, the more times you repeat something, the better you become at the task; or, to put it another way, practice makes nearly perfect.

That's why the most successful publishers form clusters of magazines or other products round a single industry that is capable of supporting rich growth – repeating proven formulas not only with new products but in new geographical areas. By the mid-1990s the Wheelers were publishing 156 world-wide guides (including Western Europe and the USA) from their base in Melbourne, with sales offices in San Francisco and London, and turning over £7.5 million.

The guides themselves, displayed prominently in bookstores, are a means of continuous promotion for the brand: Lonely Planet. That title more or less fits Patten's bill in *Successful Marketing*: 'Start with a good name, memorable and preferably illustrative of what you do.' (His own trading style is Merry Marketing. 'It invariably brings a smile to whomever I am addressing, and people remember it.')

The name is an important marketing tool, but don't exaggerate its significance. With rare exceptions, the product makes the name, not the other way round. Vacuum cleaners were called Hoover only because that was the name of the founding entrepreneur – who no doubt never expected his name to become a valuable verb.

Akio Morita and Masaru Ibuka, it is true, took great care to change their company name from Tokyo Telecommunications Corporation to Sony, which would work anywhere in the world. That was an intelligent step, but no more than an adjunct to the triumph of the transistor radio; it was no help at all when Sony engaged in a losing battle to sustain its video cassette recorder format, Beta, against the VHS rival. And that was launched by an outfit called, boringly enough, JVC.

Names acquire power by usage and attachment to successful brands – like the almighty Coca-Cola. Patten is right, though. A well-chosen name can give you a push-start. As with his own merry company, Urban Outfitters has a name that tells a story – and a profitable one. This *Forbes* 'up-and-comer' was launched by Richard Hayne after working with Eskimos in Alaska (whether he sold them fridges is not recorded).

Hayne developed the USP and the segment as a friend's MBA project: a suitably unsmart shop selling 'hippie-type paraphernalia, psychedelic posters, Indian print fabrics, scented candles and used clothing'. After twenty-three years, there were twenty shops selling annually $110 million of housewares and clothes that were either second-hand or looked it. The prices are low, but not the mark-ups.

Just like the Wheelers' guides, the stores promote themselves purposefully and consistently. Urban Outfitters maintains a costly network of young trend-spotters to keep the hippiness up-to-date. As for 'looking for something else you can supply to your devoted audience', the chain started, for instance, to explore ways of catching its grown-up hippies with a new store concept.

That's a central tenet of modern marketing. Its ace practitioners don't think in terms of markets, but rather of customers. They abhor the thought of selling one customer one product, and that's that. Instead, they aim to keep a customer for life, widening the range to enlarge the sale at every stage of that life, and changing the pitch to suit the changing preferences of the maturing buyer.

Companies selling financial services are especially keen on this prospect, but have been hampered by one not-so-little problem. They lack the technological ability to bring all their customer information together. They need a modern means, which IT will provide, of achieving what the old-fashioned entrepreneur did by instinct and with ease: that is, getting to know your customers intimately, so that you can tailor your marketing to their individual requirements.

That section of the marketing quartet poses a question that is far from simple. Are you selling to the right customers? The customers may be perfect for one-off sales of one product or service. But in these circumstances, how are you going to grow either in sales or profits? A similar supplementary question applies to those products or services. They may be excellent for present purposes, but how are you going to sell more to the existing customer base and widen it?

Then comes the issue of channels. If you are using a single method of distribution, is it limiting your sales unnecessarily? Finally, there is the matter of price, which rightly concerns Patten so much. Remember that relative price is all that matters, how your price compares with the competition, not just on the actual quotation, but in offering Value For Money (VFM).

The higher the customers rate your relative quality of product and service, the more they will be prepared to pay. You can achieve high perceived VFM at high absolute prices or low ones. If the perception of VFM is right, so is the marketing thrust: witness the rise of Urban Outfitters from the base of one $300-a-month store to the point where owner Dick Hayne became worth $90 million. The marketing quartet plays very sweet music.

It Pays to Advertise

Advertising, like owning executive jets, is commonly supposed to be a preserve of the corporate rich. On the contrary; it can be a fast-track method of joining their number. But that generally demands a very different approach from that employed by major companies like Unilever – because a little money must be made to go a very long way.

A trenchant observation about advertising by Unilever co-founder Lord Leverhulme has become a world-class cliché: that half his advertising expenditure was wasted, but he never knew which half. Giving his ad agencies a licence to lose his money didn't worry the soap king, because the returns on the total advertising investment were so vast.

The competing titans spend whatever is needed to maintain their 'share of voice', meaning their due ratio of the industry's overall spending. There is a correlation between vocal share and market share. You let either drop at your peril. In the major leagues, nobody has ever worked out a reliable way to achieve a significantly bigger bang per ad buck than the competition.

In the minor leagues, the relatively poor can't achieve longed-for results by monetary muscle, but mental muscle can work wonders, however. As in business generally, the short-cut to a brighter and better solution is often contrariness. Whatever the conventional wisdom dictates, don't go and do likewise. Go thou and do differently. That's how the Edinburgh Club, a health and fitness outfit, bucked an adverse trend.

For all the hype about keeping fit, real consumer spending on such clubs fell in the early 1990s. Obviously, the television activities of the Green Goddess and Mr Motivator have equalled the impact of much paid advertising, but the latter has been conspicuously absent. In fact, only one in seven people was taking regular exercise in mid-decade.

The conventional wisdom would preach to these converted, defining them as 'the market'. That, however, automatically limits the scope for sales. Great entrepreneurial breakthroughs often depend on turning a minority activity into a major pursuit – like George Eastman getting a Kodak camera into every hand. The famous story about two shoe salesmen sent to the same under-developed country applies here. One wires back, 'Coming home. Nobody here wears shoes'. The other demands huge shipments at once, for the same reason.

The latter logic is what appealed to George and Pauline Kerr, the owners of the Edinburgh Club. With 10 percent of a market consisting of 14 percent of the local population, doubling your share and your sales will require massive effort. It certainly won't be achieved by 'tactical price promotions', on which the Club used to rely. Nor will that help to convert the unconverted; get just 2 percent of them into the market, however, and you match the doubling.

The Kerrs' efforts to reach the unfit and fat, though, were hampered by ads that one corporate member bluntly called 'crap'. That's typical of most advertising done by smaller companies. Unable to interest a proper agency, the entrepreneur may produce the ad personally, sometimes helped by the advertising department of the chosen publication. The result is often a visual mess and a mixed-up message, with no clear strategy either for the business or the ad itself.

The latter should follow the same AIDA model as a direct mail letter, getting Attention, arousing Interest, creating Desire, and inspiring the target to take Action. That is far more easily said than done. Amateurs are unlikely to beat a professional, who will seek to ensure that both the design and the message follow AIDA to the full, and will match the message to the client's means.

When *Management Today* was launched, for example, a young copywriter had the bright idea of printing a typewritten letter from me, as the editor, supposedly to the chairman, Lord Drogheda. As I recall, the ad discussed the magazine's ambitious plans, man to man, and ended with a sentence about including a subscription form 'like this' – 'this' being a roughly drawn-coupon.

The response to this relatively small ad was huge. The copywriter concerned was Robin Wight, who went on to prove his own entrepreneurial credentials by founding WCRS, for a long time now a major force in London advertising. The member with a low opinion of the Kerrs' ads also happened to be in an advertising business, the Leith Agency, a local firm.

Acting on the Kerrs' view of their market, the agency followed through on its bluntness, putting its mouth where the Club's money was, by producing six prize-winning advertisements.

Like Wight with his letter to the chairman, the Scottish agency sought to find a different angle. *Vive la différence* applies as powerfully in advertising as in any other field of marketing.

The sameness of much TV advertising shows the difficulty of differentiation. But the Leith Agency turned the sameness trap upside down. Instead of showing lean, fit, young men and women, the ads were aimed at the fat and/or the unfit; the adipose and flabby were used as models for witty copy. 'Join the pudding club', for example, shows seven well-padded members and asks, 'So why do they use our exercise machines and follow our fitness programmes? Well, you should have seen them before they joined.'

Many more did join. From 1990 to 1995, the Kerrs more than doubled their membership (which reached 1,300 paying up to £440 a year), with profits up by 174 percent. The intake of new members more than quadrupled – and over a third of the newcomers reported that the ads aroused their interest first. In its small company way, therefore, the campaign is a perfect illustration of what marketing and advertising strategies mean.

You define your objectives and find ways to accentuate the positive factors and eliminate the negative ones. Thus, in subtle ways, the ads directly attacked a powerful objection to health clubs: fatties don't fancy being surrounded by athletic beauties. As every well-trained salesperson knows, though, objections are heaven-sent; they give you something on which to work.

Remove the objection, and the target customer is brought much nearer to purchase. With a budget of only £10,000, spent with Edinburgh newspapers, the campaign brilliantly earned its silver in 1994's Advertising Effectiveness Awards. This modest business rubbed shoulders with 'new campaigns' from giant advertisers like Courage (John Smith beer), Lord Leverhulme's Unilever (Pepperami sausage) and Playtex ('Hello Boys' for Wonderbra, of course).

These awards themselves convey an advertising message – that ads really are effective if the advertiser possesses three indispensable attributes:

1 clear aims
2 an equally clear strategy for reaching those objectives
3 clear evidence to show whether or not the aims have been
  achieved.

On all three counts, that doesn't differ from any other business
expenditure. If you have no objectives, or fuzzy ones; haven't
thought through how to get to any destination you may have
in mind; and haven't discovered the key measures that prove
how well or badly you're managing – well, failure in these all
too common circumstances cannot be a surprise.

Advertising, though, has a peculiar problem when producing
evidence of its effectiveness: what do you measure? Various
scientific (or pseudo-scientific) methods purport to measure the
pulling power of ads: customer surveys ('How did you learn
about this product?') are one way. Then, you can test either
spontaneous or prompted recall of the ads, although this only
measures effectiveness if you know the relationship between
recall and actual purchase.

A far better guide is the movement in brand preference before
and after the campaign, but that's no good to smaller advertisers.
Those total ad budgets would be exhausted by the costlier forms
of measuring – meaning that there would be nothing to measure.
The most factual yardstick, however, is the readiness of the
customers to repurchase.

Repeat customers are rich corporate possessions, but advertising can only be part of the customer retention package. Certainly
it isn't a substitute for poor or mediocre products. The Edinburgh
Club would not have kept its new members if they had been
disappointed by the quality of the premises, equipment and service. But George Kerr had concentrated on the Club since 1989
(after a gold-medal career as Austria's national team coach in
judo) and thoroughly understood his business and the clients'
needs.

Clever words and pictures, founded on reasoned strategy,
were not the only elements in the advertising's effectiveness.
Nor, self-evidently, could total spending have been the key, not
with a budget just into five figures. What does count, and for a

great deal, is consistency. The 'fatties' campaign was kept running year after year.

The principles applied are precisely the same as BA's decade of calling itself 'The World's Favourite Airline', at a cost of £400 million. The Kerrs spent their £10,000 just as wisely; the campaign was repeated because it proved effective, and its repetition created greater effectiveness still. The more an effective ad is repeated, the more strongly AIDA works.

Ads can remain imprinted on the mind long after the product has ceased to figure large: say 'Double Diamond' to most people, and they will immediately think, even sing, 'Works Wonders, Works Wonders', recalling a long unheard TV jingle. Working wonders on small budgets with similar creativity and consistency is the way in which small firms with small resources can achieve big results – if the entrepreneurs know what they want and use entrepreneurial agencies who know what they are doing.

What Business are We In?

The most crucial question in starting along the entrepreneurial trail is also by far the hardest. Out of the infinite range of possibilities, what business do you choose? The question applies equally to the company that has soldiered on for years, staying put and staying small – or smaller than its owner would truly like. The same effort, applied in a more fertile field, would generate better results.

The problem, again, is finding the new field. What business? That is a critical question, but it isn't enough. Three words need adding to make a second question. What business *are we in*? The query was made famous by Harvard Business School professor Ted Levitt, in an essay entitled *Marketing Myopia*. Companies, he argued, were short-sighted; imprisoned by narrow definitions of their markets, they failed to take a long-sighted view of the changes that technology would enforce.

In his most famous example, he cited buggy-whip manufacturers who were stranded by the advent of the horseless carriage. Had they seen themselves as making transportation accessories, not whips, their future might have been marvellous. Levitt's insight was misinterpreted by his corporate readers. They merely sought to reshape their product portfolios around some fancy, broad definition of their businesses (of which they usually had far too many).

Defining the broader business is a basic entrepreneurial requirement. It marks out the vital difference between producing and marketing. You may have a special skill, some high-tech brilliance which is certain to win customers (if, that is, the technology works). It's a mistake worthy of the whip-makers, though, to identify the business with that technology rather than the purposes for which it is used.

The Levitt question forces a business to define its market, and to understand thoroughly the workings of that market. A marvellous moment in the film, *The Graduate*, has a friend of Dustin Hoffman's screen father buttonholing the young man and offering a one-word recommendation: 'Plastics.' That gets you nowhere (even though plastics hasn't, by and large, been at all a bad business).

Far more value lies in the type of answer given by Lord Rayner in his early days as a managing director of Marks & Spencer. Asked what business he would recommend to an aspiring entrepreneur, Rayner didn't hesitate: speciality breads. The key word wasn't 'bread', but 'speciality'. It immediately suggested other questions.

1 What would be special, and why?
2 Who would be the purchasers?
3 Would better quality attract high enough prices to cover the higher costs?
4 Would a tiny proportion of the mass market provide enough turnover to make a tidy fortune in the speciality niche?
5 How would the market be supplied?

The questions are all part of the magical process known as marketing, which is summed up by the catechism cited earlier: give your customers what they want . . . in the way that they want it . . . at the time when they need it . . . at a profitable price they are prepared to pay . . . and tell your customers what they're getting – or going to get.

A neat example of pure marketing is Holiday Autos, which in a decade has grown from start-up, capitalized with only a few hundred pounds, to £40 million of private turnover. Clive Jacobs was in the bucket-shop business, selling cut-price air tickets, when opportunity beckoned. As he told the *Financial Times*: 'Car hire was the only product not being marketed extensively through travel agencies.' Jacobs and his partners moved swiftly to fill the gap.

What customers wanted was to book their car rental at the same time as the rest of the holiday, with no trouble or fuss, and at no extra cost. Car rental broking did precisely that. Jacobs started by using small rental companies in the key resorts, and went straight into profit in a £1 million first year. As sales improved, first to £2.5 million, then £6 million in the following year, large trans-European rental companies were pulled into the network, and offices were opened in Germany and the USA.

The customers were also told firmly what they were getting – car rental prices that couldn't be beaten. The use of franchising to grow the chain more rapidly emphasizes the sovereign importance of marketing in Jacobs' world, which now includes over forty-two locations. He hopes to emulate the growth to multinational gigantism of Hertz and Avis though, as they have found, the car rental business rapidly becomes over-crowded and slow-growing.

The Levitt question could have helped the giants to broaden their market. If Holiday Autos is seen as offering not car rental but easy-to-buy individual vacation services, all manner of enticing growth opportunities swim into view. That's another aspect of the art and science of entrepreneurial marketing – the Triple Play, in which you build turnover by

1 selling existing products or variants to a new body of customers
2 selling new products or extensions to the existing customer base

3 catering for new customers with new offerings tailored to
their market needs.

You can map out the possibilities with a simple exercise. Draw
a box, and divide it with lines both horizontally and vertically
into squares. The horizontal axis of this matrix consists of your
customers. The vertical axis consists of your products or services.
Where a customer takes a product, put a tick. Once that process
is complete, some squares (maybe many) will be left blank.
These are the 'windows of opportunity', through which marketing and selling efforts should be poured.

Go back to the matrix, however, and add blank lines to both
the horizontal and vertical axes. Those represent new products
and new customers, without which the company will be hard-
pressed to grow; however brilliant the customer retention, there
is always some attrition. But unless the newcomers and the new
products fit the broad definition of your market ('What business
are we in?'), you won't be able to take advantage of existing
business strengths. The market definition can, however, be
changed, very possibly with delightful results.

Stephen Williams, for example, believed that he was selling
wine. He didn't think like an entrepreneur, as he admitted to
the *Independent on Sunday*: 'I saw the wine trade then as not
particularly entrepreneurial. I felt that if I could apply my communications skills to a product I enjoyed, I should be able to
take some market share.' Christmas gift packs and cash sales to
Midlands boardrooms duly followed, but Williams disliked the
seasonal nature and tight margins of this trade.

A customer inadvertently came to the rescue. His company's
chairman was retiring. Could Williams supply a wine from the
hero's date of birth? It was 1920, and the successful sale
launched Williams in a new and thoroughly entrepreneurial
direction. Now he wasn't selling wine, but expensive celebra-
tion. The Antique Wine Company would offer somebody's birth-
day-year wine (inevitably, a very dear bottle) in a costly padded
box, complete with a copy of *The Times* from the actual date of
birth.

Advertising in expensive magazines brought in the customers;

the sale of shares (to a wealthy client) and of the previous business financed the advance to £2.5 million of sales. Like the Holiday Autos case, that of Antique Wine indicates what determines the degree of marketing success. It depends on the extent to which, having decided what business you are in, you emulate the twain by getting the right answers to eight fundamental questions:

1 What shall I make/sell, and in how many variations?
2 What prices shall I sell at and in relation to what volumes?
3 Who can I and should I sell to?
4 How will I determine when to drop an old product?
5 How will I determine when to launch a new one – and how will I do it?
6 How will I keep fully abreast of everything that my competitors are doing?
7 How will I set sales targets?
8 What standard of quality will I seek?

The last question should be a giveaway to the antiquity of these questions. They are adapted from a book which the management pioneer Lyndall F. Urwick wrote as long ago as 1933. In the late 1990s, anything but the top quality lays the business wide open to competition. Only the best is a good enough guarantee of commercial success. The so-called 'shoddy goods' strategy of low quality sold at a low price is out; the 'premium' policy of top quality at top prices has been superseded by top quality at medium or even low prices.

You can bet that when the millennium comes, people who think of themselves as entrepreneurs will still be shooting themselves in the feet by failure to act methodically along the lines indicated by the first seven questions. They will offer too many variants, fix prices according to subjective notions of what the traffic will bear and remain obstinately committed to those prices for far too long.

They will persist with existing products without even knowing the losses or profits that each line is making. They won't have any plans for new products, nor will they keep their eyes open for any opportunities that suddenly come along. They will ignore competitive activity and dismiss any new product or marketing approach on the grounds that 'it will never work'.

They will set gung-ho sales targets without first establishing, if possible by careful research, what they can reasonably expect to sell by high achievement. All this slap-dash behaviour, moreover, will convince them that they are being truly entrepreneurial. They could not be more wrong.

Navigating the Niches

The Holy Grail of the entrepreneur is supposed to be the 'gap in the market': some line of business, or unexploited location, which nobody else has discovered, and which, because it is all your very own, faces no competition. The gap sounds like the easiest approach to success. The issue is more complex than it seems, however. A fundamental business error in Somerset Maugham's story, *The Verger*, shows why.

Sacked by a new vicar because of his illiteracy, the verger wanders disconsolately down a long street, dying for a smoke. But there is no tobacconist. He reasons that other people must have felt the same need, rents an empty shop, and is on his winning way. Sunday strolls looking for similar long, tobacco-less streets generate further shop openings and a substantial fortune. (The bank manager is astonished that his rich client can't read, and wonders where the man would be if he could. The answer, of course, is verger of St Paul's, Neville Square.)

The verger's approach is all very logical. But it flies in the face of expert retailing knowledge. For preference, the experts do not (like the verger) choose an isolated 'pitch' which they will pioneer. They prefer a location where an existing business is generating heavy traffic for the trade concerned. That's why you see clusters of fast-food outlets within yards of each other, or boutiques lining up for trade, or Asian cloth houses cheek by jowl.

Similarly, the big chain stores want others to enlist for any shopping centre they are eyeing. The more stores, the more custom. If, as the verger found, there is no supplier for miles around, that could be because there are no potential customers, either. That is always a risk for gap-seekers. Their game is inherently chancy, because by definition the firm is offering something for which actual, proven demand does not exist.

The potential demand may be enormous, as two guys called Steve, Jobs and Wozniak, found when they launched the Apple personal computer on a far from expectant world. But the demand may also be derisory, as in the flop of Sir Clive Sinclair's bizarre C5 electric midget-car. Sinclair's record at spotting true gaps is uniquely rich: pocket calculators, digital watches, home computers, pocket TVs. Yet all four ventures also ended in business failure for the gap-spotter.

The flops say more about the inventor than his strategy. Failures in execution bedevilled the inventions. The pocket TV shown to the press did not work, and could not allegedly, because it was a hasty mock-up. The computers had a notorious unreliability, second only to that of the watches. The latter, anyway, used the wrong technology.

Note that Sinclair's niches didn't stay niches for long. They became global markets for large companies, mostly Japanese. Although famed as a technologist, Sinclair was more a marketing genius. He consistently avoided one risk of pioneering – that you may pick a non-existent gap – only to stumble consistently into another: that you may be stymied by the unknown hazards of the unknown product or market.

That's why, just like Burger King seeking safety close to McDonald's (and near to its general business formula), most business start-ups build on elements in the market or the technology which are known to work. The secret is to vary the point of attack, to go round the side where large established industries invariably and inevitably leave small but significant gaps.

Food amply illustrates this thesis. Major companies have covered the waterfront in all categories. But the Food from Britain organization can still count some 5,000 speciality food manufacturers who employ no more than four full-time staff (plus many part-timers). The majority earned very little: average turnover was about £250,000. Go to a food and drink exhibition and you can see them in scores selling honey-based horseradish mustard, or wild boar meat, or some other exotic goodies.

These niches are so small that imitation is worth nobody's while, and exploitation is seldom worth very much more. Some specialists, however, have transcended the limitations – even in markets where big players are dominant. For instance, packaged soups, snacks and biscuits are big company stamping grounds, but Vanessa Houlder of the *Financial Times* found three companies that have grown rapidly by differentiation.

Backed by venture capitalists, New Covent Garden Soup Company not only created a difference by putting fresh soups into cartons, but used enterprising and unusual recipes. Derwent Valley Foods found new snacks such as corn and tortilla chips to go round the side of the crisp-makers. Union Snack, which makes pretzels and flavoured pretzel products, was started by a Derwent founder, John Pike, with £2.2 million of bank money and venture capital. As he says: 'There will always be new niches opening up.'

The large company is unlikely to exploit the small niche, partly because the sales are too small to justify the effort, partly because, to quote Lawrence Mallinson of New Covent Garden, 'smaller companies can take bigger risks'. They also don't have established products to protect against the danger of cannibalization, when the new product eats into the sales of the old. 'Risk is not just about money,' according to Mallinson.

For all their caution, however, the big companies also spread their managerial energies over too many brands – so the smaller firm can direct more focused energy at its me-different product in a me-too marketplace. Me-too has its uses, however. It is the fundamental nature of a franchise operation, one of the most common points of entry for a new entrepreneur (see Chapter 2). The outlet mimics existing franchises down to the last detail of the provision and the process.

This isn't an either/or situation: there is a half-way house between the total plunge into the unknown and total imitation. The middle-of-the-road gap-seeker copies the small food manufacturers in that he looks at existing, well-established markets. Like them, too, he chooses an approach that will exploit markets in new ways. The difference is that he attacks the giants head-on, aiming at only an insignificant fraction of their trade.

I've never forgotten the attitude of one entrepreneur who attacked a giant-dominated market: just 2 percent, which the Goliath wouldn't even notice, was worth £30 million. Because his approach was fresher, more economical and customer-friendly, the challenger ended up with a highly significant 25 percent of the market. That's the first of nine proven approaches to find the small niches that pay big.

1 Neglected markets: where products and service have become ossified and customer needs have outpaced provision – in the above case, the product was wallpaper.
2 Unfilled need: like that for portable computers, for people wanting to do their work at home or when away.
3 Disadvantages in existing products: like the fatteningly high sugar content in ordinary Coke, which encouraged the enormously successful launch of Diet Coke.
4 Omissions in otherwise well-served markets: paper nappies.
5 Extensions or new formats for proven lines: Weight Watcher soups by Heinz.
6 Technological breakthroughs: that's how electronic typewriters destroyed electro-mechanical and mechanical machines.
7 Transferable successes from other markets: *Hello!* magazine being adapted from the Spanish.
8 More economical ways of satisfying wants now being met expensively: fast food of all kinds.
9 Less economical ways of satisfying wants that are being met only adequately (Haagen-Daaz and Ben & Jerrys ice-cream, Sheba cat food).

These happen to be big-time examples, but the principles they enshrine apply to every business. Whatever line you're in, look constantly for any of the nine possibilities, not only because they may provide a new and important opportunity, but for defensive reasons. When a rival introduces some new feature or service, you may shrug it off – but what if the customers want it?

Note, however, that the nine approaches, though far from similar in other respects, have one factor in common: differentiation. The first question to answer in the search for gaps and niches thus asks itself: What difference is there, if any, between this product or service and anything else on the market? That leads to eight further sets of questions:

1 What need does Plan X fill? And why has that need been ignored by others?
2 What advantage does Plan X have over other goods or services in the same market? Is this important to customers?
3 Is the general market large enough for a small, specialized product or service to carve out a small but lucrative potential share?
4 Is Plan X a one-off, or is it capable of leading to a whole family of niche projects?
5 Is there a technological or similar concrete asset that makes Plan X difficult to imitate or surpass?
6 Are there similar products or services in different markets from whose success lessons can be learned?
7 Will the cost structure enable Plan X to seem attractive on price-competitiveness alone?
8 Or does Plan X have a premium value that will sustain a premium price?

It's a fair bet that few niche entrepreneurs have consciously gone through a similar routine. They do so subconsciously, however, and they certainly won't succeed unless some of the answers are highly positive – as ad-man Rosser Reeves knew full well. He won lasting fame by coining the phrase Unique Selling Proposition.

The USP, as noted before, is something which you have that the competition doesn't – a definition which plainly applies to a gap-filling or niche-creating product. The USP can be anything from staying open for longer hours to home delivery, a no-questions money-back policy or a lifetime guarantee. Finding and concentrating on his clients' USP proved a great USP for Reeves and his agency, Ted Bates. And that's what 'the gap in the market' really means.

Export – and Thrive

Your true entrepreneur doesn't care where he sells. Overseas or domestic, it's all grist to his business mill. The comprehensive instinct is exactly right. Exports are simply sales of much the same goods or services under a different label. The ability to compete effectively overseas is a function of overall competitive prowess.

You have first to raise your sights on the four key factors of business – Investment, Innovation, Marketing and Productivity – and then enlarge your focus to cover the world. The rationale is arithmetical. A small slice from a vast cake is much more nutritious than all of a small bun. The true entrepreneur cannot possibly resist this succulent equation. If, like Britain as a whole, he only has 4 percent of the world market, taking a mere 4 percent from the rest of the globe doubles sales.

Anyway, at a time when markets are going global in many sectors, exporting is less an option than a sheer necessity. In this respect, the frontiers of success and pure survival have become the same. Any list of Queen's Awards for Industry shows the benefits that enterprising companies have reaped from regarding the world as their oyster.

Henrob, founded by Keith Jones as recently as 1985 to make specialized automatic riveting machines, is a case in point. Without overseas markets, Henrob would be a tenth of its present size. In other words, it very probably would not exist at all. The customers for the machines, used in car manufacture, are overwhelmingly resident outside the UK, big companies which dislike using small-fry suppliers.

Unlike Henrob, the RTA Wine Rack Company has no technological edge to sell – only wood-and-metal racks, retailing at £3.99, which achieve a £4.5 million turnover. That would be two-thirds smaller without exports. Managing director Tim

Arthur's family company took over the business in 1985 and
bought out its chief rival three years later. Arthur fully understands the basic economic principle behind exporting.

In 1997 he feared a slowdown in the mature markets. However, any deceleration was 'more than made up by increased
demand from emerging markets'. As he told the *Financial Times*:
'It just serves to remind you that it's a big world out there.' That
valuably obvious truth is confirmed by the thirty-three-year-old
George Costa, whose Proton Textiles gets 40 percent of its £8
million sales from abroad.

Costa's market is fabric for the booming market in football
kit. He has bucked the common 'talk of the demise of the UK
textile industry. Our experience shows there are niches that are
still active.' Sterling's 1997 strength cut back Costa's export ratio
sharply from 61 percent. But without that proportion, maintained over the previous two years, Proton's domestic niche
would have been far too small to finance its investments.

Investment, as noted, is one of the four key business factors.
Investment, Innovation, Marketing and Productivity tend to
travel together. Investment is needed to support Innovation.
That provides the technical edge for the Marketing drive, to
which the cost levels achieved by Productivity are vital – and
Productivity, to complete the benevolent circle, depends on
Investment.

The better exporting company is simply a better business all
round – witness the sustained success of J. C. Bamford with its
excavators in a market where much larger competitors roam.
Note how well the export winners illustrate the quartet. Proton's
£2 million move to a larger site, bringing its total *investment* to
£3 million, is a high figure in relation to its sales, let alone its
profits.

Henrob has thrived on *innovation*: its automatic riveting
machines aim at achieving higher efficiencies and lower costs
on the car production lines than the rival arc-welding systems.
The technological difference simultaneously gives Henrob higher
productivity and provides the *marketing* platform, which is inevitably decisive, given that selling and distribution are basic to
exporting.

Arthur's wine racks wouldn't sell 'if we did not get out there and speak to them [potential customers] personally. Our salesmen visit every major retailer in the developed world. And we make sure they speak the language.' Charles Wells, whose Bedford brewery of the same name has been active since 1876, learned Italian to cope with one of his first two inquiries, and studied US brewing techniques to deal with the second: 'We pushed out the boundaries as much as we were worth.'

Wells thus ships its export beers in kegs to supply 'British' pubs, gaining a marketing edge over rivals selling in small packs and cans. Wells had been attracted into overseas markets, not by their inherent charms, but by the hard domestic times of 1992: 'We reacted by stepping up our exports. You could say that we took it to extremes. We put more resources into it and did much better than our competitors.'

The result, inevitably, as for all the exporters, is higher productivity than the domestic market alone could ever provide. But what enables a product to win and retain an overseas market? Ask the exporters, and you get a uniform set of answers. They talk about 'quality, reliability of delivery and extensive marketing', or 'quality of product and service' – hardly earthshattering revelations.

The entrepreneur revels in the challenge of overseas markets precisely because the firm is exposed to the competition of local and overseas rivals. The latter will swiftly show up any failures of performance on any front – and those failures, especially if foreign competitors invade the market, are just as dangerous at home. The arguments for thinking world-wide are so convincing, in fact, that they pose a major puzzle.

Why do so many companies remain on the wrong side of the exporting fence, even when they fall further and further behind the competition with every passing year? That is surely the antithesis of the entrepreneurial response. Take the case of one engineering business. Over the last twenty-five years, it has seen a once-smaller foreign competitor zoom past its sales. In 1960, it outsold the competition two-to-one. On the latest results, the one-time follower outsells the former leader by 300 percent and is still expanding faster.

Worse still, another overseas rival, a mere beginner back in 1960, has grown significantly larger. What goes on in the minds of managements as they are outmanaged and outsold so consistently? Quite apart from the threat to sheer survival, the foreigners' gains in sales and profits are the British company's own lost potential income. Strangely, the free market forces sometimes fail to work on the entrepreneurial juices.

The particular business referred to above is actually a whole industry: UK Ltd's industrial gears division, a £450 million sector containing many smaller firms. If the entire British contingent doubles its sales in the next two years, it will still be as far behind the Germans as they lagged behind Britain thirty-five years ago. And the Germans will not be waiting around for Britain to catch up. Nor will the second successful rival, Italy.

This saga would be dismal enough if it stood alone. But other industries exhibit the same disease: fear of exporting. Transcending that debilitating illness is a major step across the frontier of entrepreneurial success. That truth is so obvious that export paranoia must have deep and tangled roots, even though some ways of building business abroad do not involve any leaps into the unknown.

They may lie in front of the company's nose. For instance, do any of your customers have overseas operations to which you can sell? Big companies like GKN and Pilkington are following their customers round the world. So can anybody. But that means total commitment to the exporting life, which exposes a company's whole management system. If it can't provide the pertinent information and the able managers needed for success, the firm won't fare well abroad.

Nor will it flourish at home, either; the industrial gear laggards, in fact, are being endangered by imports, which expose firms on two fronts: losing sales at home, and not compensating for the losses by gains overseas. The combination is far more dangerous than the dual threat which often intimidates proprietors or senior managers: fear of being unable to cope with big orders from abroad, and anxiety about not getting paid for whatever orders they actually manage to deliver.

On the first point, inability to cope, that stems from falling short on investment, one of the four key business factors, and a basic sin that catches laggards out at home as well as abroad. Michael Opperman, whose firm, Cross & Morse, has grown to medium size, told the *Financial Times*: 'A modern computer numerical controlled gear-cutting machine costs £300,000, and you need lots of them.' But if you don't have them, what then?

On the second point, the threat of non-payment, there are several ways of protecting the firm, from credit guarantees to factoring. The Department of Trade and Industry, which has been trying hard to lick the gear-makers into shape, is a mine of information on such relatively easy technicalities. Information about which markets are big enough, safe enough, easy enough to reach, and growing sufficiently fast is also available freely – and free.

More specific research may have to be paid for, but much highly relevant information can be found relatively cheaply by attending or exhibiting at all the right trade shows. Attendance at trade exhibitions is one of the keys turned by RTA for its humble wine racks. In other words, nothing bars the export failures from success but themselves. If you want to cross the frontiers of success, selling across frontiers is as good and rewarding a place to start as any entrepreneur can find.

The Translation of Triumph

Lucrative ideas, proved to work, can cross from country to country and continent to continent. From supermarkets and fluorescent lighting to hamburgers and sticky tape, the USA has provided the richest source of lucrative, proved products and services for the smart British entrepreneur. The transatlantic flow will never stop, but success does not translate automatically.

Few translations are more encouraging, though, than baking soda toothpaste. After a week of advertising, sales in Tesco of the Arm & Hammer Dental Care brand, previously wholly unknown in Britain, had quadrupled. The brand quickly won an amazing 5 percent of this congested and highly competitive market. It is so competitive that rivals hastily added baking soda brands to their ranges, forcing the invader to retreat to a still impressive 3 percent or so.

The rivals do not use the words 'baking soda', as Roger Parkyn gleefully notes, pointing out that the brand still has a 40 percent share of the sector which it created. Parkyn's business, then called Integrator, now renamed CKMP, handled the launch in May 1994. The launching party stuck deliberately to the unfamiliar American phrase for bicarbonate of soda, leaving the brand as the only 'baking soda' toothpaste. That preserves one element of an asset which US imports need – a Unique Selling Proposition.

That has to be the starting point. Parkyn says that there must be 'something in the intrinsic nature of the product' that will make it highly acceptable in Britain. Success in the USA does not answer that requirement. A product can boom in one market and bomb in another. How can you tell in advance which will happen? The entrepreneur always has to gamble on the public reception of the new and unfamiliar – and great care is needed in trying to hedge the bet by preliminary consumer research.

The researcher has to overcome that stubborn fact that what people say they might buy is not the same, by several long chalks, as what they actually will purchase. If a product concept, as opposed to an actual product, is being tested, the task is obviously at its toughest. When the product itself is available, however, it can be tried on local consumers to check that their reaction is as joyful as in the country of origin.

With Arm & Hammer, the preliminary consumer research worked like magic. Two-hour group discussions were followed by instant trials with brush and tube, which produced enthusiastic Ooh and Aah responses. These were duly picked up in an advertising campaign based round the exclamatory WOW! ('It must be the baking soda!') That campaign has been a wow, too; but Parkyn would be the last person to insist that advertising power is always decisive in achieving marketing breakthroughs.

The fact that a product has succeeded in another country in no way lessens the necessity to launch the same powerful, all-round marketing effort that is required for breakthroughs with an untried domestic product. Parkyn's agency believes in integrating all the activities that can make a product succeed: public relations, sales promotion, design, advertising and direct marketing.

Everybody in marketing knows that these activities work better for working together, but too few firms actually follow that logic in practice. You may not need, or be able to afford, all the elements. If you are competing in an established market like toothpaste, however, you advertise or die. Toothpaste is a major product everywhere, but the brilliant product you spotted on holiday in the States may have a relatively small presence in Britain.

If you have fallen, say, for Pace Thick and Chunky Salsa, the pride of San Antonio, Texas, and another of Parkyn's progeny, the market will not support an advertising campaign sufficiently expensive to be effective. Salsa (the hot and spicy Tex-Mex sauce) has overtaken ketchup sales in the USA, and tacos, tortilla chips and so on have been growing fast in Britain. The issue, however, is whether such a brand can cross oceans without advertising support.

Research can be misleading and ads unnecessary when products are little known, as Gustave Leven, the man behind Perrier, found when crossing the Atlantic in the opposite direction. The research showed miserably small demand. But Leven followed his own instinct, reasoning that Perrier tasted much better than New York tap water. The subsequent smash hit rested initially on word-of-mouth and public relations, which is precisely the recipe Parkyn used successfully with Pace. Sampling and PR quickly generated a 20 percent market share.

The task might seem even harder with Snyder's Pretzel Pieces, famous in the USA (especially in their home town of Hanover, Pennsylvania), but meaningless in Britain. Parkyn's firm made significant changes in the packaging to stress the authentic origins. Often material changes must be made if you want translation to work.

Equally, if you are starting small, or trying to launch a new trend, you cannot afford the diseconomies of what Parkyn calls 'the baton race effect'. In this sporting activity, advertising and other agencies pass the baton (and sometimes the buck) from one to the other, and you get (and pay for) 'strategic thinking four times over'. CKMP believes that its unified approach benefits the client. Over two years Parkyn proved his point by growing from two people and zero business to billings of £10 million and twenty-one staff.

Whether or not you employ integrated help, an American discovery is unlikely to succeed unless the launch follows an integrated marketing plan. Nor are you likely to stumble across a mass-market winner such as hamburgers or fried chicken. Like pretzels and salsa – and even baking soda toothpaste – today's American find is likely to be a minority taste. That worries Parkyn not a bit. It's better, he says, for research to find '20 percent that strongly like the product', than 60 percent who mildly like – and mildly buy.

Finding 60 percent who strongly like and strongly buy, naturally, is three times better. What is likely to cross the Atlantic now? Fast-feeding is still fast-growth in the USA; but new operators like Lone Star Steakhouse & Saloon (growth rate 78 percent annually) are stealing a free ride from McDonald's, Burger King, Pizza Hut and the rest. The proliferation of the vast fast-food chains gives an opening to smaller, fresher contenders serving slower Texan-style steak or chicken-on-a-spit.

That is a development seen several times in these pages. The newcomer goes round the flanks of the giant, whether the latter is sleeping or wideawake. Small chains like Pret a Manger and Café Rouge have already shown that, despite or because of the spread of the giants, speciality eating is a new wave in Britain. It would be unwise to bet too quickly on other US hits staying American. Are you sure that child play centres, say, or second-hand sporting goods wouldn't work in Britain?

The import may be less an idea than a broad category of marketing effort. Two-fifths of the 100 fastest-growing firms in the USA, as listed by *Fortune*, are high-technology businesses, selling to closely defined markets. If you're not a digital genius, it doesn't mean that the growth super-highway represented by switches, hubs and routers for computer networks, say, or anti-virus computer software is closed. Have their progenitors yet turned their attention to non-American markets? There may still be licences worth winning or joint ventures worth starting.

The next largest category of rapid growth is healthcare, where super-technology need not be the key; the company making those little plastic strips that footballers put across their noses, ostensibly to assist breathing, has grown at great speed. But all manner of markets can generate super-growth, some of which look most unlikely until you see how well they work.

For instance, what about buying and reselling stolen or wrecked cars from insurance companies – which is how an American firm called Insurance Auto Auctions achieved 50 per-cent annual compound growth? That is towards the bottom of the growth rates that the 100 companies chalked up over a three-year period. A list of British fast-growth businesses, how-ever, would be just as diverse and just as speedy.

The magazine *Real Business* led its 1997 list, compiled with Dun & Bradstreet, with five companies whose three-year per annum growth rates ranged from 145.5 percent to 161.2 per-cent. They won their sales increases by publishing business magazines (Nexus Media); cable laying (M & N); sign manufac-ture (Signcorp); computer software (Firefox); and costume jewellery. The latter's distributor, Cabouchon, was founded by Petra Doring, who ranks as Britain's 'number one female entre-preneur'.

Cabouchon's marketing method is basically an American import: agents give parties to their friends and neighbours, which is the way Tupperware has always been sold. Methods as well as goods have long made profitable crossings of the Atlan-tic. And one US method in particular has general application. It is well illustrated by a company called FuncoLand, which sells new and used video games to the tune of $50.5 million a year.

That figure meant multiplying nearly ten-fold in five years from a small base. In 1991 there were just three FuncoLand stores; today there are 176. What's the point of finding a growing market where you can locate customer hunger unless you exploit the opportunity *à l'Américaine*? Become the best in the business at feeding that hunger. Continually upgrade the product or service and its marketing. Use acquisitions selectively to accelerate the growth curve. And never forget the biblical preaching and FuncoLand's practice: go forth and multiply.

8

Finding the Future

The Nine-Star Entrepreneur

Many people who set out to be entrepreneurs never reach the targets they have set for themselves. They may ruefully conclude that they lack the necessary qualities. It's tempting to assume that the richly successful entrepreneur – a Richard Branson, say – is born with unique talents, like a great footballer or wonderful singer. But Branson, along with many millionaires, has a record marked by several misses as well as hits.

The unfailing Midas touch is very rare. In fact, all successful entrepreneurs have a number of attributes in common, none of which is at all magical. The *Harvard Business Review* once published an excellent study of entrepreneurial qualities by Geoffrey A. Timmons. He came up with nine such assets:

1 A high level of drive and energy.
2 Enough self-confidence to take carefully calculated, moderate risks.
3 A clear idea of money as a way of keeping score and as a means of generating more money.
4 The ability to get other people to work with you and for you productively.
5 High but realistic, achievable goals.
6 Belief that you can control your own destiny.
7 Readiness to learn from your own mistakes and failures.
8 A long-term vision of the future of your business.
9 Intense competitive urge, with self-imposed standards.

The list may look formidable; at seminars with people working in large companies, I seldom find anybody claiming more than six of the nine. The only exception was a large conference of sales people and sales managers. Their response had more to do with the salesman's professional self-confidence and bravado than with their true entrepreneurial potential. After all, none of them actually was an entrepreneur, all were hired hands.

At the other end of the scale, in the largest insurance group in Finland, nobody owned to any of the attributes except the managing director, and he only claimed one of the nine (I have always wondered which). It is true that corporate executives are unlikely to be entrepreneurial. When you do meet an obvious nine-star example, they are rarely corpocrats, and always remarkable individuals – like the young Michael Heseltine, in the days when he was an embryonic politician and an aspiring entrepreneur.

In the early 1960s, Heseltine's aspirations had produced few results, despite his nine-star rating. His Haymarket Publishing had trouble showing a profit. Its false starts, like a *Time*-style news magazine called *Topic*, and a high-prestige, non-profit glossy, *Town*, kept the business small and struggling financially. But learning all the time from his mistakes and failures (Attribute 7), Heseltine self-confidently kept on taking risks (Attribute 2) until he at last found the right market.

That market consisted of business magazines, such as *Management Today*, *Campaign* and *Accountancy Age*. He had also found a group of people (Attribute 4) who could work with him productively, and whose key members could be imbued with his monetary clarity (Attribute 3). That clarity had been reinforced by hard experience. Agonizing over how to stop your next cheque from bouncing or where to find the payroll money tends, like the prospect of imminent execution, to concentrate the mind wonderfully.

Founding father Heseltine duly followed his long-term personal vision – to become Prime Minister (alas, an unfulfilled dream) – by moving full-time into politics. Two of his key colleagues, Lindsay Masters and Simon Tindall, then built on the foundations to create the present £150 million group, which also has strong portfolios in medical publishing and leisure magazines.

Heseltine's entrepreneurial efforts thus continued to reward him with millions long after he ceased to take an active interest in the business. Would he have been any less successful if some of the nine attributes had been missing? Should others worry if they fall short on the nine-star count?

The first answer is that you can just get lucky. Tiny Rowland, selling a 30 percent stake in the House of Fraser (which he fondly expected to repurchase), 'gave me the chance on a golden plate,' Mohammed Al-Fayed gleefully noted later. But golden plates containing Harrods, which made Al-Fayed genuinely rich, are offered only rarely.

If pure luck fails, lack of any of the nine attributes may prove fateful – and even fatal. Look behind might-have-beens or bankruptcies and you will see what could have achieved success but instead accompanied failure. The missing factor might be greater drive and energy, better risk-taking, proper financial controls, less insistence on being a one-man band, larger ambitions, refusal to give up, turning error into expertise, higher standards or pursuing a dream that could be turned into rich reality.

While some people (like Heseltine) are innately gifted in some or all directions, all businessmen and women are capable of greatly improving their capability and performance on any of the nine counts. Case after case bears out this essential truth. Take drive and energy. Unquestionably, some people can work faster and harder than most others, and can drive a project forward more masterfully. Like Lady Thatcher, they may crowd more hours into their day by sleeping less. Like her, they can dominate by tirelessly exercising a driving will; but you don't have to be a Thatcher to demonstrate drive. Sir Maxwell Joseph built the Grand Metropolitan empire, now part of one of Britain's grandest multinationals, from three anything-but-grand hotels. His working days, weeks and years were short. He delegated as much as he could.

The drive and energy existed, certainly, but in his head rather than in his physical activity. His strength lay in the constant search for new opportunities and in their swift, efficient capture, all in conformity with a developing vision of future progress. Most people never get as far as thinking about the future, let alone planning that future and then acting to turn dream into reality.

The planning itself helps to provide the self-confidence required to take risks. There are major misconceptions about risk-taking, however. Sky-diving, gambling and business involve three different kinds of risk. The sky-diver knows that he has a small but inescapable chance of being killed; taking that risk is part of the excitement. The amateur gambler knows that the horse may fall, or the wrong number may come up; the professional knows the percentage chances of these events and bets accordingly – but still knowingly risks all his stake on chance.

The nine-star entrepreneur is like a professional gambler in carefully calculating the chances of success. Experience shows that most entrepreneurial calculations are far too optimistic, which raises the risks from moderate to excessive – and helps to explain why so many entrepreneurs fail. The nine-star winners, though, prefer to eliminate risk altogether and to back only what they consider to be dead certs. They may be wrong, and they may botch the execution, but they are not consciously taking risks.

Nor do all winners consciously perform the financial calculations that make them rich. Some minds can absorb balance sheets and profit and loss accounts with consummate ease, spotting black holes and lesser errors in a flash. But I have seen a figure-blind financial illiterate, forced by his boss to master budgets and management accounts, go on to direct a large private business with conspicuous, money-based effectiveness. What natural genius does not supply, hard work can.

The boss in that instance showed one side of productive people management: providing your colleagues with the skills they need to perform bigger and better jobs. Such skills do not come naturally to many entrepreneurs of the older generation. The younger ones, like William Sieghart of Forward Publishing, know better: 'a successful business is . . . about having brilliant people who flourish in the working environment around them.'

Sieghart told the Royal Society of Arts that he deliberately sought 'a consensual feminine culture', built around people who are 'open and supportive and like working together'. Without that kind of environment it is far harder to achieve the high ambitions which took Forward to a turnover of some £10 million. The ambition was to transform so-called 'corporate publishing', putting out bespoke magazines for companies, from 'the bin-end of journalism'.

That aim was realistic and proved to be achievable; but the achievement stems from an exercise that any would-be entrepreneur can and should undertake – formulating a written ambition, sharing it with others, and extrapolating the goals into the long-term future. No great techniques are required to develop either this attribute of the entrepreneur, or any of the nine; or to ensure (equally important) that the nine are developed in others.

The double process is much easier than mastering a foreign language. It only takes the application of intelligent willpower. Given that will, entrepreneurs can become masters of their own fate. Mistakes and failures become the springboard of competitive success, with self-imposed standards providing the binding discipline of both boss and business.

The results can be startlingly effective. Not only can figure-blind financial illiterates master money, but dictators can even learn to delegate and stop shouting. As well as willpower, true, it all needs effort, which some people would much prefer not to make. But that's another story – and a sadder one.

Gleaning the Globe

'Global' and 'world-class' sound like big words for big, established companies. All 'global' means, however, is that the company sells in many countries across the world on an integrated marketing platform. As for 'world-class', that means supplying products, and using processes, that are equal or superior to the best standards that can be found anywhere in the world.

The experiences of two very different entrepreneurs shows

that global, world-class virtues are not the prerogatives of the business establishment. On the contrary, the development of segmented, niche markets, and the innovations in information technology, manufacturing methods and distribution, mean that new enterprises, however small, can start by thinking very much bigger than in the past.

Even the age-old problem of making customers conscious of your existence can be tackled along big company lines: for instance, by exploiting the techniques of milking general consumer awareness, created by the media, for the specific purposes of your market niche. If the niche is right, you can create an enterprise that thinks as globally as any other and is determined to achieve world-class rank.

The Green Tyre Company of Middlesbrough has thus been exploiting the concerns of an anxious age. Its product is an environmentally sound bicycle tyre that will not puncture. It produced its first such tyre only four years ago, employs nineteen people and has a profitable turnover in seven figures. Those sales are made in twenty-two countries, because founder Colin Scarsi, aged forty-three, 'never thought of it as anything but a world company'.

His attitude sprang from the frustration of an 'awful lot of work trying to promote UK exports'. Scarsi used to work for the financial services arm of bankers Citicorp, but he had 'always fancied manufacturing'. He saw businesses that had difficulty competing. 'Was it really all that difficult?' Today he says, 'it *is* that difficult' – although you wouldn't think so from Green Tyre's phenomenal pace of development.

It all began with an article in the *Daily Mail*, reporting on the Goodyear giant's work on a puncture-proof tyre. That sounded like a wonderful idea to Scarsi, so in May 1991 he launched into his tubeless tyre project, using microcellular polyurethane. Three introductions were invaluable. One brought in a business angel, a private investor who provided funds and owns the other half of Green Tyre. Second, visiting the USA in August 1991, Scarsi found the 'mad scientists' who could turn the technology (Goodyear had only 'pottered about' with the idea) into a commercial product.

Third, the Development Corporation on Teesside did an 'absolutely incredible' job in easing the passage. Scarsi rang one day, and the next day, even though the project was still pie-in-the-sky, people from the Corporation came to see him in London. 'These boys', he said to himself, 'are keen.' In an age when the public sector is increasingly active in private business, and *vice versa*, the aid offered by the former to the latter is copious – everyone from the European Union to organizations like that on Teesside is in on the act.

It makes abundant entrepreneurial sense to take their funds and, fortunately, Scarsi fell keenly in love with Teesside – not least because, with 'ICI on the doorstep, it wasn't frightened of chemicals'. The financial aid packages were a help, though not very substantial in relation to the half-million pounds of capital required. By October 1991, however, Scarsi was 'fairly confident' that he had a business. Seven months later, the first tyre was made.

Scarsi waxes eloquent about the 'fairly unique' and 'fantastic' properties of his chemicals, which also happen to be environmentally virtuous. Hence the name: although the 'green' qualities are actually the weaker of Scarsi's two marketing cards. He has two Unique Selling Propositions. The stronger, the one which earns the tyres their premium prices (starting at double the charge for a pneumatic product), is the 'never goes flat' argument, which anybody who has ever sweated over a puncture will appreciate.

The Green issue also gives strong support. It is 'very important' in markets like Germany and Australia, and is an easier way to create a unique identity, with a potential that goes well beyond serving just a few markets. To achieve Scarsi's world ambitions, that identity had to be global: 'You've got to present your company as international' – even though at first that may well mean stretching the reality.

For a start, Green Tyre operates in six languages, and every person in administration must speak two of them. Scarsi also put a great deal of effort into product profiles, a four-minute video (made in nine languages), visiting cards, and soon. As he says, the material you take abroad is 'all they're seeing'. The

potential foreign customers are unlikely to travel to Middlesbrough, so they have to be impressed on the spot.

They must also be served on the integrated marketing platform mentioned above. The key factor, and the second global
necessity, is to have a world pricing policy. Pricing must be fairly
consistent, and you need to think of the world as a single market.
Since Green Tyres faces no domestic competition whatsoever,
that thought comes naturally to Scarsi, who points out that 5.5
million bike tyres are imported into Britain annually.

In relaunching Britain's bike tyre production, Scarsi had his
setbacks. While the first year made a profit, it was precisely
£515, and the second year made a small loss. In the third year,
although profits began to flow at around £150,000, Green Tyre
ran into capacity problems. In 1995, however, a new automated
line came on stream, which theoretically enabled the company
to treble production and thus mightily strengthen its unique
world position. At the same time, Scarsi diversified into wheel-
chair tyres, with success he describes as 'nothing less than stag-
gering'. The NHS will be buying his puncture-proof tyres for
years to come.

Allan Willett provides further stirring evidence of how the
entrepreneur can soar from small start to global status. Some
years ago, he reached the kind of levels which figure in Scarsi's
dreams. After three decades, Willett's company, Willett International, has £71 million of sales. It has increased turnover by
31 percent per annum since 1984, operating profit by 29 percent
and net profit before tax by 24 percent to hit the latest total of
£3.15 million. It operates in seventy-five countries world-wide.

This cornucopia consists of products and services for printing
variable information (including the ubiquitous barcodes) on
products, cases, trays and pallets. At his start, the business was
Green Tyre-sized, pioneering shrink-wrapping for cheese and
trying (with some difficulty) to convert supermarkets to this
novel, now universal method. That business flourished to the
point where Willett attracted the attention of a City merchant
bank.

The bankers suggested that Willett should sell his company
for £100,000 to a much larger outfit, take over as managing

director, and propel the combined business to great heights. When the grand design flopped, Willett's career could have been ruined. Fortunately, he had been negotiating a deal with a US company involved in labelling. The American boss (still a friend today) suggested that Willett take on the licence himself, and the seeds of his present triumphs were sown.

After selling all his other interests, Willett put proceeds of £711,000 into product identification, coding and labelling. Like Scarsi, he subsequently made good use of government aid, starting manufacture of industrial ink-jet printers in the Corby Enterprise Zone with grants and loans totalling £942,000. In 1987, 28,000 square feet of new freehold factory, also in Corby, was financed by tax relief. Before that, Willett had raised £2 million under the Market Entry Guarantee scheme to help him set up subsidiaries abroad.

He now has twenty-five of the latter, which he finances in an ingeniously economical manner. Once his machines, sold through agents, have provided a big enough customer base, he hires executives from local competitors and provides seedcorn capital for a new company selling the consumables. The working capital is then borrowed from local banks. The rapid international expansion has been aided not only by sensible foreign bankers but by information technology.

Willett was planning to set up regional headquarters in Asia. Then he discovered that video conferencing could accomplish exactly the same purposes at a tiny fraction of the cost – and without adding a new layer of potential bureaucracy. That's something which entrepreneurs are more likely to avoid than professional managers. The need for pros, though, must grow as the business does.

In 1990 Willett took an unusually bold step. He appointed Alan Barrell, formerly the head of Domino Printing Services, to run the company day-to-day and moved himself up to concentrate on strategy and expansion. Better still, he moved out. Stay on the premises, and people will still knock on the owner-boss's door; go several hours' drive away (from Corby to Canterbury in this case) and they will abide by the managing director.

Willett is thrilled with the results. Since 1990, sales have more than doubled and profits have risen over seven-fold before tax. There's no doubting the main moral to be drawn from the two cases: even if you're small, you can be global and world-class provided that you obey one injunction. In Scarsi's words: 'You've got to think big.'

Technology is Not Enough

The end-of-century technological cornucopia is magnificent, and growing more glorious by the minute, but it doesn't necessarily offer bigger and better opportunities than old-fashioned games like fast food, or even slow food. Management guru Gary Hamel likes to point out that between 1989 and 1996, the American market for pre-washed and packed lettuce grew from nothing to $1.1 billion. And lettuce is much safer than high-tech.

Many venture capitalists have pulled back from technological investments after some bitter losses. That is the constant fear with new technologies – that promised wonders will never materialize, or will disappoint, or will never reach the market. Notoriously, big companies seldom derive wonderful, wholly new products from heavy spending on innovation. Ironically, though, they often develop the new 'disruptive technologies' which eventually undermine their own existing products.

The majors are rarely rewarded with new wonders for a simple reason: they refuse to bring them to market. As Clayton M. Christensen's *The Innovator's Dilemma* explains (see Chapter 4), this has a perfectly sensible explanation. The major firms pursue 'sustaining technologies' which protect and expand their existing markets. That strategy is far more likely to add quickly to their cash flow, assets and profits than creating a whole new business round a new technology.

The latter approach may eventually produce a welcome addition to the big firm's riches, but it does not seem like a matter of life and death. The entrepreneur, though, lives on capturing such opportunities and dies without them, which is why smaller entrepreneurs generate the big breakthroughs, using the big company technology. But the new technologists have problems of their own which lie not with the technology, but with matching the latter to market needs.

In 1992, half the top twenty in *Fortune*'s list of America's fastest-growing companies were working in the broadly-defined computer industry. They literally ranged from A to X: from first-place Artisoft, whose niche lies in helping PCs to work together, to Xilinx at 100, making reprogrammable chips. Move on to 1994, Artisoft was still among the 100 fastest growers, but only just; Xilinx was out. Yet in 1996, it was the other way round.

The point isn't simply that high-tech is an up-and-down occupation – though it is. The argument is rather that technology is not an end in itself, and that companies of any size can shift swiftly from win to loss unless their technology remains the best available to satisfy market needs. You won't accomplish that by imitating the industries that are 'dominated by multinational companies which know what their rivals are doing and have no interest in coming out with new technologies that upset the status quo'.

The speaker, James Dyson, quoted in the *Financial Times*, had the domestic appliance industry in mind. He developed his thesis to the tune of £100 million a year by inventing the apparently impossible: a new kind of vacuum cleaner. Ever since the days of the original Hoover, vacuum cleaners had worked on the same principle, sucking dirt into a bag. Dyson's machine has no dust-bag. Centrifugal force collects the dust into a plastic container.

The advantages of this innovation swiftly catapulted the brand into top position in the UK. Dyson, a designer still aged only forty-nine, has now turned his attention to washing machines. Once again, the basic technology has not changed greatly over the years: the big makers have made incremental improvements, with not a single real breakthrough in sight.

Dyson's Law – that big companies imitate each other and hate to change technologies – offers one path to entrepreneurial riches: the entrepreneur simply jumps into the gap thus created. Another approach is to join the ranks of those who harvest the technologies that the mammoths are ignoring. Steve Jobs of

Apple, for instance, found the superb Macintosh technology in the PARC labs of Xerox, which had no intention of using its own wonders.

The abundant rewards along the beg, borrow or steal road have been exploited with products ranging from Apple's personal computers to Golden Valley's Poppops. What, you might well inquire, are Poppops? You won't ask if you're a popcorn addict and like to make the delicacy in your own kitchen, using the microwave. Nor is this a little niche product – Golden Valley Microwave Foods Inc. sells well over a billion units a year, with plenty of them in Britain, at 69p a pop.

In the beginning, however, there were no sales and no units, only a bright idea. How do you find such inspiration? You need the help of a superb piece of technology: the human being's miraculous powers of observation. Above all, keep your eyes and ears open. Brilliant technology can spring from anywhere on earth – and even from outer space.

There might seem to be no connection between NASA and popcorn, but American space technology gave the innovator of the Poppop, Jim Watkins, his marvellous notion. The piece of technology concerned would in theory enable you to put frozen corn in a packet made of thin metallic sheet. This would swiftly rise to the necessary very high temperature. Watkins only needed to make the technology work in practice. That's the hard bit – much harder than the original inspiration.

To take a big company example, Art Fry, the father of the now indispensable Post-it notes, stumbled on his Big Idea in church, wondering how he could mark the hymns more effectively. The answer – a removable and reusable piece of sticky paper – came in a flash, but it took the Post-it enthusiasts four more years of battling, often against determined, diehard opposition in their own company, 3M, before they had a winner on their hands.

What's more, the vital piece of technology, the special adhesive, had already been around for five years. Inside a big company, technological pioneers face the knee-jerk opposition of the conservatives. But there are also some big advantages. Other, more progressive people can be enlisted in the cause and, above all, there is money. Budgets were available from which the Post-it pioneers could draw cash – even if it felt like drawing blood from a stone – and there was plenty of it.

Watkins lacked the vital financial ingredient, but made up for the monetary shortage by dogged readiness to go to the brink, if not beyond. He was almost beyond when a friend advanced $100,000 to finance a last-ditch, make-or-break attempt. It did the trick. The first trick, however, is never the last. If at first you do succeed, you find that you also have to try, try again. Watkins' first product was wisely called Act One, the beginning, not the end. Act Two developed the technology so that the corn didn't have to be frozen; the next Act was then written: a demetallized package.

The gold in Golden Valley no longer belongs to Watkins. Richer by $200 million or so, he became a top executive in ConAgra, the huge conglomerate which bought his company. Such payoffs are usually the reward of much hard slogging, for the best idea in the world will not develop or sell itself. Edgar Biss discovered this after an epiphany equivalent to Fry's vision over the hymnbook. Biss was irritated by a long wait at the bank while a cashier totted up the cash takings of a local tradesman. Couldn't the loot be counted faster?

The answer sprang from his work at the time, automating a steelworks, for which up to 500 tonnes of molten steel being handled by cranes had to be measured. Biss reckoned that the same principles could be applied for the tellers. A very brainy weighing machine was needed to cope with the fact that bank-note weight varies considerably. Biss's machine, the Tellermate, compares a small number of notes against a standard sample and calculates the margin of error.

It uses this margin to calculate the larger bundles of notes added until the whole pile is cleared: forty-five seconds for an entire till, against ten to fifteen minutes without aid. Coins are automatically counted by using plastic cups: though shapes and sizes vary, weights are identical. Naturally, the banks said it couldn't be done. As the *Guardian* reported: 'Getting business to accept the Tellermate was a long struggle.'

Retailers and restaurants led the way, buying Tellermates at prices ranging from under £500 to £800, and four years ago the US market came good. Biss's company, Percell, now employs sixty full-timers in Gwent and fifteen more abroad – but note the typical technological pattern again: quick brilliance followed by hard slog, fifteen years in the Tellermate's case.

The effort required may intimidate people with less natural determination than Biss, Watkins or Fry. The latter's large company employer was singularly lucky that Fry and his colleagues showed a persistence worthy of the most determined small entrepreneur. Like Biss with the banks, Fry was always being told what 'couldn't be done' in the manufacture of Post-it pads. On one occasion, he simply proved that what 'couldn't be done' could be by doing it himself. He installed a machine in his own basement, worked for twenty-four hours non-stop, and then handed the proven process over to the 3M engineers.

One lesson of Poppops, Post-its and Percell is the same: small, committed groups of people are the best way to drive new technology into the market. James Dyson, having proved the same point with his vacuum cleaner, assembled sixty bright and mostly very young research and development people for his push into washing machines. The cleaners provide the annual millions to finance the operation – a luxury which most technological pioneers can't afford.

That isn't necessarily a disadvantage. Within his tiny, overstretched resources, Watkins was forced to be ingenious, and to do the most with the least – a brilliant contrast to the big company way of doing the least with the most. Nevertheless, for technological entrepreneurs a long, hard road probably lies ahead. So don't count your chickens before they're cashed; and that includes Dyson and his washing machines.

The Opportunity Octet

Smash-hit growth businesses are residuals. They represent the left-overs from the multitude of hopefuls which attack fast-growing markets like IT, but never reach the heights. At the start, often little distinguishes future winners from the also-rans, either in their prospects or their strategies. Should you, for example, put your faith or money in Tripod or Atcom/Info?

The first operates a 'virtual community' on the World Wide Web, the second runs Internet kiosks that are the cyberspace equivalent of phone boxes. Tripod, with forty employees, had revenues of $570,000 five years after start-up. Three years younger, Atcom/Info had five times the revenue from sixteen fewer employees. But will either ever reach the heights of Wind River Systems, whose equity is valued at nearly $1 billion?

This company makes embedded operating systems that run the microprocessors found in everything from cars to cameras. But Wind River's revenues ($64 million) bear no sensible relationship to that billion-dollar value; and its rise to relatively modest sales took sixteen years. Stock market bonanzas, though, can happen overnight. In Wall Street, the IT entrepreneurs have found the philosopher's stone that rapidly turns base metal into gold.

The gold will turn back to brass unless the real world performance matches the expectations built into the soaring share price. Study the long-term winners – like Microsoft – and you find eight principles that separate those winners from the also-rans. The Opportunity Octet is highly valuable in other businesses, too, but in IT it is decisive. Winners . . .

1 reward risk-taking and don't punish failure
2 give new ideas top, top priority
3 allow those ideas to develop freely
4 put great performance above good order
5 compete fiercely with themselves
6 enlist professional managers in good time
7 share financial rewards widely and richly
8 go for market share first and foremost.

Much of this Octet (derived from a *Business Week* study of Silicon Valley) has been strongly advised in previous chapters for all entrepreneurs. Out of sheer necessity, the IT whiz-kids have been forced to abandon traditional, hierarchical ways and have learned to live with chaos in the interests of a 'super-speed

and can-do culture'. That pair form the pure milk of entrepre-
neurism, which produces an unprecedented flow of cream in
the hands of unconventional managements.

Thus, to gain its potent market position on the Internet (8),
start-up Netscape famously just gave away its browsers. You
simply have to forget old inhibitions. For instance, competing
with yourself (2) means not being afraid to cannibalize your
existing products; if you don't eat your children, someone else
will. Al Shugart, the ace entrepreneur of the disk-drive, is only
half-joking: 'Sometimes I think we'll see the day when you
introduce a product in the morning and announce its end of life
at the end of the day.'

The Opportunity Octet are tactical necessities, but they should
rest on Four Differences which mark out winning strategies from
the runners-up and flops. Winners . . .

1 concentrate on the winning hand
2 cover every bet
3 work with strong partners
4 think really big.

How the Differences make the difference emerges from the
tale of Psion, pioneer of the palmtop computer. Dr David Potter,
formerly a professor of mathematical physics at Imperial College,
London, started off in software, and then conceived the personal
organizer. According to the *Sunday Times* wealth rankings for
1996, Potter and his wife Elaine weighed in at some £60 million,
thanks largely to his Psion holdings.

Turnover multiplied six-fold between 1986 and 1989, a year
in which market value doubled. Since then, Psion's worth has
multiplied five times. That sounds fine but, although Psion leads
its market, that market numbers only some 2 million units a
year. Even at £250 million, Psion, surrounded by IT competitors
whose worth is measured in billions, is a tiny fish in an ocean
of Great White Sharks.

Contrast Psion with Finland's Nokia, whose cellular phone
technology positioned it for vastly richer prizes and whose mid-
1997 market value was $20 billion. Once the Finnish entrepre-

neurs had spotted their winning opportunity in the cellular potential, they poured in resources to achieve a quarter of world phone sales. That meant intense concentration (Difference 1). For the sake of cellular, Nokia abandoned paper, tyres, metals, other electronics, cables, TV sets and its PC interests (sold to ICL).

The winning opportunity will probably not appear straight away. Microsoft wasn't founded to sell operating systems for PCs, and had none to its name; but when the men in suits from IBM came shopping for a system, Bill Gates seized the main chance with the avidity of the commercial Jaws he was to become. Alan Sugar did the same when his first, primitive Amstrad word processor tapped an eager market of people whose only alternative was over-priced PCs. But the Gates-style follow-up was lacking.

Concentration has never been Sugar's forte. Amstrad, even while trying vainly to become No. 1 in European PCs, stuck with hi-fi, ventured into satellite discs, and so on. Its small cellular phone business was yet another diversification, or diversion (though it inspired Psion, badly needing the technology, to bid abortively for all of Amstrad). The growth star that concentrates tends not to miss the best bets in technology (Difference 2). Thus Nokia was first with a 'smartphone' – a piece of digital equipment that also has computing power, with a keyboard and E-mail capability.

If you're not one of the Great White Sharks, and can't beat 'em, you can try joining 'em instead. Potter built a long lead in hand-held computing power. But there are now nine major alliances in so-called personal digital assistants (PDAs) which centre round an intimidating line-up of major players. The need for partners applies (Difference 3) especially in micro-electronics, because of the multiplicity of the technologies.

Even the most powerful corporate gentry cannot provide all the complex technology themselves. Microsoft has hundreds of alliances, some with tiny entrepreneurial companies. It follows that would-be growth stars should find partners early in their lives if they want to break into the global big-time. But how many British entrepreneurs have actually both harboured and nurtured that ambition?

Apricot, another UK-centred PC entry, did take a tiny stab at the USA (see Chapter 1). It was like trying to heat the ocean with a kettle of boiling water, and contravened the fourth and most important difference: *think big*. Think small, and you will miss the biggest of the new and thrilling opportunities from the IT ferment. The whiz-kids form a whole army of new, young, enterprising unknowns – greater in numbers than any industry has ever spawned – and the best of them think very big.

You can be excused a twinge of envy when start-up upstarts, running a company such as MAID, say, see their shares double in a week (thanks in that case to a deal to provide Microsoft's Internet services with business information). But other IT whizzes don't waste time on envy. If they see something or meet someone interesting, they buy in. For instance, Cisco Systems, one of the Silcon Valley leaders, has invested in thirty-four start-ups in the last three years.

That not only offers the prospect of a financial payoff if the start-up comes to fruition, but keeps the big companies abreast of the new technologies (or some of them). It's important for users to keep up with those technologies, too. The IT-linked opportunities available to entrepreneurs to magnify their markets, streamline their operations and widen their reach are fabulous. IT can open up the entire world market.

Even with less grand ideas, it must pay to have state-of-the-art information and communication systems installed. That way, even the start-up can compete for efficiency and effectiveness with multinational corporations. Not a day goes by without a new device or program being launched that has the potential to transform your business. Tell the suppliers what you want – the uses that will lift the business to a new plane – and the odds are that you will get a working solution at a workable cost, probably from an upstart.

The establishment won't plunge into unproven territory. That's why one mainframe software company was not at all interested in Dave Duffield's plan to provide software for personnel tasks. After going public in 1992, five years after foundation, PeopleSoft made Duffield worth more than £400 million. Fortunes like that are very seductive. Remember, though, that many are called, but few are chosen.

Those who are selected will almost certainly be Opportunity Octet and Four Difference companies. Ignore any of the dozen principles in Silicon Valley, and you are likely to fall short. Even if your business is far from high-tech, the IT principles could still transform it. That's because all markets now hinge on new ideas – which is why the Silicon Valley leaders stress the first member of the Octet: the right to fail.

There's no such thing as a risk-free risk. The nature of taking chances is that the dice will sometimes come up with the wrong numbers. But it's more important to keep the new ideas coming forward than to aim for an impossible failure-free record. A generally relaxed climate is also essential; paralysis by analysis will ruin innovative performance and will also militate against the most vital requirement of all – speed.

'Products brought to market within one year can boost sales by 20 to 50 percent': that's the conclusion of research, conducted by PIMS Associates, which found that innovation and exclusive know-how are so much more important than costs and productivity that they 'enable businesses to grow three to five times faster than their competitors'. In IT, that will do splendidly, thank you. And it's not bad anywhere else.

The Long-haul Payoff

Every business is sitting on a potential goldmine. Some marvellous opportunity always exists, either within the market already being served, or in another. That splendid business idea will, moreover, have staying power. But most firms never find the gold, or fail to mine the ore. A major cause is the alleged City of London disease: short-termism.

If the complaints about the obsession of City firms, especially banks, with short-term results were all true, few entrepreneurial creations would ever see the light of success. The ace short-termist is actually the small businessman, whose time horizon is often calculated in months rather than years. That is understandable when immediate financial and commercial pressures are at work, but it is a profound mistake.

The true entrepreneur keeps his eyes firmly fixed on well-conceived, ambitious long-term objectives, and maintains that steady gaze through all the vicissitudes of short-term performance. That doesn't prevent him from constructing a solid base in the here and now. Without such a base, there's no hope whatsoever of, say, expanding sales four-fold in four years, while increasing product variations from a few dozen to 60,000 in a decade.

Those are the actual results of a firm with a little-known name, R. Griggs, but a world-famous brand: Doc Martens boots. The Griggs growth rate is actually quite pedestrian (you might well say) by the standards of US-style super-growth. In achieving these stratospheric levels of performance, the business idea can be brilliantly new, like the high-tech creations of the computer nerds. Or the inspiration may be as old as the hills – or the floors.

For instance, there's a US chain of carpet franchises, Maxim, whose annual growth rate is 297 percent. That is simply unsustainable; even a much slower pace of sales expansion must eventually slow. The laws of arithmetic alone make that certain. A modest £100,000 business which, like Maxim, is quadrupling every year, will be worth over £100 billion in a decade. Ten years on, and it will own the world.

Such growth simply isn't feasible, even by Microsoft standards; the world and the market won't be big enough. The slowing growth rate, though, may reflect more than the inexorable workings of compound interest. Even new businesses that have never experienced such arithmetical headiness as a four-fold growth rate suffer from the same slowdown phenomenon. The initial chance is spotted and seized, but the entrepreneur runs out of steam – probably before the market does.

Yet golden markets can be inexhaustible, as the above-mentioned R. Griggs group has demonstrated in the ancient trade of footwear. The first Griggs, Benjamin, started making boots in Wollaston in 1901. His heirs didn't produce their first boot to a revolutionary German design until April Fool's Day,

1960. The name was Dr Martens, and the rest is history.

The secrets of success for the Griggs Group included a goodly supply of family sprigs. Growth was also fuelled by taking over other local shoemakers on a friendly basis to sustain expansion ('We've simply talked to families in the next street'). Several of these local firms were making the boots, and (as a Griggs executive explained to the *Financial Times*) it was 'getting very messy. Manufacturers were selling through different wholesalers, and High Street prices varied enormously'.

The confusion wasn't good for the customers or the brand. After buying up its neighbours, the family was able to expand sales vigorously in many markets – exports account for two-fifths of sales, mostly through an exclusive distributor, Airwair, established in 1988. Five years later the company was making 225,000 pairs a week. By 1997, the million mark had been reached.

Skinheads and factory workers, the original springs of growth, are now a minority of customers. Variations in platform soles, pink velvet or leather tartan appeal to a different breed of cat. The long-term value of the business, though, still rests on the original basis: the special comfort and youth appeal of the air-cushioned Doc Martens boots themselves, invented by a doctor who was convalescing in Munich during the Second World War.

The Griggs business, with exports alone totalling £123 million in 1996, long ago passed the frontier that separates the small company from the large. But its saga is a priceless pointer to long-term entrepreneurial goldmines.

First, mature, even over-ripe industries contain excellent new openings. Men and women have protected their feet for centuries, and decorated their footwear for almost as long, historically speaking. The market is unlimited, since anybody can be a mini-Imelda Marcos and buy more shoes than they can wear. Those that are worn will wear out and have to be replaced. Best of all, style and fashion change at regular and irregular intervals.

Just as much as changes in technology, these shifts open the door to new challengers. The saga of Doc Martens is small potatoes compared to the boom in athletic-style footwear which has enriched Nike, Reebok, Adidas and LA Gear. All four companies, however, have responded to style, technological and use changes within their self-created markets, demonstrating that maturity is no bar to innovation.

On the contrary, the basic familiarity of the product makes it easier for something decidedly different to supply a winning edge, preferably one that is hard to imitate and quick to appeal. An example of maturity, though it may look novel at first sight, is healthcare, now rivalling computers as a source of super-growth. In Britain as in the USA, providing medical needs – from hospital beds and clinics, via the doctors and nurses who serve them, to the drugs and dressings they administer – is a big, fragmented, growing business.

Healthcare is so large that even a fragment can yield a fortune. Supplying drugs to one group of 90,000 patients and finding nurses and other help for 10,000 more has given one US company $549 million in sales and growth of 110 percent annually. The clientele is implied by the title: Grancare, Inc. Whether the customers are grans or punks, the same rules apply for a company which wants to achieve the continuity of the long-running star.

Paradoxically, you don't aim at continuity. A study of winners and losers in the printing industry found that the losers did precisely that, which is partly why they lost. Among the winners, 46 percent opted for growth and an equal number for profit. Both were right. Profitable growth, not expansion for its own sake, is what unlocks the future.

With their overwhelming concern for survival, the losers were reluctant to drop any lines of business or to lose any customers. The result is that they tended to have broad product ranges and to supply customers in many industries. The winners, on the other hand, preferred to concentrate on specific product areas (like ticketing in the early years of St Ives, Robert Gavron's highly successful creation) or specific industries.

The winners not only grew faster than the continuity lovers, but, crucially, more profitably. Studies in the USA indicate that, if the high sales growth continues, but the high margins typical of early success start to dwindle, trouble lies ahead. A drooping return on capital (which is likely to follow from a decline in margins) is also ominous. Unless the business is averaging at least a 15 percent yield on equity, without much fluctuation, the growth is not soundly based financially.

The pressure to borrow will mount – and debt should be sparingly used by entrepreneurial growth businesses. Following such sage advice may well limit the pace of expansion, which may be no bad thing in itself. You won't, however, commonly find the self-discipline that deliberately restricts expansion to what the entrepreneur knows can be managed. Accepting that there are limits to growth comes hard to the gung-ho entrepreneurial mentality, and it's easy to see why. A 25 percent annual expansion in sales looks tiny compared to quadrupling, or even doubling turnover, every year.

But don't be misled: that 25 percent still doubles the business in under three years, which may be steady, but certainly isn't slow. More important, there's another paradox. An American survey of high- and low-growth companies showed that, over twenty-one years, the sluggards actually outperformed the speedsters in the stock market, with returns half again as high.

British investors who stuck with the shooting stars launched on the Unlisted Securities Market will know the feeling. Their experience wasn't quite as disastrous as that of people who backed Business Expansion Scheme companies (see Chapter 4). But in case after case, USM soaring was followed by slump. The seven-figure fortunes generated by the flotations came too early in the companies' development – and that of the entrepreneur.

The question of time horizons cannot be dodged. Two decades may seem like a century to a management whose activity is expanding by four times every year or, for that matter, every five years. But any really good idea – like Doc Martens – will have staying power, which it will need to last out the two or three decades which are required, outside high technology, to make the truly big time.

Entrepreneurs whose stamina matches that of a long-life product will manage for the long haul while optimizing the present. And they will remember, as noted earlier, that when you raise your eyes from the short-term to the long, it won't be at the expense of short-term performance, but to its advantage.

Mastering the Main Chance

There will always be entrepreneurs because there will always be new or better opportunities, and entrepreneurs are opportunity-takers. Keeping an eye on the main chance is the mainspring of their business lives (often all but indistinguishable from their personal lives). But spotting chances is not even the start: it is half the start. The key advice (from ancient Japan) goes further: 'Never let an opportunity pass by, but always think twice before acting.'

Opportunity is not only invariable, it abounds. There's nothing else but opportunity in common between running conference centres for other businesses, making fabrics for office furniture, providing stock-taking services, forecasting the business future, and so on. Each of these, covered in these pages, provided an opening that non-entrepreneurs would have ignored or rejected.

Everybody has probably had one or several business ideas of a similar nature: a product or service which (like puncture-proof, environmentally-friendly bicycle tyres) is either not being provided, or not being provided well. But there's a huge jump between seeing the possibility for a unique business and creating it. For virtually all the entrepreneurs featured, that giant leap was hazardous, with a grave threat of falling short.

The despair felt by the founders of the Harrogate Management Centre in their first, money-losing months has been experienced by many others. Persistence in the face of adversity is indispensable. Persistence beyond adversity is equally vital. The best entrepreneurs are perfectionists, for whom good is never good enough. Camborne Fabrics, with its costly efforts to improve on a 97 percent next-day delivery record, is only one example.

Those efforts reflect the continual entrepreneurial drive to create a better business with even more satisfied customers. That emphasis on customers wouldn't have figured anything like so prominently a decade ago. Customer-first policies have been preached to big companies by management gurus, but independent entrepreneurs reached the same conclusion through practical necessity. And they find it much easier to get truly close to customers.

Like being good at your business, just having customers isn't enough today. The only sure defence against the competition, to which the dissatisfied modern buyer will switch in a split second, is to turn good customer service into excellent. It's the toughest task in business, because no two customers are the same, and because no system will ever generate perfect service. Only people can – and they often fail.

That's why people have moved into the forefront of business thinking, along with the customer. Achieving the best standards of customer service, and having the business genuinely led by customer needs, means, as noted earlier, that the employees have been put first. Without that priority, ambitious targets for customer service can never be met. Training and development come in here as vital adjuncts to the entrepreneurial drive.

If you don't satisfy and train the men and women who work with and for you, they are most unlikely to satisfy the customer, still less to produce excellence. Big companies agonize over this fact, and with reason. Talk to employees in any large company, and you'll be struck by two things: the depth of their knowledge of the business and how it can be improved; and management's lack of interest in that profitable know-how.

Here smaller firms have the edge. The proprietor can get to know everybody, not just by name, but as real people with a real contribution to make. By mastering the art of being a boss, achieving a positive atmosphere and giving top priority to getting the best from people, the best of entrepreneurs will outperform any corporation on vital issues like quality. The large company concentrates too much on profit, too little on the non-financial elements that create that bottom line.

In contrast, the entrepreneur, however good at the basic business, often lacks a sound grip on the business basics – among them, stringent cash control, earning a goodly return on capital and minimizing debt. Return on capital is a ratio. Earning a decent profit is only half the battle. Keeping the capital employed as low as possible is the other half.

Achieving rapid growth carries risks. Growing revenues fast

while restraining overheads, keeping working capital low and maintaining effective controls is a demanding but perfectly feasible task. It has become much more feasible because of developments such as the personal computer, business information services of all kinds, advanced telecommunications, and fragmenting markets – all of which mean that the smaller business can go for growth with far fewer of the traditional disadvantages.

As a London Business School survey showed, however, many small companies are not keen on expansion. Even among those who were, a quarter of the study lived by the philosophy, 'I am very keen to expand the business and then find a buyer to buy me out' (which happened to the conference centre company, Style, and to Golden Valley, the maker of Poppops).

Although other business people say, 'I am very keen to expand the business and continue to run it myself', takeover may still be the end-result. That is no tragedy. Even if the entrepreneur does not stay on, making one small fortune provides the means to start on the road to another – and there's always another road. That's the real game of the businessman and woman: being enterprising, spotting and seizing those opportunities.

The game, though, has rules – rules that are written down, not in tablets of stone but in all manner of sources, including books like this. Sometimes the rules exist only to be broken, because the essence of entrepreneurship is to be different, eccentric, to think outside the box. The mind needs stimulus, and the thinking of others is a proven route to improved thought and, above all, action by entrepreneurs.

Being opportunists, they often shy away from putting their ambitions down in black-and-white. That's one of the barriers that entrepreneurs constantly place in their own paths. They also put their trust in family incompetents; they won't seek or accept constructive criticism; as noted, they never master the basics of business, like cash control; they buy bad businesses they can't afford. Ingenuity and perseverance may see them through even these gross gaffes. But there *is* a better way.

Any entrepreneur, in any business, needs to learn the fundamentals of business, the practical necessities that make dreams come true. You won't win a good franchise without that learning. But franchises involve riding on the back of somebody else's brand. The ultimate prize is to build your own identity in the marketplace, so that customers can be corralled and, better still, kept; retention being so much more profitable than replacement.

Throw in a yen for experiment – for trust, trial, error and heresy – and even small operations can match the world's best in quality of management. There is still no guaranteed protection against the traps. But falling into them, even into bankruptcy, is not necessarily the end of the world, though it may end the company. If failure is recognized as an education, the entrepreneur can start again towards his or her goals.

That, of course, means that the ambition has to exist. If you don't know where you're going, you can never get there. Paradoxically, being weak may be the door to strong success. Opening the door today demands accepting the new domination of the customer. For entrepreneurs, that is a priceless gain. The apparently weak firm with no market and an unproven product is forced to outflank large competitors and exploit their failures – which happens to be the best way to win.

That ability to create the future is the greatest contribution that the winning entrepreneur makes to the economy and to society. Such future trends often cannot be anticipated. But that does not make a case for flying blind. Accurate information about present performance, markets, technologies, techniques and trends is vital. Often, these areas of modern management are outside the entrepreneurs' own experience, but the resources of consultants and temporary management are available to supply vital needs.

It takes courage to admit to the management gap, but the entrepreneur needs more and better skills than ever before to navigate the threats and opportunities of the end-century. Much of the necessary understanding comes easily to the entrepreneur – for instance, marketing: it should be instinctive to make a beeline for the nearest attractive niche, or to seek out export markets as soon as possible. At the same time, a wider vision, or outside help, is needed to embrace the true business potential.

The broader the approach, the greater the chances of success. Overseas markets are rich potential sources of new business

ideas; developments in society can point to large commercial
sales; a new technology discarded by a giant can produce a Grand
Slam; and so on. Such strategies, however, presuppose that the
company has developed an innovative culture. If it has not, it
is hard to see how it can be called entrepreneurial or how it will
sustain success.

Innovation has precisely the same concerns as entrepreneurship. Both are ultimately about developing, improving and
delivering products and services that bring joy to the customer,
and better processes for that delivery. The benefits, moreover,
are not pie in the blue sky. The PIMS database shows that companies whose sales include over 12 percent new products gain
market share at double the rate of the 4–12 percent gang. That
is today's real reward for the opportunistic entrepreneur who
succeeds in creating tomorrow.

ENVOI

The Seven-Yes Company

There are six very basic questions that apply to any company, and which require a simple answer, Yes or No. I have posed the six queries to many audiences over the years. They sound simplistic, but strike to the heart of any business. And the results are almost invariably the same. You ask the audience:

1 Are you supplying the right things?
2 And in the most effective way?
3 And at the lowest possible economic cost?
4 Are you as good as or better than your best competitor?
5 Are you serving the widest possible market?
6 Do you have a Unique Selling Proposition – a reason for somebody to buy from you, rather than anybody else?

Even with a group of entrepreneurial managers, mostly from high-tech businesses like software, I had the usual response – the opposite of an epiphany – a tremendous letdown. In this case the negativism was exceptional: hardly any hands rose to reply Yes to any of the six questions. Why? There aren't many possible explanations.

Perhaps the unraised hands were telling the truth: the answers were overwhelmingly No. Or the audience could nearly all have been shy or modest – an unlikely story. Perhaps these managers really didn't know the answers, which, of course, is tantamount to saying No. None of these three possibilities is remotely satisfactory, which leaves just one less damning theory: that a Yes answer couldn't possibly be right because, however good you are, you can always improve.

That's the basis of *kaizen*, the Japanese doctrine of continuous improvement that changed the world. It's bluntly expressed by the 'half-way-to-the-wall' school of practitioners: every year, managers are expected to improve operations on key parameters by half the distance between the present position and the wall, which represents zero cost or time. As keen mathematicians will spot, you never reach the wall.

The wall in questions 1, 2 and 3 above is to make or supply the right things in the most effective possible way and at the lowest cost. You never get there: a Yes answer only states that you've done and are doing your damnedest. Two of the next three questions brook little argument. The widest possible market (5), in terms of global spread or products and customers, is another wall that perhaps can't be reached, but must be approached.

Being as good as or better than the best competitor (4), though, brooks no argument; subject to the warning that the best should actually be good – there's no virtue in being the Queen of the Pigs. But a company should know, thanks to stringent benchmarking and accurate customer surveys, how it compares to the competition; it can scarcely afford to be thought inferior. Comparative lags should provide the stimulus to get closer to that wall.

Similarly, how can a business expect to succeed in the marketplace if its own bosses can think of no reason for the customers to come and keep on coming (6)? This is a common failure; consultants working on the Royal Society of Arts inquiry into Tomorrow's Company were astounded to find that many chief executives could not explain what, if anything, was different about their companies.

Entrepreneurs do not have this difficulty, for the most part. Not for them the sameness of corporate vision and mission statements, and the similarity of change programmes, which is striking and deeply depressing. In cultures as in competition, *vive la différence*: the USP is what elevates one competitor or one company head and shoulders above the rest. And this book has emphasized throughout that the USP is the key to the entrepreneurial gold vaults.

Achieving a distinctive edge, however, is becoming harder and harder. Against this background, the future looks dim for firms which (like those represented in my audience of high-tech managers) are basically getting by: performing respectably, no doubt, but below the best standards, and leaving the future to look after itself.

Dimness need not mean disappearance. One of the most cast-iron predictions, for example, seemed to be that the PC industry, like the car industry before it, would coalesce into very few large competitors, with the small fry succumbing to their fate. Consolidation has indeed occurred, but surprising numbers of tiny entrepreneurs still cling around the edges of massive PC suppliers who can provide integrated solutions and enjoy large market shares.

A few of those tiny entrepreneurs will become Titans, which is what happened with Bill Gates and Microsoft. The vital phenomenon here is the sheer spread of markets. As Chapter 8 emphasizes, far smaller players than in the past are now truly global, operating in a whole range of markets from Europe to the Pacific Basin. Without their world exposure, these firms would not only be less successful, they probably wouldn't exist.

The star of that chapter was Camborne Fabrics, the Yorkshire company that delivers office furniture fabrics anywhere in the world within twenty-four hours. I've also come across a company based in Auckland (deliberately located there by non-Kiwis to take advantage of the convenient time zone) that sells advertising on escalator steps; and an American firm run from the Philippines that operated its high-tech cash register business via a world-wide PC networked to crack the Japanese hold from a cold start.

The same world-wide spread means that fringe companies can pick up orders from a much wider choice of customers. Nevertheless, firms seizing their true global chances won't be fringe operators; they will be the companies which are trying to answer all the six questions above with a Yes. Such perfectionism doesn't make for an easy life, and one reason for the abundance of No answers is that many managements, knowing that continuous improvement is highly strenuous, prefer to avoid the stress.

Once you have achieved a six-Yes status, there should not only be money available to sustain the performance, but also time. That is because all-round excellence cannot be achieved without effective delegation to teams of people who all know their jobs, execute their tasks willingly to the best of their abilities and concentrate on achieving or excelling the expected outcomes.

Those who have the opposite type of company probably, like the six-No managers in my audience, spend vastly more time putting out fires than in considering the future. What sort of future do they have? I was rebuked for the same fault after I had asked the six questions at a management meeting. A member of the audience asked, 'What about the future?' – and I tried to argue that it was implicit in the questions.

After all, if you are making the right products, they must be right at all times – including the future. But the questioner was, of course, absolutely correct. So I have added a seventh question:

Are you doing enough to ensure that in three, five and ten years' time, the answers to the above six questions will all be Yes?

The future, of course, is revealed to no one. But history's mighty entrepreneurs all intuitively sensed what lay ahead. They exploited their superb presents to achieve a far more brilliant future. They made their futures themselves – and that is the best definition of the entrepreneur.

Index